Practical DataOps

Delivering Agile Data Science
at Scale

Harvinder Atwal

Apress®

Practical DataOps: Delivering Agile Data Science at Scale

Harvinder Atwal
Isleworth, UK

ISBN-13 (pbk): 978-1-4842-5103-4   ISBN-13 (electronic): 978-1-4842-5104-1
https://doi.org/10.1007/978-1-4842-5104-1

Managing Director, Apress Media LLC: Welmoed Spahr
Acquisitions Editor: Jonathan Gennick
Development Editor: Laura Berendson
Coordinating Editor: Jill Balzano

Cover image designed by Freepik (www.freepik.com)

Distributed to the book trade worldwide by Springer Science+Business Media New York, 233 Spring Street, 6th Floor, New York, NY 10013. Phone 1-800-SPRINGER, fax (201) 348-4505, e-mail orders-ny@springer-sbm.com, or visit www.springeronline.com. Apress Media, LLC is a California LLC and the sole member (owner) is Springer Science + Business Media Finance Inc (SSBM Finance Inc). SSBM Finance Inc is a **Delaware** corporation.

For information on translations, please e-mail rights@apress.com, or visit http://www.apress.com/rights-permissions.

Apress titles may be purchased in bulk for academic, corporate, or promotional use. eBook versions and licenses are also available for most titles. For more information, reference our Print and eBook Bulk Sales web page at http://www.apress.com/bulk-sales.

Any source code or other supplementary material referenced by the author in this book is available to readers on GitHub via the book's product page, located at www.apress.com/9781484251034. For more detailed information, please visit http://www.apress.com/source-code.

Printed on acid-free paper

To Sukhpal and Buvleen.

Table of Contents

About the Author

Harvinder Atwal is a data professional with an extensive career using analytics to enhance customer experience and improve business performance. He is excited not just by algorithms but also by the people, processes, and technology changes needed to deliver value from data. He enjoys the exchange of ideas, and has spoken at O'Reilly Strata Data Conference in London, Open Data Science Conference (ODSC) in London, and Data Leaders Summit in Barcelona.

Harvinder currently leads the Group Data function responsible for the entire data lifecycle including data acquisition, data management, data governance, cloud and on-premise data platform management, data engineering, business intelligence, product analytics, and data science at Moneysupermarket Group. Previously, he led analytics teams at Dunnhumby, Lloyds Banking Group, and British Airways. His education includes an undergraduate degree from University College London and a master's degree in operational research from Birmingham University School of Engineering.

About the Technical Reviewer

Dr. David Paper is a professor at Utah State University in the Management Information Systems department. He wrote the book *Web Programming for Business: PHP Object-Oriented Programming with Oracle,* and he has over 70 publications in refereed journals such as *Organizational Research Methods, Communications of the ACM, Information & Management, Information Resource Management Journal, Communications of the AIS , Journal of Information Technology Case and Application Research,* and *Long Range Planning.* He has also served on several editorial boards in various capacities, including associate editor. Besides growing up in family businesses, Dr. Paper has worked for Texas Instruments, DLS, Inc., and the Phoenix Small Business Administration. He has performed IS consulting work for IBM, AT&T, Octel, Utah Department of Transportation, and the Space Dynamics Laboratory. Dr. Paper's teaching and research interests include data science, process reengineering, object-oriented programming, electronic customer relationship management, change management, e-commerce, and enterprise integration.

Acknowledgments

This book is based on 25 years of learning and experience working in data analytics. Many things have changed during that time, but I am forever indebted to the great managers I served under for their leadership, inspiration, and coaching. I hope to grow others in the same way.

I am thankful to have worked in organizations ahead of their time in analytics, notably British Airways, Lloyds Banking Group, and Moneysupermarket Group. A big thank you to Piers Stobbs for allowing me the opportunity to make this book possible.

Without discussions with my peers in the data leadership community across many organizations, this book would not exist. Our conversations on common challenges and experience are the inspiration and foundation for *Practical DataOps*.

The world is a better place thanks to people who rise above the hype cycle and share ideas to solve real problems. I am appreciative of Christopher Bergh, Gil Benghiat, Eran Strod, and Mike Huntyan of DataKitchen, Andy Palmer of Tamr, and many others for evangelizing DataOps as a solution to many of the modern problems organizations face turning data into value.

Writing this book could not have been a reality without the fantastic support of the editors at Apress. I am grateful to Jonathan Gennick for believing in this work and Jill Balzano for her editorial help. A special appreciation goes to Dr. David Paper as the technical reviewer for the book. His feedback made the book better than it otherwise would be. Finally, I am thankful to my family for their patience and understanding during writing.

Introduction

It is an amazing time to be working with data. Exponential growth in data collection, advances in machine learning (ML) and artificial intelligence (AI) algorithms, explosion in software libraries for working with much bigger quantities of data than was possible even a decade ago, and advances in big data technologies for storing and processing data have ushered in a transformative period for business, science, and government.

Data science aims to aid in better decision-making, leading to beneficial actions than we otherwise could achieve by extracting knowledge from data. Data science does this by applying the scientific method, algorithms, and processes to data in various forms. Data science cannot exist on its own and is part of an ecosystem of skills that includes data engineering and the broader field of data analytics.

Although there is hype associated with any technological change, and data science is no exception, many industries and fields are still at the beginning of the data-driven digital transformation. Over the next decade, machine learning, deep learning, and other data science techniques will transform every aspect of our lives from personalized healthcare to financial management to how we interface with machines, whether self-driving cars or virtual assistants.

Just as we are at the beginning of data-driven transformation, we are also only at the start of the journey to understand the best processes required to deliver our desired outcomes from raw data. Modern data science is still in the comparable transition phase between bespoke hand-crafted production and mechanized automation that manufacturing was confronting during the early 19th century.

Why This Book?

Unfortunately, the lack of maturity means there is plenty of evidence that despite heavy investment in data science returns have not been uniformly positive and the majority of organizations fail to create business value from their investments in data. According to Forrester Research, only 22% of companies are currently seeing a significant return from data science expenditures.[1] Most data science implementations are either laptop-based research projects that never impact customers, local applications that are not built to scale for production workflows, or high-cost IT projects.

Despite high failure rates, prescriptions and discussions remain the same. Many data scientists talk about how to create machine learning or AI models, but not many speak about getting them into *production*, a live reliable operational environment that serves customers. Algorithms are just the tip of the iceberg when it comes to creating business and customer value from data.

Big data technology vendors promote the latest storage and processing solutions, but few discuss how to make data readily accessible to non-IT end consumers. Solution vendors talk about the latest platforms but not how to overcome organizational barriers to using data effectively. The addition of new technology to legacy processes simply results in (very) expensive legacy processes.

Soft skills, data visualizations, and insight have been advocated to help organizations make better decisions since I started in this profession over 20 years ago without making much of a dent in value-added data productivity. Soft skills are critical to data scientists who deal with immense complexity and have to translate it into simple terms for everyone else. However, even a data scientist with the best soft skills can find it difficult to drive decisions and subsequent actions in an organizational culture that relies on human gut feeling for decision-making.

Focusing on technology, algorithms, and soft skills is not enough. If we keep hearing the same solutions but results continue to be poor, then widespread mantras associated with data analytics are likely to be wrong.

Most approaches for managing and consuming data were developed in a world where data was scarce, computer resources expensive, storage constrained, the opportunity to test and learn minimal, and digital automation nonexistent. Data was primarily required for operational purposes, so strict management was needed with tight access controls to avoid calamities. Only the largest organizations applied data analytics, typically governments, financial institutions, transportation companies, and large manufacturers, to address their most significant problems. For example, one of my earliest projects involved determining the best mix of long-haul aircraft British Airways should buy as part of a multibillion-dollar fleet renewal program. Considerable uncertainty made decisions difficult, and much time was devoted to modeling the range of outcomes and potential risk, often over multiyear timeframes.

We now live in a world with much fewer data constraints. So, data-driven decisions can be (and are expected to be) made everywhere and in much smaller increments from auto-enhancement in a photo-editing mobile app to sentence autocomplete in webmail. It is also now cheaper than ever before to generate empirical data to learn and reduce the uncertainty of decision-making.

However, most organizations still approach data science as a series of large bespoke, waterfall research projects with artificial constraints in the provision of data when instead data-driven decisions can be automated, scalable, reproducible, testable, and fast. Poor returns on data science investment are merely a result of applying 20th-century approaches to managing data, while 21st-century approaches should be embraced to deliver better decisions for 21st-century opportunities.

By late 2016, I became frustrated with the ability of our data scientists to consistently help customers and stakeholders. Although we were measurably adding value to the bottom line and helping fulfill the company's mission to save our customers money, there were still barriers and frustrations. Significant amounts of time were being absorbed helping shape business questions or indeed explaining why the problem was not worth expensive data scientist time to answer.

Data scientists were producing decision support insight without direct influence on actions. Acquiring new data and investigating discrepancies in data diverted significant resource. Our modern cloud-based analytics and data lake infrastructure were becoming increasingly difficult to maintain and optimize, limiting the speed at which we could migrate off legacy architecture. The legacy architecture and tools required specialist skills to use, resulting in data scientists becoming a bottleneck for business stakeholders or a costly resource for producing ad hoc data analysis. In summary, we were not as efficient as we could be and needed to take a radically different approach.

If you have ever been in a similar situation, this book is for you. This book aims to challenge existing approaches to delivering data science and analytics by describing a relatively new methodology that is much more relevant to today's environment and is flexible enough to adapt to future change.

What Is It?

Many other disciples have faced similar challenges as data science and analytics as they matured, needing to add value as quickly and efficiently as possible yet simultaneously dealing with high levels of complexity. The two most applicable are manufacturing and software development, which have created revolutionary approaches such as Lean, agile, and DevOps that can be adapted by data science and analytics professionals.

Out of necessity in 2017, I decided to test a different methodology to help deliver data-driven personalization, which had become a key marketing strategy but one where the business wanted to see quick results to justify further investment. Working in a web site and mobile-only company made me familiar with many of the concepts and approaches used by colleagues for software development, product engineering, and product management to rapidly turn ideas into a minimum viable product (MVP) and then iteratively optimize over time. As such, I decided to apply these approaches to the data and ML model lifecycles needed to deliver personalized experiences to our customers.

The first step was to work closely with marketing teams to mutually agree on outcome objectives and prioritize hypotheses to test. Next, we identified the data products required to deliver the objectives such as machine learning feature datasets, machine learning models, and dashboards to measure the results of experiments. Our new minimal models helped gather vital feedback from external customers.

At this stage, it was still a "string and sticky tape" process to integrate data, build our models, and deploy them, so it was necessary to increase the involvement of our data engineering team. They used their skills to improve data availability, monitor data quality, automate and speed up large parts of the data pipelines, refactor data transformations for efficiency and reusability, and implement rigorous testing and integration of machine learning outputs with downstream platforms that consumed them.

A period of continuous improvement followed because measurement of experiments gave us feedback on new hypotheses to test and data sources to integrate in collaboration with other teams. Moreover, analysis of data cycles identified bottlenecks to eliminate and quality issues to resolve with the data engineering and technology teams.

Results exceeded our expectations by a considerable degree. Within 3 months, we were able to dramatically reduce the time taken to develop new machine learning models and analyze experiments. More importantly, within 6 months, the impact on our customer and revenue KPIs was extremely positive. Achievements realized would have taken considerably longer to accomplish if we had continued with our piecemeal project prioritization and delivery approach. Without realizing it, we had accidentally started on the journey to DataOps-driven data science.

The name DataOps is a portmanteau of Data and Operations and was first introduced by Lenny Liebmann in a 2014 blog post titled "3 reasons why DataOps is essential for big data success."[2] However, it wasn't until Andy Palmer's 2015 blog post "From DevOps to DataOps" that the term was popularized.[3] Since then, interest has grown to Gartner's "Hype Cycle" for data management in 2018.[4] My goal in writing this book is to convince you that DataOps is more than hype.

As a relatively new methodology, DataOps, along with many other terms in this field, can be defined in different ways. Gartner narrowly defines DataOps as a data management practice:

> *...a collaborative data management practice focused on improving the communication, integration and automation of data flows between data managers and consumers across an organization. The goal of DataOps is to create predictable delivery and change management of data, data models and related artifacts. DataOps uses technology to automate data delivery with the appropriate levels of security, quality and metadata to improve the use and value of data in a dynamic environment.*[5]

The Ops in DataOps is a vital reminder that we must think well beyond *what* data management and data analytics are to *how* we operationalize the provision of data and resultant outputs. In reality, data delivery and data pipelines are also just one component of larger data applications involving multiple teams. Hence, DataOps must embrace application use cases, every team involved in the data lifecycle from the moment data is acquired to its consumption, and ultimate outcomes if it is to bring many benefits. For this reason, I prefer DataKitchen's wider heritage-based definition of DataOps as a combination of data analytics, Lean thinking, agile practice, and DevOps culture:[6]

- Agile practices ensure we work on the "right things" that add value for the "right people."

- Lean thinking focuses on eliminating waste and bottlenecks, improving quality, monitoring data flows, and making data cheaper for consumers.

- DevOps practices build a culture of collaboration between historically siloed teams. The practices enable data analytics teams to work more efficiently through automated processes across the whole data lifecycle to deliver faster and more reliably.

DataOps aims to benefit multiple data consumers through data-use cases from the simple data sharing to the full spectrum of data analytics popularized by the Gartner model: descriptive, diagnostic, predictive, and prescriptive. It brings together self-contained teams with data analytics, data science, data engineering, DevOps skills, and line of business expertise in close collaboration.

The goal of DataOps for data science is to turn unprocessed data into a useful data science product that provides utility to customers through a rapid, scalable, and repeatable process. A data science product incorporates data science into the operation of a service or product. Multiple times a day, we are customers of a data product whether it is a Google Maps route request or a Netflix product recommendation. It is not a one-off project. A data science product is in continuous production with constant monitoring, iteration based on experimentation, and feedback that leads to improvement. It has an owner, it is reproducible, and it solves an end goal. Users and machines can interact with data science products in multiple ways such as APIs, visualizations, or even web or mobile app interfaces.

DataOps is a solution to many of the challenges faced by data science and analytics once you realize that converting raw data into useful data products can be treated as an end-to-end assembly line process that requires high levels of collaboration, automation, and continuous improvement.

What Is It Not?

As well as understanding what DataOps is, it is also essential to understand what it is not:

- DataOps borrows best practices from agile software development, Lean manufacturing, and DevOps, but does not copy them. A fundamental difference is that, in software development, the focus is on the application code deployed at every stage. In data science and analytics, the focus is on the code AND the data at every step.

Often, far more of the complexity lies in the data than the code used to transform and model it. Hence, DataOps focuses on data, information, and model lifecycles from data acquisition to retirement and business problem definition to model deletion.

- DataOps is well suited to delivering end-to-end decision-making with machine learning. However, the methodology is not limited to machine learning and data science. Any data-oriented work that results in a data product can benefit from the approach.

- DataOps is not a product that can be bought from a vendor or cloned from GitHub. Like DevOps, successful implementation is much more about collaboration, organizational change, and best practice than technology.

- DataOps does not tie you to a particular language, tool, algorithm, or software library. Due to rapid advances and constant change in technology and algorithms, it is not possible to be prescriptive about which services and software to use. However, some solutions do support DataOps better than others, and some principles guide how they can be selected.

- DataOps does not replace data-led insight. In many ways, the DataOps methodology makes it much easier and faster to produce insight by speeding up the provision of high-quality data. However, it does make the distinction between bespoke research and automated production of a data product much more distinct. This distinction enables more conscious trade-offs in investment between the two for any given level of resource.

- DataOps is not restricted to "big data" (although in common parlance, the term is often synonymous with data analytics) and is agnostic of the size and complexity of data used. Organizations with data of any size can benefit from a methodology that seeks to increase the velocity, reliability, and quality of data analytics.

Who Is It For?

Data science cannot succeed in isolation, so an understanding of DataOps cannot be limited to data scientists and their managers. Senior leaders responsible for data and IT functions, IT professionals supporting data teams, and data engineers can all benefit from this book.

- **Data science and advanced analytics experts.** You are an analytical data expert with the technical skills to solve complex problems and employ machine learning/AI algorithms. You want guidance on how to work in an Agile way ensuring your work is reproducible and testable. You want to learn how to automate the testing and deployment of your data products. You want to know how to gather feedback from experimentation so you can learn from outcomes.

- **Analytics managers.** You manage data scientists or data science team leaders and are responsible for prioritizing and overseeing their work. You are also busy interfacing with your customers in the business, while at the same time you are a customer of other functions that provide data and IT resources to your team(s). You want to ensure you are collaborating with business stakeholders to work on the highest priorities. You want to know where to focus your efforts so you can improve the speed and quality of your team's work.

- **Chief Information Officers, Chief Data Officers, and Chief Analytics Officers.** You are in charge of an entire function and want to ensure the organization is making the most of its data asset by making data and data-driven decisions a first-class citizen. You want to understand the strategy you need to employ for people, process, and technology to do this. You want to understand the barriers your teams face and eliminate them. You want to measure the impact your teams have so you can inform business strategy.

- **Data engineers and IT professionals (developers, architects, and DBAs) supporting data teams.** You want to ensure the data analytics and data science teams have access to the data they need in a governed way, its quality is high, and lineage traceable. You want to help data science teams put their data products into production as quickly as possible, ensuring they are scalable and monitored. You want to collaborate with data scientists and data engineers to deliver supporting data infrastructure.

The Flow of the Book

The book is in four main parts. Reading chapters in order is recommended; however, most chapters can be read independently depending on your specific area of interest.

The first part is an outline of current challenges with delivering data science and why we must first start with a holistic data strategy. It outlines barriers and complications to the successful real-world implementation of data science projects, describing why analytics is so hard.

The second part moves us toward DataOps by introducing and adapting Lean thinking and agile methodology to data science together with the need for measurement and feedback to implement continuous improvement and the scientific method. The challenges in delivering value from data science are the result of three things: waste, misalignment with the business, and difficulty in productionizing data science outputs at scale. Each of these challenges can be solved by borrowing and adapting ideas used by other domains, specifically manufacturing and software development, who also manage complexity at scale successfully.

Next, in part three, we learn to move at speed and scale by building trust in data through testing, trust in users through better data governance, and rapid improvement through reproducible workflows and DevOps.

Part four offers recommendations to evaluate the technology to support DataOps objectives for agility and self-service and organizational solutions for successful DataOps implementation and increased collaboration. The final chapter concludes with the steps recommended for the application of the methodology.

Endnotes

1. Data Science Platforms Help Companies Turn Data Into Business Value, A Forrester Consulting Thought Leadership Paper Commissioned By DataScience, December 2016. *https://cdn2. hubspot.net/hubfs/532045/Forrester-white-paper-data-science-platforms-deliver-value.pdf*

2. Lenny Liebmann "3 reasons why DataOps is essential for big data success," IBM Big data and Analytics Hub, Jun 2014. *www.ibmbigdatahub.com/blog/3-reasons-why-dataops-essential-big-data-success*

3. Andy Palmer "From DevOps to DataOps," May 2015. *www.tamr. com/from-devops-to-dataops-by-andy-palmer/*

4. Gartner Hype Cycle for Data Management, July 2018. *www.gartner.com/doc/3884077/hype-cycle-data-management-*

5. Nick Heudecker, "Hyping DataOps," Gartner Blog Network, July 2018. *https://blogs.gartner.com/nick-heudecker/ hyping-dataops/*

6. DataKitchen, "DataOps is NOT Just DevOps for Data," Medium. *https://medium.com/data-ops/dataops-is-not-just-devops-for-data-6e03083157b7*

PART I

Getting Started

CHAPTER 1

The Problem with Data Science

Before adopting DataOps as a solution, it's important to understand the problem we're trying to solve. When you view articles online, hear presentations at conferences, or read of the success of leading data-driven organizations like Facebook, Amazon, Netflix, and Google *(FANG)*, delivering successful data science seems a simple process. The reality is very different.

While there are undoubtedly success stories, there is also plenty of evidence that substantial investment in data science is not generating the returns expected for a majority of organizations. There are multiple causes, but they stem from two root causes. First, a 20th-century information architecture approach to handling data and analytics in the 21st century. Second, the lack of knowledge and organizational support for data science and analytics. The common (20th-century) mantras espoused in the industry to overcome these problems make matters worse, not better.

Is There a Problem?

It is possible to create competitive advantage and solve worthy problems using data. Many organizations are managing to generate legitimate success stories from their investments in data science and data analytics:

- VP of Product Innovation Carlos Uribe-Gomez and Chief Product Officer Neil Hunt published a paper that says some of its recommendation algorithms save Netflix $1 billion each year in reduced churn.[1]

© Harvinder Atwal 2020
H. Atwal, *Practical DataOps*, https://doi.org/10.1007/978-1-4842-5104-1_1

- One of Monsanto's data science initiatives to improve global transportation and logistics delivers annual savings and cost avoidance of nearly $14 million, while simultaneously reducing C02 emissions by 350 metric tons (MT).[2]

- Alphabet's DeepMind, better known for its AlphaGo program, has developed an artificial intelligence (AI) system in partnership with London's Moorfield Eye Hospital to refer treatment for over 50 sight-threatening diseases as accurately as world-leading expert doctors.[3]

Not wanting to be left behind, most organizations are now spending heavily on expensive technology and hiring costly teams of data scientists, data engineers, and data analysts to make sense of their data and drive decisions. What was once a niche activity in even the largest organizations is now seen as a core competency. The investment and job position growth rates are staggering considering global GDP is only growing at 3.5% annually:

- International Data Corp. (IDC) expects worldwide revenue for big data and business analytics solutions to reach $260 billion in 2022, a compound annual growth rate of 11.9% over the 2017–2022 period.[4]

- LinkedIn's emerging jobs reports rank machine learning engineers, data scientists, and big data engineers as three of the top four fastest-growing jobs in the United States between 2012 and 2017. Data scientist roles grew over 650% over that period![5]

The Reality

Despite massive monetary outlay, only a minority of organizations achieve meaningful results. Case studies demonstrating quantifiable outcomes are isolated exceptions, even allowing for reluctance to disclose competitive advantages. Exponential growth in the volume of data, rapid increases in solutions spending, and improvements in technology and algorithms have not led to an increase in data analytics productivity.

There is some indication that the success rate of data analytics projects is declining. In 2016, Forrester concluded that only 22% of companies saw high revenue growth and profit from their investments in data science.[6] Also, in 2016, Gartner estimated that 60% of big data projects fail, but it gets worse. In 2017, Gartner's Nick Heudecker issued a correction. The 60% estimate was "too conservative," the real failure rate was closer to 85%.[7]

Although much of the survey data is related to "big data," I still think Nick's results are relevant. Outside of the data science field, most people mistakenly think of big data, data science, and data analytics as interchangeable terms and will be responding as such.

There may be multiple reasons for the meager rate of return and failure to improve productivity despite serious investment in data science and analytics. Explosive growth in data capture may result in the acquisition of ever-lower marginal value data. Technology, software libraries, and algorithms may not be keeping pace with the volume and complexity of data captured. The skill levels of data scientists could be insufficient. Processes might not be evolving to take advantage of data-driven opportunities. Finally, organizational and cultural barriers could be preventing data exploitation.

Data Value

There is no indication that the marginal value of data collected has declined. Much of the additional data captured is increasingly from new sources such as *Internet of Things* (IoT) device sensors or mobile devices, nonstructured data, and text, image, or semi-structured documents generated by event logs. Higher volume and variety of data acquired is expanding the opportunity for data scientists to extract knowledge and drive decisions.

However, there is evidence that poor data quality remains a serious challenge. In Figure Eight's 2018 Data Scientist Report, 55% of data scientists cited quality/quantity of training data as being their biggest challenge.[8] The rate had changed little since the inaugural 2015 report when 52.3% of data scientists cited poor quality data as their biggest daily obstacle.[9] Dirty data was also cited as the number one barrier in Kaggle's 2017 The State of Data & Machine Learning Survey of 16,000 respondents, while "data unavailable or difficult to access" was the fifth most significant barrier and mentioned by 30.2% of respondents.[10]

Technology, Software, and Algorithms

There is no indication that technology, software libraries, and algorithms are failing to keep up with the volume and complexity of data captured. Technology and software libraries continue to evolve to handle increasingly challenging problems while adding simplified interfaces to hide complexity from users or increase automation. Where once running a complex on-premise Hadoop cluster was the only choice for working with multiple terabytes of data, now the same workloads can be run on managed Spark or SQL query-engines-as-a-service on the cloud with no infrastructure engineering requirement.

Software libraries like Keras make working with deep learning libraries such as Google's popular TensorFlow much easier. Vendors like DataRobot have automated the production of machine learning models. Advances in deep learning algorithms and architectures, and large neural networks with many layers, such as *convolutional neural networks* (CNNs) and *long short-term memory networks* (LSTM networks), have enabled a step-change in *natural language processing* (NLP), machine translation, image recognition, voice processing, and real-time video analysis. In theory, all these developments should be improving productivity and *return on investment* (ROI) of data science investment. Maybe organizations are using outdated or wrong technology.

Data Scientists

As a relatively new field, the inexperience of data scientists may be a problem. In Kaggle's The State of Data & Machine Learning Survey, the modal age range of data scientists was just 24–26 years old, and the median age was 30. Median age varied by country; for the United States, it was 32. However, this is still far lower than the median age of the American worker at 41 years old. Educational attainment was not a problem though, 15.6% had a doctorate, 42% held a master's, and 32% a bachelor's degree.[10] Since all forms of advanced analytics were marginal before 2010, there is also a deficiency of experienced managers. As a result, we have many extremely bright data scientists short of experience in dealing with organizational culture and lacking in senior analytical leadership.

Data Science Processes

It is challenging to find survey data on the processes and methodologies used to deliver data science. KDnuggets' 2014 survey showed *cross industry standard process for data mining* (CRISP-DM) as the top methodology for analytics, data mining, and data science projects used by 43% of respondents.[11] The next most popular approach was not a method at all, but respondents following their homegrown process. The SAS Institute's *Sample, Explore, Modify, Model and Assess* (SEMMA) model was third, but in rapid decline as the use is tightly coupled to SAS products.

The challenge with CRISP-DM and other data mining methodologies like *Knowledge Discovery Databases* (KDD) is they treat data science as a much more linear process than it is. They encourage data scientists to spend significant time planning and analyzing for a single near-perfect delivery, which may not be what the customer ultimately wants. No attention is focused on minimum viable product, feedback from customers, or iteration to ensure that you're spending time wisely working on the right thing. They also treat deployment and monitoring as a "throw it over the fence" problem, where work is passed to other teams for completion with little communication or collaboration, reducing chances of successful delivery.

In response, many groups have proposed new methodologies, including Microsoft with their *Team Data Science Process* (TDSP).[12] TDSP is a significant improvement over previous approaches and recognizes that data science delivery needs to be agile, iterative, standardized, and collaborative. Unfortunately, TDSP does not seem to be gaining much traction. TDSP and similar methodologies are also restricted to the data science lifecycle. There is an opportunity for a methodology that encompasses end-to-end data lifecycle, from acquisition to retirement.

Organizational Culture

Emotional, situational, and cultural factors heavily influence business decisions. FORTUNE Knowledge Group's survey of more than 700 high-level executives from a variety of disciplines across nine industries demonstrates the barriers to data-driven decision-making. A majority (61%) of executives agree that when making decisions, human insights must precede hard analytics. Sixty-two percent of respondents contend that it's often necessary to rely on "gut feelings" and that soft factors should be given the same weight as hard factors. Worryingly, two-thirds (66%) of IT executives say decisions are often made out of a desire to conform to "the way things have always been done."[13] These are not isolated findings. NewVantage Partners' Big data Executive Survey 2017 found cultural challenges remain an impediment to successful business adoption:

> *More than 85% of respondents report that their firms have started programs to create data-driven cultures, but only 37% report success thus far. Big data technology is not the problem; management understanding, organizational alignment, and general organizational resistance are the culprits. If only people were as malleable as data.*[14]

It is no surprise that very few companies have followed the example of Amazon and replaced highly paid white-collar decision-makers with algorithms despite the enormous success it has achieved.[15]

The challenge in delivering successful data science has much less to do with technology, but cultural attitude where many organizations alternately treat data science as a box-ticking exercise or part of the never-ending pursuit for the perfect solution to all their challenges. Nor is the problem with the effectiveness of algorithms. Algorithms and technology are well ahead of our ability to feed them high data quality, overcome people barriers (skills, culture, and organization), and implement data-centric processes. However, these symptoms are themselves the result of deeper root causes such as lack of knowledge of the best way to use data to make decisions, legacy perceptions from last century's approach to handling data and delivering analytics, and a shortage of support for data analytics.

The Knowledge Gap

Multiple knowledge gaps make it hard to embed data science in organizations when implementation starts at the very top of an organization. Nevertheless, it is too easy to blame business leaders and IT professionals for their failure to deliver results. The knowledge gap is a two-way street because data scientists must share the blame.

The Data Scientist Knowledge Gap

Data science aims to facilitate better decisions, leading to beneficial actions by extracting knowledge from data. To enable better decisions, data scientists need a good understanding of the business domain to enable better understanding of the business problem, identify the right data and prepare it (often detecting quality issues for the first time), employ the right algorithms on the data, validate their approaches, convince stakeholders to act, operationalize their output, and measure results. This breadth of scope necessitates an extensive range of skills such as the ability to collaborate and coordinate with multiple functions within the organization in addition to their own job area, critical and scientific thinking, coding and software development skills, and knowledge of a wide range of machine learning and statistical algorithms. Moreover, the ability to communicate complex ideas to a nontechnical audience and business acumen if in a commercial setting is crucial. In the data science profession, someone with the combination of all these skills is known as a unicorn.

Since finding a unicorn is rare if not impossible (they don't sign up to LinkedIn or attend meetups), organizations try to find the next best thing. They hire people with programming (Python or R), analysis, machine learning, and statistical and computer science skills, which happen to be the five most sought-after skills by employers.[16] These skills should be the differentiator between data scientists and everyone else. Unfortunately, this belief reinforces the mistaken conviction among junior data scientists that specialist technical skills should be the focus, but this tends to create dangerously homogenous teams.

"Create me a machine translation attention model using a bi-directional long short-term memory (LSTM) with an attention layer outputting to a stacked post-attention LSTM feeding a softmax layer for predictions," said no CEO, ever.

I'm always staggered when interviewing by the number of candidates who say their primary objective is a role that allows them to create deep learning, reinforcement learning, and [insert your algorithm here] models. Their aim is not to solve a real problem or help customers, but to apply today's hottest technique. Data science is too valuable to treat as a paid hobby.

There is a disconnect between the skills data scientists think they need and what they really need. Unfortunately, technical skills are nowhere near enough to drive real success and beneficial actions from data-driven decisions. Faced with hard-to-access poor-quality data, lack of management support, no clear questions to answer, or results ignored by decision-makers, data scientists without senior data science leadership aren't equipped to change the culture. Some look for greener pastures and get a new job, only to realize that similar challenges exist in most organizations. Others focus on the part of the process they can control, the modeling.

In data science, there is an overemphasis on machine learning or deep learning, and especially among junior data scientists, the belief that working in solitary isolation to maximize model accuracy score(s) on a test dataset is the definition of success. This behavior is encouraged by training courses, online articles, and especially Kaggle. High test set prediction accuracy seems a bizarre interpretation of success to me. It is usually better, in my experience, to try ten solution scenarios rather than spend weeks on premature optimization of a single problem solution because you don't know in advance what is going to work. It is when you get feedback from consumers and measure results that you see if you have driven beneficial action or even useful learning. At that point, you can decide the value of expending further effort to optimize.

The aim must be to get a minimum viable product into production. A perfect model on a laptop that never goes into production wastes effort so is worse than a model that does not exist. There are domains where model accuracy is paramount like medical diagnosis precision, fraud detection, and AdTech, but these are a minority compared to applications where doing anything is a significant improvement over doing nothing. Even in domains benefiting disproportionately from optimizing model accuracy, quantifying real-world impact is still more important.

Getting a model into production requires different technical skills than creating the model. The most important of which are relevant software development skills. For many data scientists, who mainly have non-software development backgrounds, coding is just a means to an end. They are unaware that coding and software engineering are disciplines with their own set of best practices. Alternatively, if they are aware, they tend to see writing reusable code, version control, and testing or documentation as obstacles to be avoided.

Weak development skills cause difficulties, especially for reproducibility, performance, and quality of work. The barriers to getting models into production are not the sole responsibility of data scientists. Often, they do not have access to the tools and systems required to get their models into production and thereby must rely on other teams to facilitate implementation. Naïve data scientists ignore the gulf between local development and server-based production and treat it as a throw it over the fence problem by not thinking through the implications of their choice of programming language. This inexperience causes avoidable friction and failure.

IT Knowledge Gap

Superficially, data science and software development share similarities. Both involve code, data, databases, and computing environments. So, data scientists require some software development skills. However, there is a crucial distinction demonstrated in Figure 1-1 that shows the difference between machine learning and regular programming.

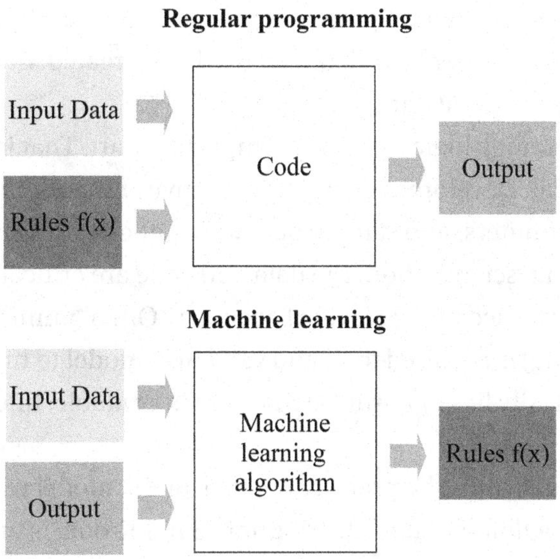

Regular programming

Machine learning

Figure 1-1. *Difference between regular programming and machine learning*

In regular programming, rules or logic are applied to input data to generate an output (Output = f(Inputs) such as Z = X + Y) based on well-understood requirements. In machine learning, examples of outputs and their input data along with their individual properties, known as features, feed a machine learning algorithm. A machine learning algorithm attempts to *learn the rules* that generate output from inputs by minimizing a cost function via a training process that will never achieve perfect accuracy on real-life data. Once suitably trained, regular programming can use machine learning model rules to make predictions for new input data. The difference between regular programming and machine learning has profound implications for data quality, data access, testing, development processes, and even computing requirements.

Garbage in, garbage out applies to regular programming. However, high-quality data is essential for machine learning as the algorithm is dependent upon good data to learn rules. Poor-quality data will lead to inferior training and predictions. Generally, more data allows a machine learning algorithm to decipher more complexity and generate more accurate predictions. Moreover, more features inherent in the data enables an algorithm to improve predictive accuracy. Data scientists can also engineer additional features from existing data based on domain knowledge and experience.

Model training is iterative and computationally expensive. High capacity memory and more powerful CPUs allow you to use more data and sophisticated algorithms. The languages and libraries used to create machine learning models are specialized for data analytics, typically the R and Python programming languages and their libraries and packages, respectively. However, once a model has been created, deployment processes are much more familiar to a software developer.

In regular programming, logic is the most important part. That is, ensuring that the code is correct is critical. Development and testing environments often do not need high-performance computers, and sample data with sufficient coverage is enough to complete testing. In data science, both the data and code are critical. There is no correct answer to test for, only an acceptable level of accuracy. Often, minimal code (compared to regular programming) is required to fit and validate a model to high test accuracy (e.g., 95%). The complexity lies in ensuring that data is available, understood, and correct.

Even for training, data must be production data, or the model will not predict well on new unseen data with a different data distribution. Sample data is not useful unless data scientists select test data as part of a deliberate strategy (e.g. random sampling, cross-validation, stratified sampling) specific to the problem. Although these requirements relate to machine learning, they generalize to all data scientist work in general.

The needs of data scientists are often misinterpreted by IT, even by those who are supportive as "nice-to-haves." Data scientists are frequently asked to justify why they need access to multiple data sources, complete production data, specific software, and powerful computers when other "developers" don't need them and reporting analysts have "mined" data for years by just running SQL queries on relational databases. IT is frustrated that data scientists don't understand the reasons behind IT practices. Data scientists are frustrated because it's not easy to justify the value of what they consider necessities upfront. More than once the question "But why do you need this data?" has made my heart sink.

It is rare to see IT processes designed to support advanced analytical processes. It starts with the way data is captured. Many developers see capturing new data items as a burden with an associated cost in planning, analysis, design, implementation, and maintenance time. Most organizations, therefore, collect data foremost to support operational processes like customer relationship management (CRM), financial management, supply chain management, e-commerce, and marketing. Frequently, this data resides in separate silos, each with its strict data governance strategy.

Often, data will go through an *ETL* (Extract, Transform, Load) process to transform it into structured data (typically a tabular format) before loading it into a data warehouse to make it accessible for analytics. There are some drawbacks to this approach for data science. Only a subset of data makes its way through the ETL where it is typically prioritized for reporting. Adding new data items can take months of development. As such, raw data is unavailable to data scientists. Raw data is what they need!

Traditional data warehouses usually only handle structured data in relational schemas (with data split across multiple joinable tables to avoid duplication and improve performance) and can struggle to manage the scale of data we have available today. They also don't handle modern use cases that require unstructured data like text or sometimes even machine-generated semi-structured data formats like *JSON* (JavaScript Object Notation). One solution is the creation of data lakes where data is stored in raw native format and goes through an *ELT* (Extract, Load, Transform) process when needed, with the transformation being dependent on the use case.

When a data lake is not available, data scientists must extract the data themselves and combine it on a local machine or work with data engineers to build pipelines into an environment with the tools, computing resource, and storage they need. Requests to access data, provision environments, and install tools and software are often the responsibility of separate teams with varying concerns for security, costs, and governance. As such, data scientists need to work with different groups to deploy and schedule their models, dashboards, and APIs. With processes in place incongruent with data science needs, costs are greatly elevated.

The entire data lifecycle splits across many IT teams, and each in isolation makes rational decisions based on its functional silo objectives. Such silo objectives do not serve data scientists. For data scientists who need data pipelines from raw data to final data product, significant challenges arise. They need to justify their requirements and negotiate with multiple stakeholders to complete a delivery. Even if they are successful, they will still be dependent on other teams for many tasks and at the mercy of backlogs and prioritization. No one person or function is responsible for the entire pipeline leading to delays, bottlenecks, and operational risk.

Data security and privacy are cited occasionally as obstacles to prevent access and processing of data. There are genuine concerns to ensure compliance with regulations, respect user privacy, protect reputation, defend competitive advantage, and prevent malicious damage. However, such concerns can also be used to take a risk-averse route and not implement solutions that allow for the safe, legitimate, and ethical use of data. More typically, problems occur when data security and privacy policies are implemented without undertaking a thorough cost-benefit analysis and fully understanding the impact on data analytics.

Technology Knowledge Gap

Although technology is not the only barrier to the successful implementation of data science, it is still crucial to get tooling right. Figure 1-2 shows the typical hardware and software layers in a data lifecycle from raw data to useful business applications.

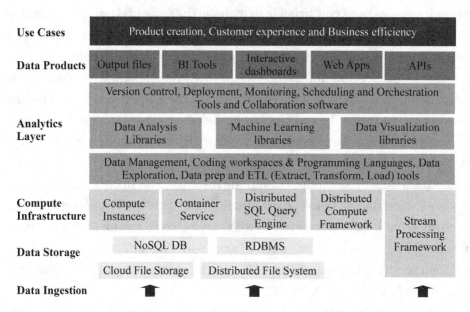

Figure 1-2. *Typical hardware and software layers in the data lifecycle*

Many software and hardware requirements need to come together to create data products. There must be a holistic understanding of requirements and investment balance across all the lifecycle layers. Unfortunately, it is easy to focus on one part of the jigsaw to the detriment of others. Large enterprises tend to concentrate on the big data technologies used to build applications. They obsess over Kafka, Spark, and Kubernetes, but fail to provide their data scientists sufficient access to data, software libraries, and tools they need. Smaller organizations are more likely to provide their data scientists with the software tools they need, but may fail to invest in storage and processing technologies, leaving analytics processing isolated on laptops.

Even if they do get the investment in tools right, organizations can still underestimate the supporting resources needed to build, maintain, and optimize the stack. Without sufficient talent in data engineering, data governance, DevOps, database administration, solutions architecture, and infrastructure engineering, it is next to impossible to utilize the tools efficiently.

Larger organizations also tend to make the mistake of treating data science as an "old-world waterfall" technology project, where expensive infrastructure or buying high-priced tools is needed before you can start using data. This belief comes from the last century when your only option for handling large-scale data and apply analytics was to purchase expensive on-premise systems from companies like Oracle, Teradata, IBM, or SAS. The problem is that waterfall technology projects are slow, expensive, and highly likely to fail for data science activities. Even if they do deliver, technology moves so fast that the final solution may be obsolete when released. You do not need a multimillion-dollar enterprise Hadoop cluster to get started. You need just enough functionality to prove value before investing further in technology and people.

Leadership Knowledge Gap

Most C-suite execs don't seem to understand data science even though they tend to be very numerate, or even IT literate. One reason might be that they tend to read the latest Harvard Business Review and treat it as gospel. They do know that successful companies like Google, Amazon, and Facebook have lots of data so they must store it too. They seem to believe that hiring smart data scientists with PhDs in Astrophysics is then all that is needed to make magic happen, create value from data, and increase money flows. Money does stream, but, as we have seen from the evidence, in the opposite direction. Storing data is a cost, and data scientists are not cheap.

The fear of missing out and sometimes pressure from investors and boards to appear at the forefront of progress lead senior executives to jump from bandwagon to bandwagon. "Single Customer View," "big data," "Hadoop," and "Customer 360" are just some of the buzzwords to explode and fade in recent years. The latest buzzword in data science is artificial intelligence (AI), which is the ability of machines to perform tasks somewhat like humans in terms of ability to learn, problem-solving, and rational decision-making. The market intelligence research company, CB Insights, has analyzed 10 years of earnings calls transcripts from public companies. They report that AI overtook "big data" as the analytics buzzword in mid-2016. Since then, they have measured tremendous growth in mentions of AI (it was discussed around 791 times in just Q3 2017), which is up 25% quarter-on-quarter.[17]

It is not only C-suite execs that have an interest in the next big thing. Journalists power a hype machine for their purposes. Vendors rebrand the same product as big data-driven, then machine learning-driven, and now AI-driven to keep riding the wave.

Consultants have a stake in inflating the positive benefits of employing new approaches and minimizing the actual costs and complexity of implementation. Good vendors and consultants should be explicit about the difficulties of working in the data science realm and provide real answers to solve real problems.

Without data representation in the C-suite, data science and its techniques must appear to be a dark art. Unfamiliarity makes it difficult to separate hype from reality and truly understand the requirements needed to maximize the benefits of data. AI, for instance, is not a magic black box. It is just a collection of algorithms that a good strategy can bring to life. Figure 1-3 shows the relationship between AI, machine learning, and deep learning.

Artificial intelligence (AI)			
The ability of machines to perform tasks that require at least human intelligence levels of learning, problem-solving and rational decision-making			
	Machine learning (ML)		
	Algorithms that give computers the ability to learn rules from data		
If-Then rules	Unsupervised Learning algorithms	**Reinforcement learning (RL)**	**Deep learning**
Knowledge-based expert systems	Semi-supervised Learning	ML Algorithms that enable an agent to learn by trial and error using feedback from actions in an environment	Large neural networks with many layers that excel at text, vision and speech recognition
	Supervised Learning algorithms		

Figure 1-3. *The relationship between AI and machine learning*

Artificial intelligence is not new. AI algorithms were developed soon after digital computers became available in the 1950s. They remained primitive until machine learning (and associated processing power) started to flourish in the 1990s. Machine learning is conceptually a subset of AI where algorithms that can learn from data are considered intelligent. However, it is the recent rapid advances in reinforcement learning and deep learning, both subsets of machine learning, that have propelled AI into the mainstream.

In reinforcement learning, an agent takes action in an environment, receives a reward (positive, neutral, or negative) as feedback, and moves to the next state. The agent learns the rules to maximize cumulative rewards by learning from the action, reward, and state loop. An example is DeepMind's AlphaGo that beat the human champion of the game of Go. Deep learning uses neural networks with many layers and specialized architectures to solve complex problems. Deep learning is what many people today consider AI, which is the ability of neural network algorithms to solve human perception problems utilizing natural language processing, image recognition, voice processing, and real-time vision analysis, approaches, or abilities.

AI is real. Its benefits are real. It is not a simple rebranding of statistics, machine learning, or neural networks, but a superset of approaches. However, an AI strategy alone will not magically fix terrible products, ineffective marketing, and broken processes that have deep problems. Neither is it something you can implement without the right foundations in place. An organization that struggles to embed simple statistical measurement and forecasting will have difficulty making machine learning work, and an organization that cannot deliver success from everyday machine learning will not find it easy to take advantage of deep learning. A lack of leadership understanding of AI leads to unrealistic expectations for short-term achievements and unawareness of the investment needed not just in people and technology but process and culture change.

Data-Literacy Gap

Data literacy is necessary to make decisions from data and/or trust automated machine decisions. Data literacy is the ability to read tables and charts of data, understand them to draw correct conclusions, and know when it is potentially misinforming. It also includes the capability to communicate meaning to others from data. To deliver maximum benefit from data and make data science successful, advanced data literacy is needed. Advanced data literacy includes knowledge of experimental design, statistical literacy, an understanding of predictive analytics, the ability to make sense of "big data" using machine learning, and capability to extract meaning from unstructured data like text, images, audio, and video.

Unfortunately, advanced data literacy is extremely rare in organizations. The supply of people with advanced data literacy skills should rise, but even then, I am not hopeful the skills will ever be widespread. The challenge is not restricted to data, but applies to any technical domain. Every week, I come across examples of colleagues carrying out manual processes that with basic or intermediate coding skills could be automated. The benefits in most cases would be at least a tenfold improvement in productivity from such automation. However, despite the ability to code on personal computers being widely possible since the early 1980s and the wide availability of free training material, most people see coding as too complicated, not their job, or even a threat. AI and machine learning excite a few people, but my typical colleague does not want to develop advanced analytical literacy skills any more than the average data scientist wants to learn accounting.

The lack of advanced data literacy causes significant problems. Colleagues with just enough knowledge to be dangerous can make the wrong decisions. Simpson's paradox (drawing the wrong conclusion from aggregating data) and survival bias (basing results on those who made it through a filtering process and not the original cohort) are just two pervasive examples. Many analytical pitfalls for the unwary go undetected where a good data scientist will catch.

Competent data scientists will make sure the problem is appropriately structured, apply the right techniques, and draw the correct inferences. Imagine you run a test on your web site to measure the conversion impact of changing the color of the "Order Now!" button. Half the web site visitors at random will see the existing green button (the champion) and half the new red button (the challenger). After a day of testing, the click-through rate on the red button is 33% and the green button 32%.

The product manager is keen to declare another winning optimization and roll out the red button, but the data scientist is not convinced. She wants to know the volume of visitors to run a statistical hypothesis test to ensure the results are not due to chance rather than click-through rate or all the visitors. Some of the visitors seeing the red button may be recently returning and have thereby previously seen the green button. As such, they should not be considered the same as visitors viewing a red button for the first time. Click-through is not typically where the company makes money because many customers click-through to find out shipping costs. It is easy to influence clicks, but real sales are much harder to achieve. She can run a statistical significance test on the sales rate for visitors who were new to the purchasing cycle during the experiment to verify that there is no evidence a red button is better than green.

Data scientists think critically so as not to take results at face value. In one of the first examples of data science in the popular press, US retailer Target was able to determine that a teenage girl was pregnant before the father did.[18] They trained a statistical model on purchases made by women before signing up for Target baby registry and used the model to send targeted coupons for baby merchandise during pregnancy. A father complained to Target about the coupons his daughter received before later apologizing when he found out she was pregnant. A win for statistical modeling? Our data scientist is not impressed, and not just because of the creepiness of the campaign. She knows you can achieve the same result with no data or model. You mail *everyone* baby-related coupons. At least one of the recipients is bound to be pregnant and not to have told her father. Instead, she wants to know the accuracy metrics of the model like the false-positive rate (how many people were wrongly predicted to be pregnant when they were not) before deciding if it is successful.

Relying on basic data literacy alone tends to result in the suboptimal use of data. Often, people think they are making data-driven decisions when in reality they are making hypothesis-driven decisions. A typical example is using a single dimension of data, or rule-based criteria, to make decisions regarding a specific objective (e.g., men between the ages of 25 and 34 are the most likely to submit fraudulent claims, so we should spend our audit budget on them), which is putting the data cart before the objective horse. A data scientist understands that finding customers most likely to submit fraudulent claims is an objective for a predictive modeling problem that can then be used to evaluate all available data to calculate a far more accurate likelihood of fraud at an individual customer level. Predictive modeling and other advanced techniques are opaque to those without advanced data literacy, so it is easy for them to reject the data scientists' solution as too complicated.

When I am ill, I do not attempt to self-medicate. I visit a health professional for advice and trust their experience and knowledge-based recommendations. Relying on experts is also a typical behavior in organizations. Accountants produce financial reporting, procurement specialists conduct supplier negotiation, and production managers direct manufacturing. Rarely do decision-makers challenge or second-guess specialists. However, basic data literacy is widespread enough in most organizations that many decision-makers think they "get it." They believe they are accurately evaluating the data alongside gut instinct to make informed decisions and they are exploiting the data entirely to make correct decisions. Unfortunately, without advanced data literacy, they tend to be way off the mark.

The absence of advanced data literacy is why democratizing data has limits. While more information is better than less, moving data from an Excel spreadsheet to a visual Business Intelligence (BI) tool will not automatically lead to better decisions, just as showing me CT scan images and blood test results will not help me cure myself. I do not have the skills to diagnose and make the right decision on medication and procedures.

Lack of Support

Hiring bright people and leaving them to add business value is a recipe for failure. Data scientists are charged to figure out their objectives and problems to solve, find data, get access, clean data, install software, and find hardware to run their data-oriented jobs. Possibly because many in the organization see data science as just a bigger version of exploring data in Excel workbooks, too many companies have not realized the need to change and take advantage of a new world of data-driven opportunity. IT departments have historically locked down access to software, systems, and data to enforce governance and security standards, and most continue to do so. Data management and data science are not mutually exclusive. The right data management makes data science more effective. The wrong data management suffocates it.

Education and Culture

A common expectation is charging data scientists to be solely responsible for educating the business to make it data-driven. However, data scientists tend to be relatively inexperienced in business process compared to the people they work with and can thereby struggle to change the culture. There may be success influencing individuals (champions) to facilitate data-driven decisions, but if they leave, the cycle must start again with their replacements. Turning data scientists into teachers is not a good use of their time, and we do not expect this of other professions. Advanced analytics training needs to be provided centrally to those who want it. As this will always be a small minority of individuals, if you are serious about becoming a data-driven business, you have to hire like Google. That is, find advanced analytical people who happen to make good product, commercial, or marketing managers.[19]

Creating a data-driven culture must be led from the top down by example. In addition to investing in people and technology, senior executives must be seen to make decisions based on data and demand to see the same behavior from their direct reports. They must measure the subsequent actions and request to see metrics published. This type of role modeling will cascade down the organization. Unfortunately, this rarely happens. Senior executives are in their roles due to their experience and judgment. Often, they demand others to make data-driven decisions while they continue to make gut instinct decisions that have served them well in the past. This behavior sends the wrong signals about the importance of data in decision-making.

Unclear Objectives

Data, insights, decisions, and actions are not synonyms. Data is raw information. Insights are an accurate understanding of that data. Those insights should lead to a decision to do something different and result in beneficial action. A common problem is treating data science as a pure research activity. Data scientists are told to scour data looking for "interesting insights" or answer "interesting questions" without a clear goal. The conventional wisdom is that given freedom data scientists will find nuggets of insight and automagically turn them into money. There are several problems with this approach.

Insight not closely aligned to a business objective and defined use case faces significant barriers to driving a human decision that leads to action, given the cultural difficulties in getting managers to act on data and IT obstacles in productionizing data products. At best, such insight delivers an ad hoc decision support report that may, or may not, lead to action. Desperate to demonstrate their helpfulness, data scientists answer increasingly low-value business questions that the business intelligence teams or self-service data analytics should answer. The organization sees little impact on *Key Performance Indicators* (KPIs) and questions the benefit of the expensive data science team.

There is another reason insight should not be the focus. Let me share an insight from when I was at Dunnhumby. The founders realized early on that if they produced data-driven customer insight for ten million customers, they were not going to get paid ten times more money than if they produced customer insight for one million customers. However, they would get paid ten times more if they used data to sell ten million targeted grocery coupons instead of one million. Dunnhumby was one of the first companies in the world to monetize data on an industrial scale using Tesco and Kroger loyalty scheme data to sell individually targeted media instead of producing decision-support data insights for management as other agencies did at the time. They had discovered the importance of scaling data-driven decisions.

You can use the same data for multiple purposes. Cloud resources can scale massively, and data pipelines can be automated, but people are limited by the hours they can work. Organizations need to be looking for ways to scale the impact of their data scientists. The problem with time spent producing data-driven decision-support insight is that it does not scale. If you want to double the benefit, you have to double the hours spent. Treat pure insight like any lab-based pure research. It should be allocated a research and development (R&D) budget from data science resources with specific long-term strategic goals.

If insight is not the product but the beginning of a process, why is it still given so much focus? The reason is simply legacy. There was very little digital automation in the past, so data analytics attempted to influence human decision-making. Data analysts explored data, presented a document with recommendations, and moved on to the next problem. Analysis results remained on the computer or in a written report, but this is no longer the case. Opportunities for automated machine decisions surpass those from human decision-making. The watershed moment came nearly two decades ago when Google's automated PageRank algorithm demolished Yahoo's human-edited directory of the Web, which was at the time the most visited web page on the planet.

Leaving It to Data Scientists to Figure Out

A typical journey for a data scientist is full of frustrations. A data scientist has a business problem to solve, and one of the first steps is to evaluate the available data in the organization. She finds it is difficult to discover useful data sources, as they are typically not well documented. After some conversations with subject matter experts, she identifies some potentially helpful anonymized data sources, but finds she does not have permission to view them and completes a data access request from IT. IT helpdesk does not understand why anyone would want to analyze data stored outside the data warehouse, but following some explanation, she gains access.

Our data scientist works with samples of the data locally, as it is the only analytical environment to which she has access. The lack of *metadata* (data about the data) and data governance causes her to spend considerable time identifying what the data items mean, scrubbing test data, and reformatting date-time fields. Eventually, she builds an excellent predictive churn model, and the product owner is excited at the prospect of accurately identifying customers at risk of lapsing and is keen to test proactive retention strategies.

For the model to be useful, it needs to run daily on a more powerful machine with minimal manual intervention and automatically output recommendations to the CRM system. Our data scientist realizes the model will need to run on an on-premise virtual machine in the datacenter so requests resources from IT. IT helpdesk does not understand why anyone would want to run an experimental nonoperational application on a server, but after some escalation agrees to add the request to their backlog.

Three months later, the server is provisioned. Excited, our data scientist accesses the machine but finds that she can't install the languages and libraries she needs as security protocols block the Internet. She requests the installation of the R programming language along with libraries and tools she needs. IT helpdesk does not recognize the software and can't understand why the "application" cannot be written using the languages other developers use, namely, Java, JavaScript, or C++. After months of further escalation and investigation, IT determines that the R programming language and libraries requested are not a security threat and agrees to install.

Our data scientist can now configure connectivity and secure access to the internal systems she needs, but during model building realizes she needs to request another library. Another request to IT helpdesk and some weeks later, she has her library. Eventually, there are results to share, and the business stakeholder is pleased with the reduction in churn and an increase in revenue achieved by retaining targeted customers with renewal incentives.

Everyone agrees there is a case for moving from the experimental development model to a productionized operational version maintained by the data engineering team. The development model code was a lift and shift of the laptop code and needs refactoring for operational use. The data engineering team are not comfortable with R code in production so decide to recode in Python. They request the installation of the Python programming language along with the packages and tools they need. IT helpdesk does not recognize the software and cannot understand why the "application" is not written using the languages other developers use, Java, JavaScript, C++, or R....

So it goes on, barrier after barrier, delay after delay, which means a lot of data analytics remains on local machines or shadow IT emerges. Laptop analytics and shadow IT are undesirable for two reasons. First, they encourage terrible development practices. Second, it is less likely that work ends up in production where it can impact consumers. People want to do their job, so workarounds appear that are worse than the problems the original controls were trying to prevent.

Summary

In this chapter, we encountered the problems we are trying to solve. While there are significant achievements, there is also abundant evidence that many organizations are not generating the ROI they expect from their investment in data science. The core causes are knowledge gaps (occasionally chasms), outdated approaches to managing data and producing analytics, and a lack of support for data analytics within the organization.

Data science teams focus too heavily on the algorithms and not the end-to-end skills they need such as collaboration with stakeholders and software development best practice to productionize a data product and get feedback. As data science is a relatively new field, IT does not appreciate the differences with regular software development and the importance of providing high variety, veracity, and volume of data. Organizational silos split the data supply chain across departmental silos and introduce unnecessary friction to data scientists who need efficient data pipelines.

Data scientists are left to overcome barriers themselves, discover data, access data, clean data, and negotiate for computing resources and software with no dedicated support. There is an underappreciation of the breadth of tools, software, and supporting resource needed for the data science stack, which results in inefficient technology use.

Senior leadership does not understand data science leading to unrealistic expectations and a blind spot for the investment needed in process and culture change. It is left to data scientists to make the organization data-centric while senior leaders fail to role model data-driven decision-making. Lack of advanced data literacy leads to bad decisions and disregard for data science recommendations. Without clear objectives or questions to answer, data scientists focus on producing insights instead of scalable data products. In the next chapter, we will start to solve some of these problems.

Endnotes

1. Carlos A. Gomez-Uribe and Neil Hunt, "The Netflix Recommender System: Algorithms, Business Value, and Innovation," Advanced Computing for Machinery, January 2016. *https://dl.acm.org/ citation.cfm?id=2843948*

2. Jim Swanson, Digital Fluency: An Intelligent Approach to A.I., April 2018. *https://monsanto.com/news-stories/articles/ digital-fluency-intelligent-approach/*

3. Clinically applicable deep learning for diagnosis and referral in retinal disease, Nature, September 2018. *www.nature.com/ articles/s41591-018-0107-6.epdf*

4. Revenues for Big Data and Business Analytics Solutions Forecast to Reach $260 Billion in 2022, Led by the Banking and Manufacturing Industries, According to IDC, August 2018. *www.idc.com/getdoc.jsp?containerId=prUS44215218*

5. LinkedIn's 2017 U.S. Emerging Jobs Report, December 2017. *https://economicgraph.linkedin.com/research/LinkedIns-2017-US-Emerging-Jobs-Report*

6. Data Science Platforms Help Companies Turn Data Into Business Value, A Forrester Consulting Thought Leadership Paper Commissioned By DataScience, December 2016. *https://cdn2.hubspot.net/hubfs/532045/Forrester-white-paper-data-science-platforms-deliver-value.pdf*

7. Nick Heudecker, Gartner, November 2017. *https://twitter.com/nheudecker/status/928720268662530048*

8. The Figure Eight 2018 Data Scientist Report, July 2018. *www.figure-eight.com/figure-eight-2018-data-scientist-report/*

9. CrowdFlower 2015 Data Scientist Report *https://visit.figure-eight.com/rs/416-ZBE-142/images/Crowdflower_Data_Scientist_Survey2015.pdf*

10. The State of Data Science & Machine Learning, Kaggle, 2017 *www.kaggle.com/surveys/2017*

11. Gregory Piatetsky, "CRISP-DM, still the top methodology for analytics, data mining, or data science projects," KDnuggets, October 2014. *www.kdnuggets.com/2014/10/crisp-dm-top-methodology-analytics-data-mining-data-science-projects.html*

12. What is the Team Data Science Process?, Microsoft, October 2017 *https://docs.microsoft.com/en-us/azure/machine-learning/team-data-science-process/overview*

13. The Fortune Knowledge Group, "ONLY HUMAN: The Emotional Logic of Business Decisions," June 2014 *www.gyro.com/ onlyhuman/gyro-only-human.pdf*

14. NewVantage Partners, Big data Executive Survey, 2017. *http:// newvantage.com/wp-content/uploads/2017/01/Big-Data- Executive-Survey-2017-Executive-Summary.pdf*

15. Spencer Soper, "Amazon's Clever Machines Are Moving From the Warehouse to Headquarters," Bloomberg, June 2018 *www. bloomberg.com/news/articles/2018-06-13/amazon-s-clever- machines-are-moving-from-the-warehouse-to-headquarters*

16. Jeff Hale, "The Most in Demand Skills for Data Scientists," Towards Data Science, October 2018 *https://towardsdatascience. com/the-most-in-demand-skills-for-data-scientists- 4a4a8db896db*

17. On Earnings Calls, Big Data Is Out. Execs Have AI On The Brain, November 2017 *www.cbinsights.com/research/artificial- intelligence-earnings-calls/*

18. Kashmir Hill, How Target Figured Out A Teen Girl Was Pregnant Before Her Father Did, Forbes, February 2012 *www.forbes. com/sites/kashmirhill/2012/02/16/how-target-figured- out-a-teen-girl-was-pregnant-before-her-father- did/#6b47b6496668*

19. Drake Baer, 13 qualities Google looks for in job candidates, Business Insider, April 2015 *http://uk.businessinsider.com/ what-google-looks-for-in-employees-2015-4*

CHAPTER 2

Data Strategy

The previous chapter revealed multiple problems that may lead to the failure of investments designed to make organizations data-driven. To avoid becoming a statistic in a Gartner or Forrester report on poor returns for data analytics, organizations need to identify solutions. However, before diving into minutiae and delivering specific tactics, it is much better to take a 30,000 feet view and start with a data strategy.

DataOps should be part of a well-thought-out data strategy that lays the foundation for a transformation. Actually, all organizations that want to use data for data-sharing or analytical purposes need a data strategy. The only variation will be the depth of strategy and complexity of use cases. A start-up's data strategy might not need the same detail and span as a multinational corporation, but it should still define a means to prepare for the future.

Why We Need a New Data Strategy

Strategy planning gets a bad reputation for producing vague high-level documents with well-meaning mission statements, matrix diagrams, and ambitions that are forgotten as soon as everyone involved goes back to their desk. However, without a proper strategy, there is a risk of constant reactive firefighting, implementing uncoordinated tactical solutions that misalign resources and waste investment, foregoing opportunities, or, worse, becoming irrelevant. A good strategy makes organizations proactive, aligns teams, pinpoints problems to fix, identifies what not to focus on, and tells them what actions to take to prepare for future opportunity.

To create a good strategy requires an understanding of where you are, objectives for where you want to be, and a plan to reach those objectives. It is also essential to grasp why a new data strategy fit for analytics and distinct from an IT strategy, or even a traditional data strategy focused on governance, is needed.

© Harvinder Atwal 2020
H. Atwal, *Practical DataOps*, https://doi.org/10.1007/978-1-4842-5104-1_2

Data Is No Longer IT

The story starts with the first era of computing. Some of the first users of digital computers were telephone companies, and they serve as an example of how data use has evolved. Early computers like the LEO III were used by telephone companies to calculate bills correctly.[1] The computations were simple. All that was required was call time, duration, and destination, together with a list of tariffs. Once the calculation was complete, and the bills produced, the data no longer had any value. Data stored on punch cards or tapes could be safely archived or destroyed.

Computing advanced through the second era of microprocessors and the third era of personal computers connected via internal networks, but the fundamentals remained the same. Computers and storage were still relatively expensive and, although Management Information Systems (MIS) started to make reporting available, they were still primarily used for operational tasks like inventory management. As a result, IT evolved very rigorous procedures not to waste computing resource and to bulletproof operational processes because getting important tasks such as stock control, orders, and billing wrong was unacceptable. There was a painstaking focus on systems architecture, analysis of solutions and requirements, systems design, code reusability, and documentation even before development began. There was a tight control of system access as unintended changes could be disastrous. Data sharing was limited to applications with specific business processes, but data still had little or no value once those processes completed.

In the fourth era of enterprise computing, data started to be used increasingly for analytical purposes, which spurred the popularity of data warehouses. However, the development of data warehouses still followed past principles. A data warehouse was treated as another operational system with Big Design Up Front (BDUF) to meet specific requirements, long development cycles for change requests, and restricted access. The heritage of IT departments was to treat data as secondary to the systems that process data and the logic applied to it.

The telephone company of the 1960s captured data from landline usage, but this data was a relatively small amount compared to the modern telco. The telco obtains data on broadband usage, location of its mobile phone subscribers, viewing habits of its cable TV viewers, clickstream data from its web site, customer interactions with its CRM system, inventory levels in its stores, location of its engineers, comments on social media, and hundreds of other data items.

The different systems (inherent in telco) *serialize* (convert data into storage or transmission format) and persist data in multiple formats, some of which are structured tabular data, but more as semi-structured machine-generated formats like JSON or XML (eXtensible Markup Language) or unstructured text, audio, and video. Data storage and compute are now very cheap, so telco stores data in multiple data silos such as transactional stores, operational data stores, file systems, software-as-a-service systems, and data warehouses.

A small proportion of the telco's data will make its way to data warehouses and marts. Many teams need to share and combine data across many systems to support multiple and sometimes complex analysis such as fraud detection, financial modeling, offer prioritization, marketing effectiveness, cross-sell modeling, customer lifetime value modeling, regulatory feeds, product affinity, product demand forecasting, A/B testing, cohort analysis, sentiment analysis, churn analysis, and so on.

Data is a critical asset for analytical decision-making long after operational processes like sending a bill complete. Analytical outputs drive business decisions for multiple use cases such as marketing mix, network planning, promotions, pricing, web site/ app optimization, workforce planning, financial forecasting, product propositions, and so on. In most cases, analytical outputs do not need to be perfect, but only achieve an acceptable level of accuracy. This "less than perfect" output is hard for those not acquainted with data science to understand and accept.

Do not underestimate the magnitude of the revolution taking place. Data is now more than an IT application input and by-product. It is an incredibly valuable raw material. Data science and data analytics are now competitive requirements. The difference between doing data science well and badly can be the difference between rapidly taking over the world, and to quote Mike in Hemingway's *The Sun Also Rises*, "gradually, then suddenly" going bankrupt.

Just as any raw material needs processing and refining before it becomes finished product so too does data. The complexity in the volume, variety, veracity, and velocity of data has led to the development of new "big data" technologies to handle it. The multitude of analytical approaches and diversity of use cases require much more flexible and agile use of data. Last century's systems and code-first thinking are not fit for the data-centric world. A new philosophy to treat data as an asset and first-class citizen is required.

The Scope of the Data Strategy

There are many sources, types, and use cases for data, which means the first step is to define the scope of the strategy. The scope cannot be too narrow as it is not easy to isolate analytical data requirements from operational applications. Since the strategy must be data-centric, the data lifecycle and the people, processes, and technology it needs to function form a natural basis for the scope.

The data lifecycle is the stages a unit of data passes through from birth (data acquisition or generation) to death (archival and deletion). While nearly everyone in data management agrees on the start and end points of the data lifecycle, unfortunately, there is no consensus on the stages in between. The European Data Portal defines as few as four stages: collect, prepare, publish, and maintain.[2] A more widely cited definition by Malcolm Chisholm defines 7 phases of a data lifecycle: data capture, data maintenance, data synthesis, data usage, data publication, data archival, and data purging.[3] Since a paradigm is required not just for data governance but a conceptual model for the entire data strategy, a version of the data lifecycle with the following stages is needed:

- **Capture**. The initial step of data materialization within our organization. Data can be acquired from external sources, entered by humans into devices, or generated by machines.

- **Store**. Once captured, files, databases, or occasionally memory persists data in different data structures, data models, and data formats.

- **Process**. Data is processed as it moves through its lifecycle. It will go through ETL, cleaning, and enrichment processes to make it usable in the next stage.

- **Share**. Stored data needs to be shared or integrated between systems to use it effectively. Sharing includes more than transactional data generated by operational systems but also covers intermediate analytical outputs and one-off extracts.

- **Use**. The value from data comes from refining it and fulfilling a use case. The use can be simple data sharing or the outputs of descriptive, diagnostic, predictive, and prescriptive analytics. Consumers of the outputs can be internal or external to the organization.

- **End-of-life**. Whether it is due to regulatory requirements, cost, or declining value, eventually, data must be retired. The process begins with data archival and ends with *data purging* (the permanent deletion of data).

It is essential to know that the stages in the data lifecycle are not linear between capture and end-of-life, which is one of the reasons why people define it in multiple ways. Figure 2-1 shows the stages of the data lifecycle and the flows of data between them.

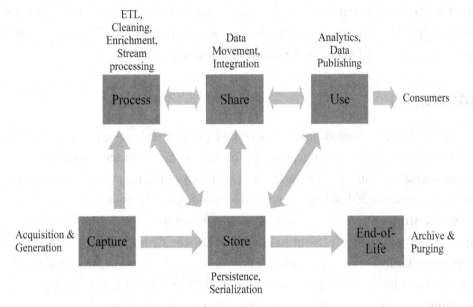

Figure 2-1. *The stages of the data lifecycle*

Data can loop through the phases multiple times. For instance, a loop can be stored, shared, processed, stored, used, shared, and reused. Neither does data have to pass through all stages. The purpose of the data strategy is not to tell us how to capture, store, share, process, or use data but inform the path to take for improvement.

Timeframe

Ideally, the data strategy synchronizes with the timespans of the organization's strategy. However, there can be exceptions. If shorter than 2 years, the strategy will be too focused on short-term objectives and reactive. It is also far harder to make effective improvements in people, processes, and technology in such a short timeframe. Waiting for the end of the strategy period to find out if it is working well or failing badly is not a good idea. So, there must be regular measurement and review.

Reviews are an opportunity to change the way organizations deliver objectives, re-prioritize them, or completely pivot in another direction. Still, the high-level goals of the data strategy should not be chopped and changed frequently as this wastes work. However, lower-level tactical initiatives may change often. As such, the data strategy should facilitate lower-level rapid change if reviews suggest there is a need. For instance, if reviews suggest an objective or objectives are too tactical or poorly formed. A strategy timespan longer than 5 years will result in more uncertain predictions about future technological, analytical, and business change, which increases the probability of objectives changing midway, wasting effort and resources.

Sponsorship

A data strategy is not an algorithm, buzzword, IT project, technology or application, collection of data in storage, department or team, or project or tactic. A data strategy is a set of organization-wide objectives leading to highly efficient processes that turn data resources into outcomes that help the organization fulfill its mission.

For a data strategy to be successful organization-wide, it needs high-level and visible executive sponsorship, ideally from a Chief Data Officer, Chief Information Officer, or Chief Analytics Officer. The sponsor must be someone who believes the organization needs to be data-driven. They must also have the influence and authority to gain the commitment and involvement of leadership teams responsible for processes across the data lifecycle. Crucially, they must also be someone who can engage the business users of data and gain their input. The sponsor can delegate many of the day-to-day activities, but they must be responsible for the overall success of the strategy, lead regular reviews, help eliminate blockers, and communicate updates.

Start with Situational Awareness

There are many different ways to develop a data strategy. The data strategy process and outputs must be intuitive and straightforward for there to be any chance of successful implementation. No strategy is going to be fit for purpose without awareness of context. Decisions about data strategy and subsequent actions become a lot easier and less risky to make when you know your organization, customers, partners, and competencies as well as trends.

The first step is to undertake situational analysis (an understanding of the environment you operate in), which informs strategic objectives for where you want to go. Spend around half the time allocated to the strategic planning process on situational analysis. The analysis focuses on five areas: the organization, people, technology, processes, and data. The data strategy must fit with the overall organization plan, so there must be a clear grasp of the program and what is driving it. The strategy entails an understanding of people, not only people resources aligned to the data lifecycle but also internal customers of data and stakeholders. Development of the data strategy also requires insight into the technology and processes deployed across the data lifecycle. The final step is a deep dive into the data asset that flows through the data lifecycle. The sections are not linear, so they can be completed in parallel or any order.

There are two other dimensions to add to the situational analysis. Situational awareness cannot be restricted to internal analysis only but must include the external environment. The world is not a 2D Boston Consulting Group (BCG) Matrix. It is not even 3D. The world exists in four-dimensional space. The data strategy must also account for time in the form of trends.

Caution   It is crucial during situational analysis not to come up with solutions and objectives. The situational analysis aims to make plan development more robust not to be the plan. The first time you produce a situational analysis, it can take time, but don't give up. It becomes easier to create with each iteration.

The Organization

Questions drive situation analysis. The answers to some questions may readily exist as outputs from other organizational strategic exercises or reports. Other times, insight is gathered from subject matter experts to answer questions. At a minimum, it is necessary to know:

- What are the organization's mission, values, and vision statements?

- What are the organization's strategic objectives and strategic scope? What are the KPIs the organization cares about, and what are the trends?

- What are the organization's strengths, weaknesses, and distinct competitive advantage in terms of product ease of use and range, price, distribution, marketing, service, or processes? Who are the leading competitors, and how do they compete against you?

- What is its product portfolio performance (by product/market segment), how is it evolving, and what is the growth strategy?

- Using gap analysis, where business unit results differ from stated objectives, what are the root causes? Is it lack of skills, wrong structure, wrong systems, or something else?

- Who are the customers for the products, and how do they differ from ideal customers? What are customer needs, and how are they satisfied? What are future customer needs, and how can we identify them? How do customers find us, and what are their pain points in dealing with us? How do we continually improve our relationships with customers? Are they loyal, are they happy, and how do they see us?

- What political, economic, social, technological, and environmental opportunities and threats do we need to consider?

People

An understanding of how prominent business decision-makers use data analytics is required:

- Who are the key leaders and at what stage of the data-driven organization buy-in process are they?

- What are significant stakeholders saying about data analytics and data teams in the organization?

- Which internal leaders are more likely to use data analytics and make data-driven decisions? Who should be the ideal customers for data analytics be?

- Why do internal consumers use data, what are their needs, are requirements fulfilled, and what are their future needs?

For teams involved in the functioning of the data lifecycle, it is necessary to understand the role types, allocation of resources, and how well people are retained and develop skills:

- What is the type and amount of work within the organization compared to available talent supply and demand? Against each role (e.g., data scientist, data engineer, Business Intelligence (BI) developer, or systems architect), roughly measure the amount of full-time equivalent (FTE) allocated to different tasks such as stakeholder management, development/migration, data cleansing, modeling, monitoring, measurement and reporting, and process improvement.

- Is talent aligned with business objectives, stakeholders, and customer needs identified earlier? If not, where are the most significant gaps?

- How well does the organization retain and engage people in teams that support the data lifecycle? What are the turnover rates, why do people leave, and what are levels of job satisfaction and engagement? How well are we growing data talent, and what are the growth paths and changeover points for people?

- Do we have the right learning and development opportunities to build new capabilities and strengthen existing skills?

Technology

It is essential to know the current and planned data technology capability of the organization:

- What are the current and proposed data architectures for the data lifecycle?

- What is the capability and capacity to store and process data? Is there access to scalable computing resources such as elastic Virtual Machines (VMs), *Platform-as-a-Service* (PAAS), or container management solutions like Kubernetes, Mesos, or Docker Swarm. Is there the ability to process streaming data? Is scalable storage such as cloud storage or distributed storage available? What capability to store nonstructured data or non-relational data in NoSQL databases exists?

- What languages and applications do people use in each stage of the data lifecycle?

- What are the latest developments and trends in data-related technology?

- Who are our technology partners? What are their strengths and weaknesses?

Processes

An understanding of the organization's level of data engineering, data analytics, and data science process maturity is vital:

- How well are data analytics projects planned and prioritized? How aligned are plans to the organization's objectives, stakeholders, and customer needs?

- How effectively are the benefits of work tracked? How efficient is the feedback loop to new opportunities? How good is the ability of analytics teams to sell their work? How well do they drive business and customer change?

- How strong is the data analytics capability at delivering data preparation, plots and interactive graphs, web analytics, statistics, machine learning, deep learning, stream analytics, natural language processing, and graph/network modeling? How quickly can we create and validate AI models? Do we have access to a wide range of algorithms? Are models explainable?

- How efficient are ETL processes? What types of data and code testing do we undertake? What is the capability to schedule processes?

- How rigorous is development lifecycle management? Is there effective revision control, configuration management, QA, release and deployment management, operations monitoring, knowledge management, and collaboration?

- How easy is it to deploy data products across customer touchpoints? How long does it take to generate and update reporting? How easy is it to launch experiments? How quick is it to update existing data products?

- How thoroughly do we review and revalidate our output and processes? How often do we reuse existing developments?

The Data Asset

It is crucial to know how well the organization manages data, how accessible it is for multiple use cases, and if it can be enhanced:

- How well is data governed? How is sensitive data secured and privacy protected? Is nonsensitive data easily accessible? Do we have the right *data owners* (individuals ultimately accountable for data quality) and *data stewards* (individuals responsible day-to-day for data quality)?

- How well is current data integrated, and how easy is it to integrate new data? Can *data lineage* (the origin, movement, and processing steps of data) and *data provenance* (the historical record of the data and its source) be tracked across the data lifecycle? How quickly can data be provisioned to end users?

- How effective is *master data management* (MDM) (management of critical data like products, accounts, and customers)? How well is *Reference data* (set of values transactional data can take) maintained? How well is metadata managed so data can be easy to locate and understand?

- Are *data quality assurance* (discovering anomalies in data and cleansing them) and *data quality control,* (determining if data meets a quality goal) successful in ensuring data is fit for its purposes? Is *data integrity* (accuracy of data across the data lifecycle) maintained?

- Is data structured and persisted for the appropriate use case such as a relational model, flat tables, cubes, files, or streams? Is there the ability to process streaming data?

- Does the organization have unique data only it can exploit? What data are we not capturing/storing that we should? What are the useful external data sources we are not using?

At the end of the situational analysis exercise, you will have an excellent understanding of your organization, customers, partners, and competencies. With knowledge of where the organization is and the direction of travel, you can then decide how this fits with the desired future path for data analytics and set realistic objectives for the data strategy. The next step is to determine that future path for data analytics.

Identify Analytics Use Cases

Often, the data strategy discussion starts with "What's our AI strategy?" or "What's our big data strategy?" These questions have nothing to do with improving the organization. The data strategy must align with the company's mission, vision, strategy, and KPIs for it to be useful. An organization's objectives typically cascade down from mission to vision to financial objectives to departmental objectives down to specific objectives for teams (e.g., social media objectives or sales objectives).

Missions, Visions, and KPIs

A mission statement is the organization's overall purpose. It defines what the organization does for its customers, how it rewards owners, and the way it motivates employees. It may also demonstrate corporate social responsibility.

The vision statement is aspirational and focuses on what the organization hopes to achieve or become, typically at or beyond the end of the strategic planning horizon. Organizations often write it in the form of a headline.

The mission and vision statements guide the organization's strategy and KPI objectives, which is where the data strategy intersects. Aligning early means avoiding options with a low probability of buy-in or impact. A minor challenge to alignment is that organizations differ in how they manage strategy and measure targets.

The most common way organizations manage strategy is via a balanced scorecard strategy map. The scorecard will contain multiple strategic goals and objectives tracked in the form of KPI measures against targets alongside the project initiatives designed to hit those targets. The strategic goals are categorized into perspectives, typically targeting improvements in financial, learning and growth, customer, and process outcomes.

Examples of KPIs associated with goals include revenue, market share, margin, net promoter score, the launch of new products, employee satisfaction, defect rates, clinical outcomes, crime rates, and R&D development.

Another approach commonly, but not exclusively, used by digital companies to manage strategy is *OKRs* (Objectives and Key Results). OKR is a goal system invented at Intel and popularized at Google in the form of "we will achieve *objective* measured by *key results.*" OKR objectives are ambitious, memorable, and motivating descriptions of what the organization wants to accomplish (e.g., increase customer lifetime value). Key results are metrics that measure progress and success toward an objective. They are value-based outcomes, not activity-based outputs (things you effect, not things you do). Each objective typically has 2 to 5 key results. Examples include reduce monthly churn from 3% to 1%, increase average subscription size from $99 to $149, and increase annual renewals from 60% to 75%. OKRs typically have a short quarterly cadence, which makes them very agile but also tactical. OKRs can operate with different tempos at different levels of the hierarchy, typically 1 year at the organization level, a calendar quarter, or, less, at the team or initiative level.

The data strategy must be closely aligned to the organization's strategic goals and objectives, regardless of the system used to create them, balanced scorecard, OKR, SMART (specific, measurable, achievable, relevant and time-bound) goals, or something else. The organization's analytical initiatives must support the organization's mission, vision, goals, and objectives, and the data strategy must make delivery of those analytical initiatives as efficient and well-governed as possible.

Ideate – What Could We Do?

Generating multiple options for potential analytical use cases is crucial for comprehending the changes to make and ensuring the data strategy is fit for purpose. Although it is not possible to know all the different ways the organization may use analytics in the future, it is still necessary to be as exhaustive as possible in generating realistic use cases. The volume of options is more important than precision at this stage.

Make sure the broadest range of options for using data is considered by ensuring there is coverage of the four main ways data analytics can help organizations: new product creation, better customer experience, improved operational efficiency, and data publishing, which includes data monetization. To help produce the potential analytical initiatives, also consider the four different types of analytics. Figure 2-2 shows the different types of data analytics: descriptive, diagnostic, predictive, and prescriptive.

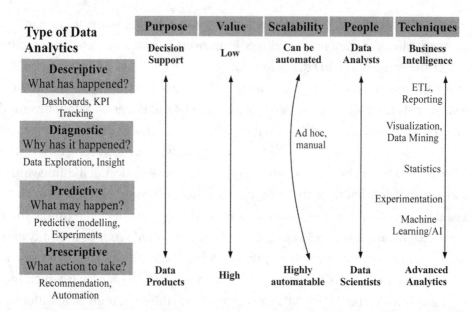

Type of Data Analytics	Purpose	Value	Scalability	People	Techniques
Descriptive What has happened? Dashboards, KPI Tracking	Decision Support	Low	Can be automated	Data Analysts	Business Intelligence
Diagnostic Why has it happened? Data Exploration, Insight			Ad hoc, manual		ETL, Reporting Visualization, Data Mining
Predictive What may happen? Predictive modelling, Experiments					Statistics Experimentation Machine Learning/AI
Prescriptive What action to take? Recommendation, Automation	Data Products	High	Highly automatable	Data Scientists	Advanced Analytics

Figure 2-2. *Types of data analytics*

Although the data strategy must support all types of analytical use cases, the highest value comes from automating prescriptive analytics. Suppose a business has a KPI to reduce financial losses from fraud. Descriptive analytics can be used to aggregate data and produces tables or reports to generate information on historical levels of fraud. Diagnostic analytics can help find patterns and relationships in data to yield insight into why fraud occurs. Predictive analytics can determine the likelihood of a customer or transaction ultimately resulting in a fraudulent financial loss. Prescriptive analytics can recommend the best decision to minimize the cost of fraud. Choices include declining a transaction or customer application, requests for further information, or dynamically changing the offer.

Automating the prescriptive analytics process can have a more significant impact than automating other forms of analytics as it makes possible action in real-time and at scale. Automated prescriptive analytics can also create a considerable benefit by removing gut instinct from decision-making. However, it is also the most complicated analytics to deliver because it requires infrastructure to produce decisions in real-time, an experimentation and monitoring framework to measure the impact of decisions, machine learning models to make predictions, and a highly efficient data supply chain to provide machine learning training and scoring processes with high volume, quality, and variety of data.

The potential analytical initiatives should be described in the form of short, succinct statements such as achieve *the strategic goal or KPI by* delivering an *analytical initiative* using *data and techniques* to *the benefit of the analytical initiative*. A "real-world" example would be "to meet the organization's cost reduction goal, deliver a predictive maintenance solution (using data from machine sensors and machine learning models) to reduce cost from unplanned downtime by $10 million." Ideating back to strategic goals and KPIs ensures alignment with the big goals of the organization.

Quantification of potential benefits ensures trade-offs can be made between initiatives, and against costs. Ideally, the benefits should be estimated using results from similar past actions or small experiments. If this is not possible, then make a prior estimate using subject matter expertise and externally available data. However, the estimation of benefits is not enough. The initiative must be measurable if rolled out for it to even be considered. As initiatives are delivered and results measured, data becomes available to update benefit estimates, increase the accuracy of benefit forecasts, generate better ideas, and improve prioritization from a build-measure-learn process.

Benchmark Capabilities of the Data Lifecycle

A common pitfall when defining strategies is to confuse strategic decisions with tactical decisions. Strategic decisions are long-term and more difficult to change, while tactical decisions are short-term and cheap to alter. While an inaccurate machine learning model can be fixed or ditched at a relatively low cost, not correcting poor data quality is a strategic mistake leading to much higher detriments from poor decision-making and lack of innovation.

People are often so lost in daily minutiae that they can struggle to raise their heads even a few inches to see the more significant, longer-term picture. "Build a machine learning model for product recommendation" is not a 5-year strategy; it is a tactic. "Improve the way we capture, store, process, and share data to make it 10x faster facilitates the creation of machine learning models that can use the output across customer touchpoints, which results in increased sales and retention" is a strategy. Applying tactical solutions to strategic problems (a phenomenon called strategic drift) may cover over cracks for a while, but won't fix root causes or improve the effectiveness of the data lifecycle.

So far, the strategy process has produced an understanding of the organization's context and a set of potential analytical initiatives. Now, the knowledge must help identify the strategic changes required to the data lifecycle to deliver initiatives reliably at speed and scale.

Gap Analysis – What Needs to Change?

To identify strategic changes to the data lifecycle within the organization, the gap between current capability and the ideal journey each unit of data should make through the lifecycle to deliver potential analytical initiatives must be ascertained. This comparison pinpoints strategic decisions to make to each lifecycle stage and improvements needed in better supporting people, processes, and technology to deliver the analytical initiatives efficiently. The situational analysis conducted earlier is designed to make this process easier.

For each analytical initiative, make a backward pass, one stage at a time, through the data lifecycle to better understand requirements compared to how well each unit of data currently moves through it. For example, imagine a retailer with both a physical and online presence. One of their analytical initiatives may be "To achieve the organization's revenue goal, deliver a product promotion recommendation solution, using customer, transaction, and product data in machine learning models to increase revenue per customer from $250 to $275." The business aim is to generate incremental revenue through personalized promotions on products relevant to the customer.

In the use stage of the data lifecycle, data scientists need to combine data from multiple sources into product offer recommendations using machine learning models. Data scientists require Python packages on fast computers with plenty of RAM to build models. The organization needs to serve product offers in real-time to the web site and mobile app when customers are logged in and recognized via an API. The retailer also needs to make the same recommendations available to their email and direct mail marketing systems through the supply of batch files. Data scientists need to schedule, deploy, and monitor models in a production environment. Data analysts need to create reporting using BI tools to track results. However, although data scientists can currently develop models on their laptops, the hardware specification is a constraint, and they have no way of deploying models without relying heavily on other teams.

In the share stage of the data lifecycle, data needs to move from multiple systems into a single system preferably in the format data scientists need (e.g., denormalized flat files for structured data). Data scientists want data from numerous sources as it is likely to improve the accuracy of their models. They also need to identify data, its location, and its content. Unfortunately, data scientists only have access to two isolated data warehouses, which contain anonymized customer and transaction data for the registered web site and app customers or members of its retail loyalty program. As the development of the two data warehouses was independent and the customer details are anonymized, there is no useful or easy way of joining them. Other potentially helpful data sources exist such as comprehensive product detail data, product review data, and marketing campaign data, but they are not accessible or lack metadata and business glossary information to make it impossible to know what the data represents.

In the process stage of the data lifecycle, data needs to move in a series of steps as quickly as possible from one state to another. Data scientists need data engineers to build ETL pipelines from data sources to the target systems they use to create and run their models and get measurements. During processing, data needs to be transformed into the required format, it must be cleaned, and sensitive data needs to be masked or removed. Currently, there is no resource to build automated ETL pipelines that data scientists need. So, they must manually query, extract, and combine the data they need themselves from data warehouses and data marts. Data analysts need to produce reporting, but aggregate counts in data warehouses don't match counts direct from source operational systems. Without the ability to trace data lineage in data warehouses, it is not possible to explain differences with source systems.

In the store stage of the data lifecycle, data is at rest in files or database storage. Data scientists need data in business *event data format*, which is data with a timestamp, event name, event type, and details of the change in state that triggered the event. They are interested in many kinds of events such as new customer registrations, web site visits, clicks, email opens, and sales transactions. Event data allows for very granular analysis, multiple techniques to be applied, and the ability to "time travel" and recreate the state of customers at any past point in time. Unfortunately, the data scientist's primary data source (the data warehouses) only contains aggregated and summarized data. Some raw event data exists in archives of original JSON format, but data scientists don't have access to an analytical NoSQL database with which to load and analyze the data quickly.

In the capture stage, data scientists need to acquire and generate additional data. They need to capture new event data to know when to expose customers to their product offer recommendation for measurement purposes. There are potentially useful external data sources such as geo-demographic data that can augment internal data to make their models more accurate. Alas, capturing new data currently requires a lengthy software development lifecycle (*SDLC*) process to supply it, and the value of new data is much harder to quantify vs. competing projects for the same resource.

The process is repeated for all analytical initiatives (or at least all of those with sufficient estimated benefit) to ensure no gaps are missed. At the end of the exercise, there should be a good understanding of ideal requirements at each stage of the data lifecycle and divergence with current capability.

Define Data Strategy Objectives – Where Do We Need to Go?

With a better understanding of requirements and current capability, the organization can begin to consider objectives for the data strategy. As a start, make a forward pass through the data lifecycle, and at each stage, determine the data strategy objectives needed to simultaneously close as many identified gaps as possible.

Every organization is different with its specific strengths and weaknesses. However, Chapter 1 highlighted many common data analytics challenges across organizations such as poor data quality, inaccessible data, lack of scalable computing resources, skillset gaps, poor metadata management, no access to suitable software, and difficulty getting data products into production. The following paragraphs are not a comprehensive guide but typical of the objectives at each stage of the data lifecycle based on the continuation of the retailer example from the previous section.

The objective for the capture stage of the data lifecycle is to make it as easy as possible to acquire new data in a way that makes its journey through the rest of the lifecycle as frictionless as possible. The retailer must consider the short-term cost of capturing additional data against the long-term benefit of using it. Developers need to give equal weight to how analytics will use captured data as they do for operational purposes. A data item captured to fulfill an order may only be used by the operational system once, but potentially, the data can be used hundreds of times over many years for analytical use cases.

The store stage objective is to save as much potentially useful data as possible in locations, formats, and storage solutions that benefit the process, share, and use stages. The retailer cannot just rely on traditional relational database management systems (RDBMS) data warehouses. The retailer needs to store raw unstructured, semi-structured, and structured data to support multiple analytical use cases including deep learning and natural language processing. The retailer also does not want to lock itself into fixed data structures when storing data (schema on write). Instead, it needs to decide what data to use at the point it needs to use it (schema on read). The retailer needs to ensure that it protects data privacy and only people and systems who need to access sensitive data can do so.

The retailer's objective for the process stage of the data lifecycle is to process data streams or stored data in any format as efficiently as possible to produce output that it can reliably share for use. The retailer needs to decouple data processing engines from storage, so it can handle raw data in multiple formats, whether binary, CSV, JSON, Parquet, or another file type. Raw data needs to be turned into production data as quickly as possible. There must be high levels of data quality assurance and the ability for data consumers to track data lineage.

The share stage objective is to make sharing data between users and systems as simple as sharing code between developers. The retailer wants to get rid of data silos and have the ability to integrate data from multiple data sources.

The retailer's objective for the use stage of the data lifecycle is to ensure it has the hardware and software resources to combine data, create data products for the analytical initiatives it has identified, deploy them in production, and monitor performance. The retailer needs the capability to provision elastic compute, data storage, networks, APIs, and other infrastructure resources in minutes or seconds rather than the weeks and months it currently takes.

At the end-of-life stage of the data lifecycle, the objective is to hold data for as long as it is useful rather than constrain it by artificial capacity limits, and any data that is archived needs to be easily retrievable. The retailer also needs to ensure compliance with any regulations that limit the duration for which it can hold data, including the right of data subjects to have their data deleted.

Setting data strategy objectives for each stage of the data lifecycle makes it easier for everyone to know what they should be doing, rather than aiming for a perfect but rigid end-to-end architecture and data management process. Figure 2-3 shows the alignment between the organizational and data strategy, along with the steps to generate objectives for the data strategy.

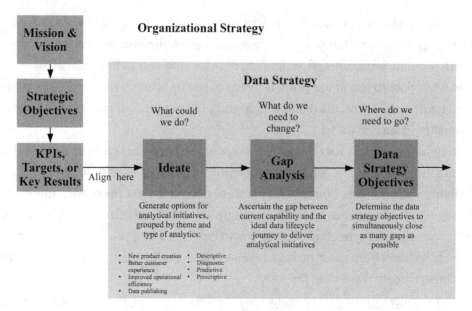

Figure 2-3. *Data strategy objectives creation and alignment to organizational strategy*

Deliver the Data Strategy

The data strategy objectives ensure the organization sets the right goals, but to move in the right direction and reach those goals requires a roadmap of data strategy strategic initiatives to close the gap between current capability and the desired future state. A strategic initiative is a project with a resource budget committed to achieving a strategic objective.

Define Data Strategy Initiatives – How Do We Get There?

Each of the data strategy objectives defined for the data lifecycle stages requires the creation of multiple data strategy initiatives (actions that will achieve our goals). Some data strategy initiatives will be short-term, some long-term, and others will be stages in a sequence of initiatives. The following are some illustrative data strategy initiatives for the example retailer.

To achieve the capture stage data lifecycle objectives, there is a data strategy initiative to ensure that developers make data analytics a first-class citizen. The initiative requires developers to gain sign-off from analytics before they consider projects done, capture data in event data format where possible, and conform to defined naming, format, and value representation standards. Another data strategy initiative involves the acquisition of external data to enhance internal data.

For the store stage data lifecycle objectives, a data strategy initiative includes creating a source archive of raw data in its native format in cloud storage. Hadoop is no longer a solution because it merely replaces multiple data silos with a technology silo. Cloud storage is cheap and accessible, not just by reporting tools and SQL queries but also for programmatic access to connect with as many tools as possible. In addition to the source archive, there is a data strategy initiative to create a centralized analytics data warehouse in the cloud that combines structured and semi-structured data from multiple existing sources. A data governance strategic initiative ensures restricted access to sensitive data by system or user role without locking people out of other data.

To achieve the retailer's process stage, data lifecycle objectives and data strategy initiatives are created to improve data quality and enable users to track data lineage and provenance. Other strategic initiatives include implementing *Change Data Capture* (CDC), tracking inserts, updates, and deletes on legacy data warehouses so data can be updated quickly in the cloud without the need for slow batch copying of data. Moving analytics to the cloud enables data storage to be separated from compute so the retailer can dynamically scale ETL processing to deal with seasonal swings in transactions.

To deliver the share stage data lifecycle objective, the retailer has data management strategic initiatives to create a metadata management solution, implement an MDM solution, and generate a data catalog to make it easier to discover and integrate data. In the cloud, there is a data strategy initiative to develop common aggregations and derivations on the centralized analytics data warehouse. These aggregations and derivations enable multiple users across the organization to reuse the same logic without reinventing their own.

There is a data strategy initiative to deliver self-service capability for the analytics teams consisting of data scientists, data analysts, and data engineers to reach the objective for the use stage of the data lifecycle. The initiative will allow analytics teams access to a range of cloud services, including computing and storage services, data ingestion, data processing, and data preparation tools. Data scientists will also gain access to the software tools and libraries to develop reproducible data products they can schedule, deploy, and monitor independently.

So far, the strategic initiatives are focused on the individual stages of the data lifecycle, but the aim is not to create fragmented projects and solutions. The objective for each of the data lifecycle stages is to remove blockers and bottlenecks to benefit the other stages or organizational goals. Regular reviews, transparent plans, and open communication facilitated by the data strategy sponsor reduce risk of fractured perspectives. However, there is still a need for further projects to support the entire data lifecycle. The retailer needs to align the processes, technology, and people across the data lifecycle with the strategic initiatives.

The retailer requires new skills to support the data strategy. Successful data governance requires data stewards and data owners, data scientists need software development skills, and data engineers need cloud computing skills. There is a data strategy initiative to train internal people or hire externally to meet new demands. To streamline ownership of initiatives and prioritization, a reorganization initiative moves teams involved in the functioning of the data lifecycle into one reporting line under a *Chief Data Officer* (CDO).

The retailer needs to change processes to increase the speed, scale, and reliability of data flow through the data lifecycle. There is a data strategy initiative to create service-level agreements with ownership for performance and availability. There is also an initiative to introduce agile software development methodologies to the data scientists and data engineers.

For technology, there are strategic initiatives to migrate analytics to the cloud and decommission legacy "on-premise" hardware to create a strategic architecture. Although the initial effort to migrate data to the cloud is high, involves duplication of data, and introduces latency due to additional data transfers, the advantages outweigh the costs. The cloud gives the retailer a single platform to manage easily scalable services and provides future-proofing as it can use additional functionality as the use cases increase in complexity. Over time, as more of the retailer's operational workloads migrate to the cloud, latency and duplication of data become less and less of a problem. A tools initiative ensures the retailer's technology selection process prioritizes requirements of the data strategy objectives and initiatives.

Execution and Measurement Plan – How Do We Know if We're There?

With the data strategy objectives and initiatives developed, the organization needs to create a realistic execution plan to deliver them and measure outcomes. Figure 2-4 summarizes the final steps in the data strategy development process.

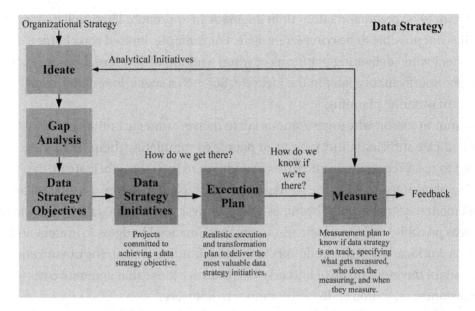

Figure 2-4. *The data strategy initiatives, execution, and measurement steps*

There are options for how to deliver the data strategy execution plan. An organization can produce traditional waterfall project plans with early agreement on how to achieve objectives, gather requirements beforehand to require fewer approvals in future, easy progress tracking, and more straightforward integration of components as the design is complete early on. The downside of this approach is that early requirements gathering and little feedback until the end risk spending much time developing a solution that is not fit for purpose when handed over to users. Even worse, analytical initiatives that rely on delivery of the waterfall project will not be able to start until it's finished.

The preferred approach to delivering the execution plan is to take an iterative, timeboxed, and agile approach to delivery. With limited people, money, and time, there is always a need to prioritize. By ensuring the plan is consistently delivering complete functionality during every timeboxed phase, the organization can continue to work on the most valuable analytical initiatives for the capability it has at that point. The ability to re-prioritize between timeboxes means people always work on the most valuable data strategy strategic initiatives first rather than everything in an all or nothing approach. For example, early in the process, improving data quality and data integration will help multiple analytical initiatives and better use limited resources rather than devoting resources to create capability for a narrow application of deep learning.

As the data lifecycle is improved, the organization can deliver more advanced data strategy and analytical initiatives and iterate on those already in production. However, it is important to be pragmatic rather than dogmatic in approach. There will be scenarios where it is not possible to be completely agile. For example, limited stakeholder involvement when delivering platforms or when working with external vendors could lead to poor performance later in the lifecycle. So, such a scenario requires some elements of waterfall planning.

A common reason why organizations fail to deliver strategic initiatives is that they do not dedicate sufficient time, money, or people to completing them. Teams are expected to resource strategic initiatives in addition to their day job. Instead, day-to-day operating plans must build in the strategic work. Sufficient resource must be set aside to implement the strategy, or it becomes a side-of-desk activity that falls by the wayside. As soon as possible, create realistic resourcing and financial budgets to understand the impact on workloads and the trade-offs to make. If funding is tight, the organization may need to adapt the sequencing of initiatives to prioritize those that generate costs savings by, for instance, migrating off legacy commercial software.

The quote "Culture Eats Strategy for Breakfast!" is commonly misattributed to Peter Drucker. Regardless, it's an important reminder that a good strategy alone cannot carry the day. We also need to take people with us. Many of the changes required to deliver a modern data strategy such as the idea that you don't have to format, transform, and fit data to a relational model before using it are a radical shift from traditional approaches and need careful communication. Part of the execution plan is a data strategy communication plan to explain, align, and motivate colleagues touched by the changes. Alongside the communication plan, the data strategy sponsor needs to ensure that individual personal objectives and incentives align with the data strategy value-based outcome measures. Otherwise, there will be unintended blockers to change.

In addition to the execution plan, there must be a measurement plan to know if the data strategy is on track. The measurement plan should use whatever framework is used by the rest of the organization, such as balanced scorecards, OKR, KPIs, or another method. The measures must be value-based outcomes, not activity-based outputs. Otherwise, there is an inducement to spend time and effort to deliver projects regardless of benefit. The metrics must include measures of speed and agility as well as service-level measures for quality, availability, and reliability. The measurement plan should not just specify what gets measured but also who does the measuring, when they measure, and what happens if strategy execution is well behind or ahead of goals.

Waiting until the end of the data strategy timespan to measure and readjust the data strategy objectives and initiatives is too late. Review strategic initiatives every month or quarter and objectives every year. At the end of the year, the measurements will feed into the next iteration of the situational analysis, ensuring realistic goals and targets are set.

The purpose of the data strategy objectives and initiatives is to deliver benefits from analytical initiatives to achieve the organization's goals. Hence, there is also a need to track the benefit of analytical projects to both to understand their return and the returns of the data strategy initiatives. Having a good measurement plan in place reveals what works well and what doesn't work well. It stops resources from being wasted and allows the organization to optimize the strategy continuously.

From the measurement plan, the ultimate result is three feedback loops: slow, medium, and fast. The fast loop provides learning from analytical initiatives. The medium feedback loop supplies learning from data strategy initiatives. Finally, the slow loop delivers learning on the data and even organizational, strategic objectives. Each feedback loop helps optimize our organization's effectiveness at meeting its goals over different timeframes.

All the components needed to develop an effective data strategy are now covered. Figure 2-5 shows all the steps taken to create a single iteration of the data strategy, which is aligned with organizational objectives and underpinned by robust situational analysis.

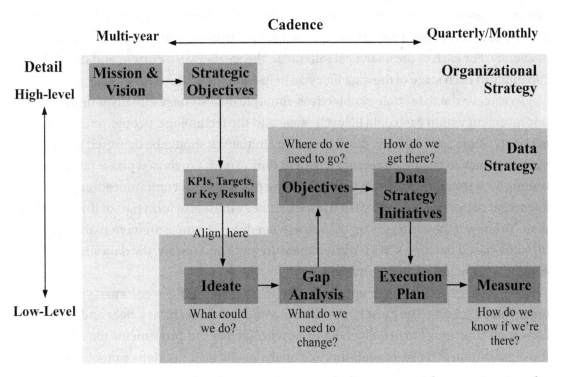

Figure 2-5. *Data Strategy development steps and alignment with organizational objectives*

The approach delivers a data strategy adaptable to change in business strategy, customer needs, technology, and regulation. The method itself is agnostic of the organization's type, industry, or data analytics maturity level.

Summary

This chapter described the need for a data strategy fit for modern analytical uses of data that goes well beyond a traditional focus on operational usages of data or simple data management. There is now as much production data need for analytics as there is for operational applications (the historical domain for IT). A well-planned, well-executed data strategy ensures an organization takes actions that maximize the ability of analytics or data sharing to help accomplish its mission well into the future.

Development of the data strategy centers on the end-to-end data lifecycle and requires sufficient executive sponsorship and buy-in to deliver change. Comprehensive situational awareness is crucial to ensuring that the data strategy leads to successful outcomes aligned to the organizations' mission, vision, objectives, strengths, weakness, and the external environment in which it operates. The situational analysis also makes it possible to understand what needs to change to deliver potential analytical initiatives efficiently. For each of the analytical initiatives, the gap between current and desired capability in each stage of the data lifecycle helps determine the data strategy objectives.

To achieve the data strategy objectives, multiple data strategy initiatives drive improvement within each data lifecycle stage and the technology, people, and processes across its whole span. Ideally, the data strategy initiatives should be delivered using an agile approach to ensure incremental benefit during each timeboxed phase rather than waiting for a waterfall project to deliver at some future date. A communication plan and alignment of personal objectives to the data strategy must also form part of the execution plan. To know if the strategy is on track, there needs to be a measurement plan based on value-based outcomes. With regular measurement and review, the data strategy is continuously adjusted and optimized.

This strategy development approach can be adapted to whatever format your organization prefers. The most important outcome is that you have a clear and consistent strategic plan to deliver data lifecycle efficiency improvements that help the organization achieve its goals through analytics. Tactical solutions cannot solve the problems associated with producing successful data science and analytics. A data strategy must be the starting point. The next chapter begins to look at how the DataOps approach can successfully deliver many of the objectives of the data strategy, starting with Lean thinking.

Endnotes

1. LEO III completed in 1961, Centre for computing history *www.computinghistory.org.uk/det/6164/LEO-III-completed-in-1961/*

2. Putting in place an Open Data lifecycle, European Data Portal *www.europeandataportal.eu/en/providing-data/goldbook/putting-place-open-data-lifecycle*

3. Malcolm Chisholm, "7 Phases of A Data Life Cycle," Information Management, July 2015 *www.information-management.com/news/7-phases-of-a-data-life-cycle*

PART II

Toward DataOps

CHAPTER 3

Lean Thinking

Many of the problems in delivering data science are the result of waste. Sometimes, identifying waste is obvious, including wasted time waiting for data and provisioning of systems or wasted effort cleaning data. However, sometimes waste is not obvious to see. Such instances are squandering expensive, hard-to-recruit talent, or working on the wrong things for the wrong stakeholders.

Waste also exists in manufacturing operations, supply chains, and product development. These fields have successfully adopted a philosophy, *Lean thinking*, to eliminate as much waste as possible, improve quality, and increase speed to market. Lean thinking allows us to analyze data analytics and data science activity to see the waste inadvertently generated by existing organizational processes.

Introduction to Lean Thinking

During the early 20th century, cargo cults developed on Melanesia, New Guinea, and other parts of the Western Pacific Ocean. The indigenous tribal societies came into contact with Western goods like radios, clothing, canned foods, and guns for the first time. Not understanding the manufactured products, cult members believed if they imitated the rituals of the foreigners bringing the "cargo," they too could acquire it. Cult members went to great lengths to copy outsider behavior, creating mock airstrips and control towers; lighting pretend runways and lighthouses; making headsets, radios, and even planes from wood; and staging parade ground drills with sticks for guns.

Unsurprisingly, most cargo cults fizzled out when they failed to deliver the goods. The cults are a warning that copying rituals and practices blindly without understanding underlying principles leads to mediocre results. Lean thinking is a philosophy (or mindset) with values and principles. To apply Lean thinking correctly entails understanding the Japanese origins of the philosophy.

© Harvinder Atwal 2020
H. Atwal, *Practical DataOps*, https://doi.org/10.1007/978-1-4842-5104-1_3

Origins at Toyota

Today, Toyota is the largest motor vehicle manufacturer in the world, overtaking General Motors, which had held the top position for 77 consecutive years ending in 2009. The path of Toyota Motors Corporation from a division of the Toyoda Automatic Looms Works to the dominant position it holds today was not smooth. Toyota struggled during its early years and was on the verge of bankruptcy in 1950. A consortium of banks rescued the company on the condition it let go of excess workers. Kiichiro Toyoda, the founder of Toyota Motor Company, had avoided making layoffs and in the face of labor unrest stepped down as President.

Although Toyota was in a dire situation when Kiichiro left, he laid the foundations for future success. Kiichiro wanted Toyota to "catch up with America," then by far the dominant motor industry in the world. However, productivity levels in Japan were a fraction of US levels, and copying Detroit's economies of scale through a mass production model was not an option. Kiichiro needed to find different approaches to close the productivity and cost gap. By studying Henry Ford's production and management system, especially the conveyor belt system, he discovered one method that would give Toyota an advantage in the decades to come, "*just-in-time.*"

Just-in-time (JIT) involves making just what is needed, when required, eliminating the need to carry inventory, while being much more capable of handling the complexity building a variety of products requires. JIT was the antithesis of contemporary beliefs for how an efficient manufacturing process should operate. For instance, Henry Ford leveraged the conveyer belt system to mass-produce as many cars as possible to bring down unit costs and selling prices without due consideration for market demand. He was famous for saying "... customer can have ... any color [car] so long as it is black." This adage is definitely not JIT.

Taiichi Ohno was a brilliant engineer who moved to the Toyota motor company from a sister Toyoda company in 1943. He continued Kiichiro's challenge to "catch up with America," gradually developing the *Toyota Production System (TPS)* through a process of experimentation. Taiichi used observations of other companies and his experience of working on the machine shop floor to add further, radically different ways of organizing production to just-in-time flow.

Toyoda's automated looms were designed to shut down automatically if they detected a broken thread. This concept was extended to a "stop cord" at Toyota where any worker could stop the line if they found a defect. Stopping a line would get an operator fired in America, but in Toyota, it was a mechanism to make problems highly visible for investigation and prevention. Taiichi studied the way the American Piggly Wiggly grocery store handled inventory, stocking just what they needed by reordering based on a visual stock replenishment signal. The study led to a pull system at Toyota where each process only draws what it needs from the previous process, which then only produces what it needs to replace. The pull system was in contrast to traditional push systems, which produce products based on future forecast demand rather than actual consumption.

As an ex-shop floor manager, Taiichi would make inexperienced managers go to the *gemba* (Japanese for the place where work takes place) and perform root cause analysis to fix problems using the *5 whys technique*. Sakichi Toyoda, the founder of Toyoda, originally devised this technique. The method involves asking "why?" repeatedly five times to find the source of the problem and the solution to stop it from happening again. Whereas Kiichiro saw inventory as dead money, Taiichi took it a step further. He aggressively reduced inventory to reveal hidden waste such as stocks that customers aren't going to buy, distribution systems that lose track of inventory, and spare production to cover defects introduced by processes.

Taiichi saw the Toyota Production System as far more than a nonstock production system. In his book, *Toyota Production System: Beyond Large-Scale Production*[1], Taiichi refers to TPS as a system for the absolute elimination of waste. He identified seven wastes, known as *muda* (uselessness in Japanese), that added no value between the customer placing an order and Toyota receiving the cash. The seven wastes are as follows:

- **Overproduction**. The most significant waste is producing too much or too early. It results from making large batch sizes with long lead times and leads to an irregular flow of materials. It is also a primary cause of other forms of waste.

- **Waiting**. Materials or components waiting for processing are a waste of time.

- **Transportation**. Moving material from one location to another for processing adds no value to the product.

- **Overprocessing**. Doing more than is required by a customer, or using tools that are more expensive or complex than needed, results in higher costs and unnecessary asset utilization.

- **Excess motion**. Making people and equipment move more than necessary wastes time and energy.

- **Inventory**. Work in progress (WIP) and finished products in storage result from waiting and overproduction. Excess inventory ties up capital, has to be tracked or gets lost, hides defective processes, requires storage, becomes superseded, and may need offloading.

- **Defects**. Inspecting production, rework, or scrapping all consume resources, introduce delays, and impact the bottom line.

TPS also identifies two other forms of wasteful practices to be eliminated. *Mura* is an irregularity or nonuniformity that causes unevenness in workflow causing workers to rush then wait. *Muri* is unreasonableness that requires workers and machines to work at an unsustainable pace to meet deadlines or targets.

While TPS covers operations, Toyota also developed a unique approach to product development. The *Toyota product development system* differs from the TPS and focuses on the processes, people, and tools required to create new models much faster than competitors. Toyota typically designs a new vehicle in as little as 15 months, which compares very favorably to the industry average of 24 months. James Morgan and Jeffrey Liker identified the 13 management principles of Toyota's product development system in the book "The Toyota Product Development System: Integrating People, Process and Technology."[2] Some of the fundamental principles are as follows:

- **Set-based concurrent engineering**. Instead of picking a single design to refine early on, Toyota front-loads the development process and explores multiple options concurrently. They converge on the optimal solution by gradually narrowing the design space. This process means options are left open for as long as possible and decisions made at the last possible moment.

- **System design by a chief engineer**. A chief engineer is both project leader and senior engineer during product development. She is responsible for the business success of the product and ensuring that functional development teams integrate their work into the project successfully. The chief engineer is expected to fully understand customer needs and the system-level design needed to take the product from concept to production.

- **Develop expert engineers**. Toyota develops engineers to have specialist knowledge of their area. They are expected to gain deep mastery of their field before they join the development team in a specific role.

- **Learning and continuous improvement**. Toyota schedules three 2-hour sessions after each project for reflection (known as *hansei* in Japanese) to understand how to improve processes and increase personal growth.

- **Align through simple visual communication**. Communication is expected to be as simple as possible within the organization. Toyota uses multiple visual tools to communicate and solve problems such as templated *A3 reports* (named after the paper size they use) and *Team boards*.

Implementation of TPS initially met resistance within Toyota, but by the mid-1960s, it gave the company a significant lead over Nissan (its main domestic competitor). However, TPS was still ignored outside Toyota until the 1970s when the economic slowdown encouraged other Japanese manufacturing companies to copy its features successfully.

By the early 1980s, US and European auto manufacturers, consumer electronics companies, and computer builders came under intense competitive pressure from cheaper, more reliable, and better designed Japanese products forcing many to the brink of failure. In response, western companies scrambled to implement their initiatives to improve quality and efficiency such as Six Sigma, total quality management (TQM), or variants of TPS throughout the 1980s. The Toyota product development system, seen internally within Toyota as the source of its competitive advantage, took much longer to be replicated by others. It was only during the 1990s that it started to influence the way other companies developed products.

Lean Software Development

It was the 1990 release of the book *The Machine That Changed the World*[3] that gave the name Lean Production to Toyota's TPS (which had been commonly known as JIT production). Lean thinking became increasingly popular and started to make its way beyond manufacturing to include Lean supply chains, Lean order processing, Lean healthcare, Lean airlines (low-cost carriers), and, highly relevant for data analytics, Lean software development.

Mary Poppendieck was a process control programmer in a US videocassette manufacturing plant in the early 1980s when the company began to be dramatically undercut by Japanese rivals. The plant decided to copy the new Japanese JIT approach to stay in business. There were no domestic consultants to offer support, so the implementation was done through a "learn by doing" procedure until it succeeded.

Mary continued to apply a Lean approach as she progressed to manage the IT department at the plant and then moved into product development. After leaving the plant, she found herself leading a government IT project and was shocked to come across the waterfall methodology for the first time. Contrasting the mediocre success rate of the waterfall approach with her prior successes, Mary Poppendieck decided to write a book to counter the prevailing orthodoxy on how to manage software projects with her husband Tom in 2003. The book, *Lean Software Development: An Agile Toolkit,*[4] became an immediate success by tackling the problems that gave software development a poor success rate.

Mary and Tom Poppendieck realized that, despite some differences, the software development process could be considered analogous to manufacturing product development and the Toyota product development system. The most significant difference is that software, unlike a vehicle, is not just developed once, but expected to be modified multiple times over its life. So, making it easy to change is a high priority.

Learnings from the Toyota product development system apply to frequently changing products because it takes an empirical evolutionary approach to new product development. The original Prius product concept did not deterministically specify vehicle dimensions or a hybrid engine, but only a fuel economy target and roomy cabin requirement. Only late in the cycle did the development team choose the hybrid engine fresh from the research lab, which is something they could not have done if they followed traditional vehicle development approaches. The Poppendiecks believed software development should also pursue an evolutionary empirical process as the best way to deal with constant change. From the Toyota product development system and TPS, the Poppendiecks developed Seven Principles of Lean software development.

Principle one is *Eliminate waste*. For Toyota, any steps that don't add value between the customer placing an order and the company receiving the cash is considered waste. In software development, the clock starts ticking when you receive a request to meet a customer need (e.g., a new product feature) and stops when the updated software is deployed to address the need. Software development waste comes in many forms including partially done work, building features customers didn't ask for, multitasking between projects, waiting for others to review and approve, defects that need fixing, superfluous processes to follow, or excess motion through travel because development team members and managers are not colocated.

Principle two is *Build quality in.* According to Toyota, there are two types of inspection. First, inspect for defects after they occur. Second, inspect (control variables) within a process, that is, control for defects as the product is being made. To achieve high quality, create processes that make it hard for errors to happen in the first place making inspection for defects redundant. If early elimination of mistakes is not possible, products should be inspected immediately after small process steps to prevent them from undergoing further processing (resulting in more defects later in the process). The idea is to avoid passing on poor quality. Stop the line when defects are discovered so the cause can be found and fixed straight away. Lean software developers take a *test-driven development* (TDD) approach. With this approach, they write unit and acceptance tests before development code is written and integrate code and test as frequently as possible. If the code fails the test, they do not add any new code but roll back changes and fix the problem.

Principle three is *Create knowledge.* The Toyota product development system is designed to generate and integrate as much knowledge as possible. Engineers are expected to schedule time for learning and *kaizen* (continuous improvement of processes in Japanese). Engineers are expected to communicate as simply as possible and work with colleagues in an *obeya* (a war room in Japanese) to speed up communication and decision-making. Software development is a knowledge creation process. Knowledge creation occurs during the development process and from customer feedback. Lean software developers codify knowledge gained from other developers to pull information as needed for future products. A Lean organization also develops knowledge to improve the development process itself. Development teams set aside time for experimentation and process improvement.

Principle four is *Defer commitment.* Toyota uses set-based concurrent engineering to experiment with multiple options leaving choices open until they must make a decision. Detailed plans *a priori* are not seen as healthy. Taiichi Ohno believed businesses that did not change plans in response to circumstances could not exist for long. So, Lean software developers should not spend large amounts of time gathering detailed requirements to create meticulous designs months in advance. They should aim to make reversible decisions based on changing business requirements and customer feedback and, if that is not possible, timetable irreversible decisions for the last possible moment using all the information they acquire up to that point.

Principle five is *Deliver fast*. It took Toyota just 15 months from formal board approval of the clay model design in September 1996 to start mass production of the Prius in December 1997. This speed was at a time when the standard for developing new models in the United States was 5–6 years. Like Toyota, Lean organizations do not believe speed and quality are mutually exclusive. Instead of slowing down to be careful, Lean software developers continually improve their processes to increase quality and ability to reliably add features their customers value. Achieving improvements in quality and reliability are not possible without eliminating a considerable amount of waste. Lean developer agility and waste reduction give the organization a cost and speed to market advantage.

Principle six is *Respect people*. In the Toyota product development system, people doing the work are empowered to make decisions for themselves. Teams are expected to self-organize to meet goals, be dedicated to developing deep technical expertise in a specific area, and be led by an entrepreneurial chief engineer who creates the vision, sets the schedule, and makes trade-offs. Lean organizations believe the best ideas for improving process come from the gemba (the place where value is created in Japanese). In software development, the people doing the work day-to-day are experts in a way their managers cannot be. Frontline workers have the best perspective on improving methods of working, while managers are in a better position to train teams, ensure people have the resources to succeed, and build the system to keep work flowing. Lean software development teams are small cross-functional teams with in-depth domain knowledge that are accountable for taking a product from hypothesis to launch and then implementing continuous improvement with autonomy.

Principle seven is *Optimize the whole*. Toyota is careful to ensure the flow of work through the whole system is optimized even if parts of the system are suboptimized. Mary Poppendieck discovered this counterintuitive lesson implementing JIT at a tape plant. Previously, running the plant's most expensive machinery at full utilization (to maximize ROI) caused inventories to build up. Upon implementing JIT, the stocks disappeared and the total efficiency of the whole plant increased despite introducing idle capacity for the most expensive machines. Software development is also full of negative feedback loops. The pressure to add new features causes testers to become overloaded, which delays the detection of defects. Delay only allows developers to add more defects, which means more work for testers. Thus, the problems snowball. Lean organizations optimize the whole system. There is no point wasting time optimizing part of the process if there is a more significant bottleneck somewhere else. Optimizing the whole may seem like common sense, but teams in their silos making independent process improvements may pile extra workload pressure on downstream teams without increasing total throughput.

By concentrating on economies of flow instead of economies of scale, TPS was the antithesis of conventional wisdom for generating manufacturing efficiency since the time of Henry Ford. In the same vein, Poppendiecks' ideas for delivering new software products were a radical departure for how to release software (dating back to the first days of computing). The Lean software development movement has been hugely influential in shaping modern agile software development, which we will discuss in the next chapter.

Lean Product Development

Another Lean movement has made an equally significant impact on product development in the last decade based on the ideas formulated by Eric Ries in his 2011 book, *The Lean Startup*.[5] Don't let the title of the book fool you. The concepts apply to nearly any new internal or external product or service development and organizations of all sizes and industries. Although the movements started by Ries' book are called *Lean startup* or *Lean product development*, they combine ideas from other fields. Ries synthesized Lean thinking for software development and product development with the concepts of entrepreneur Steve Blank and design thinking to create an approach fit for developing products under conditions of uncertainty.

Until recently, both startups and software development followed the same patterns for taking an idea or requirement to a finished product. Startups began with an idea and spent months and years building and refining a "perfect" product, while developers spent months and years gathering requirements, building detailed designs, coding, and testing a "perfect" release. When ready, the startup would release its product to an expectant public, only for the public to, more often than not, fail to excite because the product did not meet their needs.

In a similar vein, software developers would deploy their software only for users to reject it because requirements gathered months ago no longer fit the current purpose. In both cases, failure was based on a legacy belief that software products must be perfect and complete before release to customers. This legacy belief is grounded in expensive computing and costly developer time as well as difficulty (and costs) related to making frequent software changes. Many of these costs and constraints no longer exist. Lean thinking argues the efforts involved to create a better development process are worthwhile if a better product can be delivered.

The reason startups fail is because they base their ideas on assumptions that may not be correct. Spending months building a product or feature based on untested assumptions is a waste of time. Ries argued that the way for a startup to maximize its chances of success is to use the scientific method. Instead of abandoning all process and taking a "just do it" approach when faced with an uncertain probability of success for a new service or product, use a methodology to test the vision continuously.

Ries advocates the *Lean startup methodology*, which is a set of methods to quickly discover if a proposed business model or product is viable, and if it is, iteratively improving it in short development cycles. The starting point is the belief that every new product is an experiment to answer the question "*should* this product be built?", not "*can* it be built?" Ries based the methodology on a set of core concepts and principles, *validated learning, build-measure-learn cycles*, a *minimum viable product* (MVP), *split testing, actionable metrics,* and *pivots*.

If every startup is an experiment, it is important to test its basic assumptions sooner rather than later through validated learning. Validated learning is a unit of progress generated by evaluating a hypothesis on customers to validate an idea. The first stage of validated learning is to create an MVP to gather the maximum amount of feedback on the initial assumptions from customers as soon as possible. Feedback tells you if customers value your idea and provides a basis to test and refine further assumptions in a series of build-measure-learn cycles. Each set of learnings should generate additional ideas for improving the product.

The best way to validate hypotheses is to build a feature from the concept, run split test experiments to measure the cause-and-effect relationship of adding it, and learn from the metrics. The metrics must be actionable, that is, align with your goals *and* help decision-making. Examples of actionable metrics include per customer revenue, repeat purchase rates, and volume of transactions. The opposite of actionable metrics are vanity metrics. Although they make you feel good, they neither help you achieve goals nor assist decision-making. Running an expensive marketing campaign and measuring the increase in web site visits or social media likes don't tell you if spending more on similar campaigns will lead to higher profitability or drive you to bankruptcy.

At some point in the experiment, optimizations delivered by the build-measure-learn cycles reach a point of diminishing returns where customer feedback metrics don't validate initial assumptions. At this point, the startup needs to decide if it accepts the situation or if it believes it can reimagine the product. Testing a new direction and hypothesis is known as a pivot. A pivot is not an admission of failure. Persevering with an idea customers do not value is a failure. Many famous companies have successfully pivoted during their history. Nintendo had many previous lives as a playing card maker, vacuum cleaner manufacturer, instant rice producer, taxi company, and even a "love hotel" chain before settling on electronic games and consoles.

Lean Thinking and Data Analytics

Data analytics and data science have the characteristics of both a production system and a product development system. The flow of data from initial capture to use by consumers resembles the flow of raw materials through a manufacturing process to create a finished product. It is not just the development of end-use outputs, such as dashboards or machine learning models, that are analogous with product development. The intermediate processing stages should also be considered as part of the product rather than projects. Projects have an end. Products (hopefully) have a long shelf-life before replacement or redundancy. Processing tasks like ETL pipelines, data cleansing, and data enrichment routines typically run for a very long time even if they must change over time.

Lean principles derived from manufacturing, software development, and startups are highly relevant to data science and analytics. The starting point is to stop thinking of independent layers of technology and functions when creating data analytics solutions to thinking of the flow of data instead. Figure 3-1 shows the flow of production data to meet use cases as opposed to the traditional view of the horizontal hardware and software layer diagram demonstrated in Chapter 1.

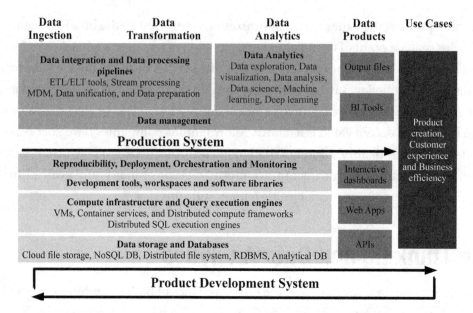

Figure 3-1. *Data analytics as production and product development systems*

Seeing Waste

Most teams are too busy delivering outputs or maintaining systems to stop and think about how and why they work the way they do. Organizations are happy to apply the scientific method to data use or product development, but very rarely employ it to improve their activities. They passively accept there is a "way to do things here." In data science and analytics, there is much waste when you look closely. The seven wastes Poppendiecks identified can be used to find and eliminate such waste.

Partially done work is the first waste. It is the equivalent of inventory in the manufacturing process. Partially done work doesn't help an organization make decisions or improve the customer experience. So, it is a waste. Data analytics is complicated, but not thinking about interpretability or explaining solutions clearly to stakeholders can delay implementation unnecessarily. Other examples of partially done work include documented requests that data engineers or data scientists haven't started work on, untested code and data pipelines, unmonitored pipelines or models, work that needs recoding from one language to another (e.g., R to Python) for production, and failing to track the benefit of the data product.

However, the biggest wastes are work that doesn't go into production. For example, work stuck on a data scientist's laptop because it does not fit into the overall application (or codebase) or the business never considers it to make a decision using gut instinct instead. There is no partial credit for technically excellent work that is never used. Either the work gets used or it is waste.

Extra features are the counterpart to overproduction in manufacturing and considered the worst waste if they do not help data consumers make decisions. Additional features in a data product should not be confused with *data features*, which are individual attributes of data observations. Examples of surplus features are charts and metrics on dashboards that are not actionable, unused data derivations, or data item extracts that cannot help solve the problem under scrutiny. Sometimes, extra features are a result of stakeholder requests for everything but the kitchen sink because they don't know what they need. Other times, they are the result of excited data team members who want to try out cool new functionality instead of just solving the problem. There should be a deep predisposition against adding new features unless there is a definite and immediate need. Development should start with an MVP that can be iterated to add new features later as needed.

Extra processes result in an unnecessary effort that does not create value. This category of waste is very varied. Extra processes include duplication of data and transformations in multiple data stores across the organization, using a complex algorithm when a simpler one would have worked as well or relearning the task because knowledge is not captured and reused. Unreproducible work due to lack of *configuration management* (the management of source code, software, data, and other assets during the development of the data product) is another major cause of time waste among inexperienced data science teams. Writing bespoke code to create system connectors and manage ETL pipelines instead of using an off-the-shelf tool is superfluous effort by data engineering teams. As an ex-manager of mine once said, "documentation is like sex, any is better than none." However, too much bureaucracy can also be a bad thing. Creating documentation that is not looked at, producing detailed project plans and estimates that are impossible to adhere to, and providing status updates that decision-makers do not use are extra process wastes.

Data analytics and data engineering are sophisticated disciplines that require deep focus and concentration to solve problems. *Multitasking* imposes high switching costs as we move from one task to another and wastes time. Research by the American Psychological Association shows even short mental blocks caused by context switching can cost up to 40% of someone's productive time.[6]

Multitasking also wastes the potential early contribution of work. James Womack and Daniel Jones illustrate the impact through a simulation of mailing ten newsletters. Mailing each newsletter requires four steps, fold paper, insert the paper into an envelope, seal the envelope, and stamp the envelope. Working in parallel on each newsletter involves sequentially performing an operation (fold, insert, seal, or stamp) ten times before moving to the next operation. If each operation takes ten seconds, then the first newsletter is complete after 310 seconds. However, if newsletters are tackled in sequence, the first newsletter is complete after just 40 seconds, then another every 40 seconds after that. Not only is the first newsletter produced faster, but any problems with paper folding, envelope size, sealing envelopes, and the stamp are detected much earlier. So, we need to focus on the fewest possible assignments at any point in time to identify problems and deliver work early.[7]

Waiting for people, data, and systems is a massive cause of waste in the data analytics process. Examples of waste include time spent finding and understanding data, waiting for approvals, waiting for people to be assigned, waiting for software and systems to be provisioned, waiting for data to be made available, and waiting for jobs to run on slow machines.

Excess motion from separate and disperse teams causes waste from handoffs and travel. Every handoff (tasks handed from one team or team member to another) leaves behind tacit knowledge of the data, which is very difficult to capture in a document. If we only retain half the knowledge after each handoff, only 6.25% of the original understanding is retained after just four handoffs. Knowledge transfer is done most effectively through face-to-face discussion and interaction. Traveling to do this becomes a barrier to dialog and can add days of waste over the course of a year.

The seventh waste is *defects*. Correct problem definition is surprisingly hard in data analytics. Solving the wrong problem, usually due to poor communication and unaligned expectations, is considered defective work. Data, as well as code, can have bugs. And, poor-quality data is the number one challenge cited by data scientists. Defects in data and code lead to wasted effort finding and fixing problems. Writing good code on top of bad data is merely a case of garbage in, garbage out. The aim should be to uncover all defects in the data as soon as possible. The later a problem is detected, the more expensive it is to fix, especially if your customers find it. Data engineers should include a set of mistake-proofing tests so poor-quality data does not enter data pipelines. Whenever we discover a new defect, stop the line, fix the problem, and add a new test so the error cannot cause a problem again.

Often added to the original seven is an eighth waste called *not-utilizing talent*. With the plummeting cost of data collection, data storage, computing, and software, people are the most expensive and valuable resource in the data analytics process. So, the maximum use of their talent should be a priority. Good data analysts, data scientists, and data engineers are hard to find and expensive to hire, but their skills are often wasted. Too often, people lack training and direction, are given tasks like reporting or data cleaning below their ability and qualification level, are not engaged in decision-making processes, or are not trusted with self-service access to systems and data.

Value Stream Mapping

Lean thinking tools encapsulate Lean mindset values and principles. Many of the tools began in manufacturing but are equally applicable to data analytics. Value stream mapping is a Lean tool for visualizing waste in processes. The process starts by grouping similar types of work together, such as building dashboards or creating machine learning models, and choosing a typical project for each group.

A horizontal timeline is drawn from the customer's point of view starting at the point a need is recognized (or when a request is submitted) and ending when the data product is in production. On the timeline, plot significant steps involved in the end-to-end process without excessive detail. Plot activities that add value above the horizontal timeline and wasteful activities below. Figure 3-2 shows an example value stream map plotted for the predictive churn model introduced in Chapter 1.

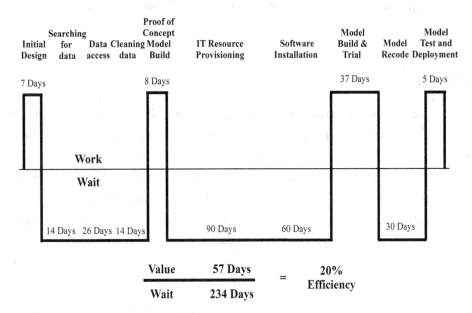

Figure 3-2. *The value stream map for a predictive churn model*

The finished value stream map answers two questions. First, how long does it take to create a data product? Second, what proportion of elapsed time is spent adding value? This added value is known as the process cycle efficiency. As shown in Figure 3-2, it took a total of 291 days from the time our data scientist received the initial request to deploy the model in production with 20% process cycle efficiency. Seeing the overall picture helps identify necessary delays as well as wasteful ones. Not all waiting is waste. The churn model ran as a split test experiment with customers for a month to measure benefit.

The irony is that business stakeholders want results yesterday and often do not wait for statistically robust experiment results. Yet, they do not show the same intolerance for avoidable waiting in the rest of the process. None of the teams involved, except the stakeholder who requested the churn model to improve customer retention, may have realized how much time was wasted waiting. The teams will be busy working on multiple other tasks in parallel, laboring under the false impression of being productive and efficient. Often, there is no single value stream owner, so visualizing the waste across it makes it easier to convince everyone involved that something needs to change.

Value stream mapping should also be used to measure the process cycle efficiency of production data flows from capture to use. The map identifies waste from waiting for data to be provisioned and processed as each unit of data passes through the data lifecycle. Typically, delays occur when there are handoffs between systems owned by different teams.

Deliver Fast

The first time you undertake value stream mapping, you will almost certainly realize you can move more quickly. The faster you go, the more you can learn and the better the results you can achieve. In traditional organizations, deliver fast means cutting corners and asking teams to perform heroics by working late nights and weekends. This stores up problems and leads to "deliver slow" in the long run as all the burnout, hacks, and shortcuts show up as time delays in the process. Code and data defects add delay, technical debt makes it slow to manage changes, and too many tasks in the process produce queues that further slow down the flow.

The American statistician W. Edwards Deming was highly influential in changing the perception of Japanese products from inferior copies to market-leading high-quality goods in the post-war era. It was Deming who introduced the Japanese to *statistical process control (SPC)* to monitor processes and detect significant variation early enough and prevent bigger problems. Deming also made Japanese managers think of production as a system from suppliers through to customers that requires continuous improvement.

Deming stated that a system has fixed maximum capacity and potential for quality. So, you can't push more through the system without negative consequences. Wishful thinking, fear, and financial incentives can't change the maximum capability of a system. Only improving the system itself can make a positive difference. Lean has thinking tools and measures, cycle times, and queuing theory that can help improve the system and make teams deliver faster.

Since waste shows up as a time delay, the best way to quantify performance is to measure the *average* end-to-end cycle time. For data product development, this measure begins from the moment a need is recognized or a request submitted to deployment in production for all development activities. For production data flows, measurement is from the point of capture to first use for all units of data in the data lifecycle. The faster an organization can make good decisions from data, the better it can serve customer needs.

The mathematical study of queuing or waiting lines is queuing theory, which is a significant branch of the operations research disciple that makes business decisions using advanced analytical methods. Since data product development and production data flows involve queues in an end-to-end process, queueing theory can help us reduce the average cycle time it takes work to exit the process.

Queuing theory tells us that a flat arrival rate, a small steady processing time, limiting utilization below capacity, reducing the number of items in the queue, and multiple servers lead to lower average cycle times in a system with fixed capability. Both requests for new data product development and newly captured data tend to arrive in bursts. We can hold requests in a backlog and release them steadily to teams doing the work. Parallelized processing can evenly process newly captured data with horizontally scaling computing resource or algorithms, which is the equivalent of adding multiple human servers to assist a line.

Variation in the size of work negatively affects cycle time as large batches of work lead to high variation. There is a greater risk of something going wrong on a 6-month project than a 6-hour piece of work. For instance, anyone who has dealt with the aftermath of failed data loads knows that a 6TB file transfer is a much different project than a 6MB transfer.

Although data analytics is not software development, the concepts of *releases* and *iterations* are useful to adopt. Releases result in shipping a consumable product to customers. Iterations are smaller units of work between releases that are sometimes, but not always, released to customers. The solution to highly variable work size is to make release cycles of complete development as short as you can handle, determine how much work can be done in the cycle, and never take on more than the cycle can handle. Instead of delaying a release, leave work out for future iterations, accept a less accurate machine learning model, use fewer data items in a pipeline, use a more straightforward dashboard, or produce only headline data insight.

Small complete chunks of work create a reliable, repeatable velocity and help determine the team's capacity. Instead of lots of partially done work, create a lot of smaller units of complete work. For data pipelines, instead of processing large batches of data, move to mini or micro-batches or even streaming data using an event-driven architecture that responds to data as soon as it arrives.

Managers often ask teams to squeeze in one more task without asking for anything else to be dropped believing the way to get more done is to pile on more work. Queueing theory shows that average cycle times surprisingly interact with utilization rates. Road traffic does not go from usual speed to immediate standstill when road utilization goes from 99.9% to 100% of capacity. It starts to slow down long before that point as more and more vehicles join the highway.

Beyond 80% utilization, average cycle times begin to increase exponentially. This slowdown effect is why most computer servers contain slack or are set to scale well below 100% of capacity. While this thinking is healthy for operations, the math has not made its way to the rest of the organization. Many managers do not realize that creating large projects and utilizing everyone at 100% is the surefire way to deliver anything slowly.

To deliver fast, we need some spare capacity in our servers, databases, data pipelines, and people. One way to achieve this with people is to allow time for side projects and self-learning that is not time-critical. Another way is to unclog the system of work that will never be done. Items of work in the system absorb energy that can be better spent producing useful output. Work has to be reprioritized, reestimated, and have status updates even when making no progress. Instead, we can cut out all the items you will never get around to doing and all those items that are nice to have but not critical. If what remains still exceeds the capacity of your system, it is a justification for additional resource.

Pull Systems

Pull systems are Lean thinking's solution to limit work to the capacity of the system and to deliver on-demand. They derive from Toyota's systems for managing parts in the supply chain. It is difficult to forecast the demand for parts accurately, but a shortage of even a single screw can bring an entire production line to a halt and lead to a massive cost of delay while teams wait for delivery of the missing piece. The temptation is to overproduce parts to minimize the cost of delay and *push* them into the production process whether they are needed or not.

Instead of attempting to forecast the number of components required or carry excess stockpiles, Toyota created a system where assembly line stations visually send a signal when they need new parts. The visual cue is a *Kanban card* that contains details of the component to *pull* from the supplier. The card passes to the supplier who makes to order the exact replenishment quantity in the sequence as cards arrive and dispatches it back with the card. By progressively reducing the number of cards in the system, Toyota can decrease work in progress and reduce all three forms of waste, muda (uselessness), mura (unevenness), and muri (unreasonableness).

Instead of having managers push work to teams, Lean teams break large work into smaller consumable batches of work and add them to a queue. Teams pull from the queue to begin work. The length of the queue should only be large enough to even out the pace of work. Anything larger generates waste by creating partially done work, increasing average cycle times, and gives stakeholders the impression you are working on their requests when the team has not prioritized the work. Accepting a customer request but not starting a piece of work may have significant negative impact on relationships after a couple of months of radio silence or sending positive vibes than a realistic conversation upfront.

Pull scheduling has many advantages over push scheduling. The workflow is even, teams never pull more work than they can deliver, and pull systems give us more options. Options are precious rights without obligations because their value increases with uncertainty. A financial option always trades at a premium to its intrinsic value because there is a chance in future that the underlying asset price will change enough to make the option more valuable. The more volatile the underlying asset price, the more valuable the option because the potential for profit is higher.

In the real world, we are willing to pay more for a flexible airline ticket, which is an option to change flights than a nonrefundable non-changeable ticket because we know plans are unpredictable and the cost of last-minute tickets is high. Options thinking also applies to product development as Toyota discovered with set-based development and Eric Ries with MVPs and split testing of new features. MVPs are options to develop a better product if the initial version is successful, and split testing provides low-cost options to roll out new features if customers value them.

In pull scheduling, as soon as the team has the capacity, they have the option to decide what to work on next based on the latest priority and value information without disrupting existing work in progress. In a push system, with a fixed path for tasks and overloaded teams, there is far more disruption if plans change much like missing a flight with a non-flexible ticket.

Data pipelines can also be push or pull based. The popular distributed streaming platform Apache Kafka is a good example of pull-based design benefits. Kafka uses a publish-subscribe pattern to read and write streams of data between applications. Producers of data do not directly send it to consumers of data (known as subscribers). Instead, the application producing data sends a stream of records to a *Kafka topic* (a category of data) hosted in a *Kafka broker* (a publishing server). A topic can have one, many, or no applications who subscribe to consume its records.

The developers of Kafka considered a push-based system with brokers pushing data to consumers, but this has downsides. The broker decides the rate at which to push data for all subscribers and can easily overwhelm one or all of them if they cannot consume the data quickly enough. A push-based broker also has to decide whether to push new data immediately or batch it up. Pushing single records at a time can cause them to queue at the subscriber, wasting the purpose of trying to reduce latency. Instead, the developers opted for a pull system. In a pull system, the subscriber can decide the optimal record batch size and fetch frequency to reduce latency and can catch up at any time by fetching unprocessed data from the topic if it falls behind the rate of data production.

Lean thinking makes it possible to identify waste and manage the flow of work and data to deliver as quickly as possible. However, to produce a new machine learning model or data pipeline rapidly from idea to deployment in one complete releasable batch still requires the creation of a system that makes it possible. The first stage is to identify the significant barriers in existing processes and start to dismantle them.

See the Whole

Lean thinking encourages us to step back and see the whole picture to increase performance rather than make isolated improvements. The *theory of constraints (TOC)*, introduced by Eliya M. Goldratt in his 1984 book *The Goal*[8], views the performance of a system as being limited by its most significant constraint. Just as a chain is only as strong as its weakest link, the biggest bottleneck limits output of any system. Eliminating the largest bottleneck causes the next biggest limitation to become the constraint for the *whole system*.

The theory has implications for prioritization. Instead of trying to solve every problem, concentrate resources to systematically find and remove only the biggest bottlenecks in the whole process. Any other improvements are just an illusion. There is no point buying data scientists the fastest, most expensive laptops if it takes them months to gain access to data. And there is no point migrating an ETL process to Apache Spark to dramatically speed it up if it feeds a reporting process refreshed weekly.

Constraints fall into four categories: physical, policy, other nonphysical, and people. Physical constraints are typically equipment related. Policy constraints are rules and measurements that prevent the system from achieving its goal. Other nonphysical constraints can include a lack of clean data. People constraints include lack of resource and skills, but also intensely held beliefs and inertia that limit the consumption of data analytics. Policy and people constraints are the most common and hardest to overcome because they are deeply entrenched. Constraints are the reason hiring an army of data scientists without unblocking their obstacles is wasting their talent.

The theory of constraints has a methodology for finding and eliminating constraints known as the five steps. Step one is to identify the major constraints. Value chain mapping can help here. Other methods include asking team members, looking for areas where work often has to be expedited through escalation (or hounding), and looking for accumulations of partially done work. Step two is to maximize throughput using the resources you have including checking and fixing the quality of work or data going into the bottleneck, upskilling employees or offloading work, and processing on to other teams and systems that are not so constrained.

Step three is to subordinate the rest of the system to the constraint. Since the rest of the process has by definition spare capacity, it should continuously work at the same pace as the bottleneck and never overload it or fail to deal with its output. Subordination may require people and processes who are not part of the bottleneck to slow down, which can seem counterintuitive. If this fails to "break the constraint," that is, move it somewhere else, then step four is to elevate the constraint. Elevate by investing additional resources in the bottleneck, hire more people, provide additional training, switch to new technology, capture more data, or bypass human decision-making. The final step is to repeat the process as part of a continuous improvement cycle. Either the constraint is broken and a new constraint needs eliminating, or more work is necessary to remove the existing bottleneck.

It is natural for people to want to jump from step one (identify the constraint) to step four (throw more resources at the problem), especially as policy constraints are the most common form of restriction. However, throwing more resource at a problem initially slows things down as it takes time for new people and systems to become operational. Instead, we should tackle policy constraints head-on.

Policies and rules become accepted mantra, and organizations adhere to them long after forgetting the reason for implementing them. Often, these policies are a result of accommodations of historical constraints that no longer exist. For example, we no longer need to accommodate the risk of accessing nonsensitive data, limited processor power, expensive storage, slow networks, lack of memory, or code that is hard to change. Policy constraints often put departments into conflict so are rarely solved from within. It usually takes an external party to come in and point out the problems, but sometimes, those who are responsible for the policy are unaware of its impact on the flow of work and can be persuaded to change it.

For the removal of constraints to be effective, we must be sure we are solving the root problem and not the symptoms. The theory of constraints incorporates a set of tools to solve problems called *thinking processes* to answer three questions. What to change? What to change to? How to change? The tools are used to follow a multistep buy-in process, gain agreement on the problem, achieve consensus on the solution, and overcome obstacles to implementation.

Root Cause Analysis

There are two different techniques you can use to find a root cause to answer the "What to Change?" question correctly, *current reality tree (CRT)* from the theory of constraints and 5 whys from Lean thinking. 5 whys is suited to finding a relatively simple root cause of symptoms with few interactions with other root causes. CRT is more structured and designed to uncover relationships between issues.

5 whys determine the root cause of a problem by repeating the question "why?" and iteratively using the answer to form the basis of the next question. The process starts by assembling a cross-functional team familiar with the process to investigate and define a clear problem statement. A facilitator asks the team "why?" as many times as needed to identify the root cause of the problem. Toyota believed asking "why?" five times was needed to make the root cause clear, but that is not a hard and fast rule. The facilitator should ask as many questions as necessary to get beyond the symptoms. The facilitator also has an important role to play in keeping the team focused and avoiding the blame game.

At the end of the process, the facilitator helps the team identify countermeasures to fix the root cause problem and assigns responsibilities. For example, the team can use the 5 whys to find the root cause of the long cycle times for data science product development by asking questions like this:

- **Why is the average cycle time so long?** Before using data, it can take weeks to clean.

- **Why is it taking so long to clean data?** Because there are many defects in the source data including missing data, data type mismatches, duplicate records, transformation logic errors, and truncation of data.

- **Why are there so many defects in the data?** Not enough testing takes place to ensure defective data does not enter pipelines or databases.

- **Why is there not enough testing?** IT teams do not see data quality as a high priority.

- **Why do IT teams not see data quality as a top priority?** IT teams do not understand how consumers use data and the problems poor data quality causes.

The final why leads to a root cause the team can act upon. Even with the same problem statement, the root cause may be different if the knowledge of the people involved is different. The problem may also have multiple root causes, and the only way to identify them is to ask a different sequence of questions each time. An alternative approach if the system is involved is to use a current reality tree.

A CRT is a tool to identify cause and effect relationships via a visual diagram. The assumption is that we can trace every problem in an organization that appears as a symptom back to a much smaller number of core root causes. Fixing these core root causes results in multiple connected and dependent problems disappearing.

To construct a CRT, a small group with knowledge and experience of the organization and its systems agree on a list of no more than five to ten problems (*undesirable effects (UDEs)*) to analyze. The UDEs must have a measurable negative impact, be clearly described, and should not be a list of missing solutions. An example might be lack of training in data science methodologies. Other examples of UDEs may include a high turnover of data engineers, managers making decisions based on gut instinct, data scientists spending excessive time cleaning data, or taking a long time for data science products to reach production. The team may also choose to set a boundary for the system represented by the CRT. An example might be scope of authority or influence.

The team graphically constructs the CRT using a chain of cause and effect reasoning from the UDE using if/then logic (*if* this occurs, *then* this effect results) where ellipses represent an *and* condition. The chain of reasoning links UDEs, and during the process, additional intermediate undesirable effects need to be added to join everything together. The process continues until the approach converges on a few core root causes. Figure 3-3 shows a simplified CRT for three UDEs with two core root causes.

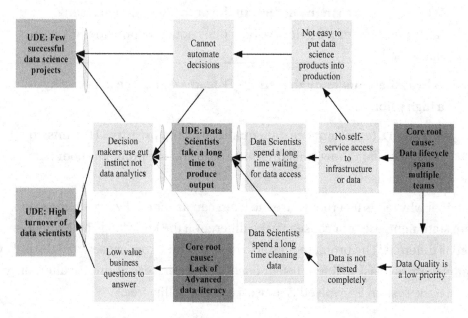

Figure 3-3. *A simplified current reality tree*

The CRT itself does not tell you how to handle the core root causes. There are other thinking processes for that. But, it does identify where to focus effort and avoid the suboptimization trap of resources wasted trying to solve multiple UDEs.

Summary

Lean thinking revolutionized the whole global manufacturing sector, the entire industries such as air transport and software creation methodologies, and the route startups take to success. Lean thinking can also transform data analytics, which most organizations do not yet recognize as a production system or product development system in its own right. A mental shift is required to think of data products rather than data projects, and data flows rather than layers of technology or organizational functions. Once our perspective changes, it becomes possible to apply the Lean thinking mindset and the scientific method to improve process efficiency significantly.

For a production system and product development system to be useful, an understanding of what our customers value is needed, so time and effort are not wasted building something they do not want. Unfortunately, when it comes to data analytics and data science, our customers often do not know what they need, or in the case of data engineering, what solution works best. The Lean startup methodology deals with the uncertainty by first building an MVP and then iteratively improving the product through validated learning and feedback. The faster we can learn, the more successful we can be. So, sustainable increase in delivery velocity should be a high priority if not outright obsession.

To deliver what our customers need as efficiently as possible, any wasteful steps that do not help us achieve our goals must be removed. A value stream map is an eye-opening way of identifying waste in our processes whether it is production data flows or data product development. All avoidable waste eventually shows up as additional time delays in processes. Average end-to-end cycle times for data flows and data product development can be reduced by eliminating the eight categories of waste, which are partially done work, extra features, extra processes, multitasking, waiting, excess motion, defects, and not-utilizing talent.

Once recognizable forms of waste are eliminated, the flow of work can increase. Traditional management methods to deliver fast such as piling on more work, wishful thinking, creating fear, or dangling the carrot of incentives can only work in the short term because they pile up problems for the future. The only way to deliver fast sustainably without compromising quality is to improve the capability of the system to deliver.

Queuing theory tells us the most efficient way to reduce average cycle time is to break work up into small uniform size batches and not take on more tasks than we can handle. The objective is to move a piece of work from start to deployment as quickly as possible so we don't end up with partially done work. The theory of constraints tells us the biggest bottleneck limits the output of the entire system. The theory also tells us it is pointless trying to solve multiple problems in isolation. We need to optimize the whole. Resources should concentrate on eliminating only the most significant constraints using root cause analysis tools to ensure we fix core problems, not symptoms. Root cause analysis may require a cross-functional effort from those with the knowledge and authority to make changes and can be the most prominent implementation challenge to overcome.

With improved flow, we can move to pull scheduling which evens out the workflow, prevents overcommitment, and provides options for what to work on next. The beginning of projects is the worst possible time to make plans and commitments because it is when we have the least information about the entire process. By deferring commitment until the last possible moment, we can pull work from a queue based on the most up-to-date information from which we have to make decisions.

Lean thinking is a mindset so it is never "done." It requires the constant effort of continuous process improvement, kaizen, and continuous performance measurement to aim for perfection (creating valuable data products and data pipelines with zero waste). In the next chapter, we take a close look at Agile development, which is a set of methodologies for rapid software delivery closely related to Lean principles.

Endnotes

1. Taiichi Ohno, Toyota Production System: Beyond Large-Scale Production, March 1988.

2. James Morgan and Jeffrey Liker, The Toyota product development system: Integrating People, Process and Technology, March 2006.

3. James Womack, Daniel Jones, and Daniel Roos, The Machine That Changed the World, October 1990.

4. Mary and Tom Poppendieck, Lean Software Development: An Agile Toolkit, May 2003.

5. Eric Ries, The Lean Startup: How Constant Innovation Creates Radically Successful Businesses, October 2011.

6. Multitasking: Switching costs, American Psychological Association, March 2006, *www.apa.org/research/action/ multitask.aspx*

7. James Womack and Daniel Jones, Lean Thinking: Banish Waste And Create Wealth In Your Corporation, July 2003

8. Eliyahu M. Goldratt and Jeff Cox, The Goal: Excellence In Manufacturing, 1984.

CHAPTER 4

Agile Collaboration

The agile software development movement arose in 2001 as a reaction to traditional software development approaches, which struggle to deal with uncertainty. The founders of the movement chose the term *agile* to exemplify their view that software development must be adaptive and responsive to change. In addition to adaptiveness, it is how people work together that makes agile different from other software development approaches. Agile teams are expected to be cross-functional and self-organizing and to collaborate closely to come up with a solution.

Like software development, data science and analytics has to deal with tremendous uncertainty. The uncertainty goes beyond the engineering effort required for software development. Data science is applied research with ever-changing data that requires an iterative approach with hard-to-estimate effort to deliver results. Agile approaches seem well suited to deliver data science and analytics. Some attempts have been made to devise agile data science methodologies including Russell Jurney's publication of Agile Data Science 2.0 complete with its agile data science manifesto.[1] However, before applying agile approaches to data science and analytics, it is essential to understand the agile mindset, frameworks, and practices.

Why Agile?

Agile software development practices are now the dominant approach to delivering software. In Stackoverflow's 2018 Developer Survey of over 100,000 developers around the world, 85.9% of professional developers stated they use agile software development approaches in their work.[2] The rapid adoption of agile software development practices is a direct result of the problems with previous project management methodologies.

© Harvinder Atwal 2020
H. Atwal, *Practical DataOps*, https://doi.org/10.1007/978-1-4842-5104-1_4

Waterfall Project Management

Traditionally, organizations used the *waterfall* project management approach to deliver plans. The waterfall model originated in the construction and manufacturing industries where the cost of late change is excessive or design changes are not even possible once work starts. The model entails freezing requirements early. After all, it is not easy to increase the number of floors in a building after its foundations are complete.

Waterfall project management takes a sequential approach with requirements defined upfront. The project is planned in its entirety followed by design, build, test, and implementation phases. Progress flows only one way in waterfall project management from one stage to the next, which is analogous to the way water only cascades in one direction (downward). The waterfall model is a form of predictive project management. Requirements are fixed, but resources and time required to deliver them are estimated variables.

The waterfall model was the earliest SDLC approach used for software development. As software became more complex, limitations of the waterfall model started to become apparent. Gathering accurate requirements is difficult because customers do not precisely know what they want at an early stage. It is hard to accommodate change easily because once a step is complete, there is no going back. So, customers are kept well away from developers to avoid rework and missed deadlines.

The final stage of a waterfall project delivers working software. However, at this point, the world has moved on and the original requirements are typically out of date. It is tricky to estimate resource and time requirements for complicated software. So, project managers create detailed project plans to appraise them and allocate tasks in command and control fashion. Not only are the estimates very likely to be wrong, but telling software developers precisely what to do and when may be demotivating and likely lead to shortcuts. As a result of the shortcomings inherent to the waterfall approach, software is prone to late delivery, bugs, or miscalculating customer needs.

Agile Values

As a reaction to overly planned and micromanaged waterfall software development, lightweight frameworks emerged in the 1980s and 1990s including *Rapid Application Development* (RAD), *Dynamic Systems Development Methods* (DSDM), *Scrum*, and *Extreme Programming* (XP). These software development frameworks are adaptive rather than predictive project delivery approaches. Time and resources are fixed variables and features change according to what the customer wants.

However, these lightweight adaptive project management approaches failed to gain much traction until 17 leading developers met at the Snowbird ski resort in Utah during February 2001 to discuss commonalities between them. Apart from coining the umbrella term agile, they came up with the *Manifesto for Agile Software Development*. Many now refer to it as the Agile Manifesto, which includes four core values based on their experience of successful teams and projects.

"We are uncovering better ways of developing software by doing it and helping others do it. Through this work we have come to value:

- **Individuals and interactions** over processes and tools

- **Working software** over comprehensive documentation

- **Customer collaboration** over contract negotiation

- **Responding to change** over following a plan

That is, while there is value in the items on the right we value the items on the left more."[3]

Agile teams focus more on intrateam communication and worry less about the tools and practices they use. Delivering software that does what the customer wants is more useful than providing a detailed specification document to describe it. Treating the customer as part of the team recognizes that customers cannot accurately define requirements at the start of the project and embracing continuous collaboration ensures their involvement throughout the process. Plans are rarely perfect. So, it is essential to change direction and deliver what the customer wants instead of working to deliver an outdated plan.

In addition to the four values in the agile manifesto, the 17 original signers also came up with 12 principles to guide practitioners implementing and executing with agility[4]:

- Our highest priority is to satisfy the customer through early and continuous delivery of valuable software.

- Welcome changing requirements, even late in development. Agile processes harness change for the customer's competitive advantage.

- Deliver working software frequently, from a couple of weeks to a couple of months, with a preference to the shorter timescale.

- Business people and developers must work together daily throughout the project.

- Build projects around motivated individuals. Give them the environment and support they need, and trust them to get the job done.

- The most efficient and effective method of conveying information to and within a development team is face-to-face conversation.

- Working software is the primary measure of progress.

- Agile processes promote sustainable development. The sponsors, developers, and users should be able to maintain a constant pace indefinitely.

- Continuous attention to technical excellence and good design enhances agility.

- Simplicity – the art of maximizing the amount of work not done – is essential.

- The best architectures, requirements, and designs emerge from self-organizing teams.

- At regular intervals, the team reflects on how to become more effective and then tunes and adjusts its behavior accordingly.

Agile software development is *not* a methodology. It is more than a framework like Scrum and XP and their practices such as sprints and pair programming. Agile software development is the umbrella term for a collection of independent frameworks and practices that follow the values of the Agile Manifesto. Many of these frameworks and practices predate the Agile Manifesto or borrow from other philosophies such as Lean thinking. Like Lean thinking, agile is a mindset. It takes more than adopting a few token agile practices to improve project delivery.

Agile Frameworks

Agile encompasses a variety of methodologies that implement the values of the Agile Manifesto. The 12th annual state of agile report listed Scrum, Scrum/XP hybrid, Kanban, and *Scrumban* (a Scrum and Kanban hybrid) as the most widely used agile frameworks by delivery teams. However, the *Scaled Agile Framework* (SAFe) is by far the most popular methodology for scaling agile practices across multiple teams in the organization.[5]

Scrum

Scrum is the most popular and well-known agile framework. Scrum suits iterative product development and applies to non-software development projects too. Scrum is straightforward in theory, but hard to master in practice.

There are three key roles within a Scrum team. A *Product Owner* is responsible for outcomes and prioritization. The *Scrum Master* is accountable for team focus, coaching, removal of impediments, and application of Scrum principles and practices. A three- to nine-person cross-functional development team is responsible for deciding how to get work done and complete it.

The development team is egalitarian and self-organizing. Not even the Scrum Master tells them how to deliver. The Product Owner, together with the team, creates a prioritized task list known as the *product backlog*. Work takes place in *timeboxed* iterations called *sprints*, which are fixed lengths of 1, 2, or 4 weeks, but no longer than a month as short iterations reduce risk. A sprint starts with a *sprint planning* session where the product owner and team agree to pull a sprint's worth of work from the product backlog into a detailed list of tasks known as the *sprint backlog* to achieve a *sprint goal*. Once the sprint backlog and goals are agreed upon and the development team fixed, no further changes can be made except under exceptional circumstances by the product owner.

Each day, the team, Scrum Master, Product Owner, and team meet in a short standup meeting known as a *daily Scrum* where every team member updates the group on the previous day's achievements, plans for that day, and impediments to progress. At the end of the sprint, the team is required to deliver a complete tested new feature known as a *shippable increment*, which is demonstrated to the Product Owner and other stakeholders during a short *sprint review* meeting. The meeting is an opportunity to review the final output against original sprint goals. The final sprint event is a *sprint retrospective* when the team looks back on the sprint and identifies actions for improving the way future sprints run. Figure 4-1 shows the agile Scrum lifecycle.

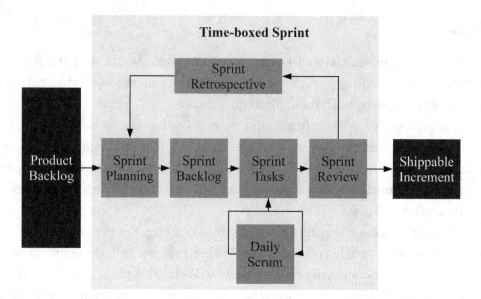

Figure 4-1. *The Scrum agile lifecycle*

Scrum uses further artifacts to manage delivery in addition to the product backlog, sprint backlog, and shippable feature. Work is controlled via a *task board*, which can be a physical board drawn on a wall or whiteboard or implemented in software tools like JIRA. Although Scrum task boards started with five columns, the most common format now has just three columns ("To do," "In progress," and "Done"). Index cards or sticky notes, each representing a task, are added or moved to the appropriate column of the task board to reflect their status. The purpose of the task board is to visually disseminate information efficiently and create a focal point for collaboration, especially during the daily Scrum.

Progress on Scrum projects is tracked on a *burndown chart* that plots work remaining in tasks, effort hours, and team days or another measure against days for a sprint burndown (or sprints for a release). Task boards and burndown charts are examples of *information radiators* in agile terminology, which are highly visible charts where all team members can see the latest information at a glance. The concept of information radiators has its roots in visual control systems used in the Toyota Production System.

XP and Scrum/XP Hybrid

Scrum is a framework for managing product development. It is not a process, technique, or method for building products, which makes Scrum ideal for combining with other frameworks such as XP and Kanban. Many teams implementing Scrum are combining practices from XP.

It is the focus on technical practices that differentiates XP from most other agile frameworks. XP has a set of 13 primary practices grouped into team, planning, programming, and integration practices. How teams work together is a big part of XP, so four of the practices relate to teams that should be no bigger than 12 people. The first practice is *sit together* where teams communicate in an open space large enough to accommodate the whole team with barriers or divisions where appropriate. The next practice is *whole team* where a cross-functional group working as one unit possesses all necessary skills for the project to be successful. The third practice is an *informative workspace* where information radiators allow an observer to get an idea on how the project is going within 15 seconds of walking into team space. The final team practice is *energized work* where teams must work at a sustainable pace to avoid burnout.

Pair programming is unique to XP and is the first programming practice. Two people sit side-by-side at a machine, and each takes turns to code while the other watches and reviews. By continually discussing approach, the code typically has fewer bugs and is more efficient. *Test-first programming* (synonymous with TDD) is the next practice. It involves writing a failing automated test before writing the code to get early feedback on issues and decrease bugs. The code is then written to pass the test, which is usually a *unit test* that checks the smallest testable unit of software like a function. Instead of expending substantial effort on the design before implementation, XP teams create conditions to minimize the cost of change. One way to do this is to invest in the design every day, making changes at the last responsible moment in proportion to the need for change in a practice known as *incremental design*. Restructuring existing code without changing its behavior, known as *refactoring*, takes place relentlessly in XP and supports incremental design by keeping code simple.

Planning practices in XP start with *user stories*, which are short descriptions written by or for users to describe a meaningful use for the product. The concept of user stories originated in XP to replace large requirements documents with just enough detail for early estimation of benefits, costs, and constraints. XP does not prescribe a specific format for user stories although the "role-feature-reason" template invented by Connextra in the United Kingdom is the most common structure.

The *weekly cycle* practice is the iteration equivalent of a weekly timebox in Scrum. The team holds a planning meeting at the start of the week to review progress, have customers pick stories to work on for the iteration, and break stories into tasks that individuals can embrace responsibility. The goal is to have deployable software at the end of the week. Longer-term planning takes place through the *quarterly cycle* practice.

During a quarterly planning meeting, the team meets to plan the *theme* or themes for the quarter. A theme is a significant focus area that can be addressed using stories that are usually aligned with larger organizational goals. The team then decides which stories to add to the quarterly cycle to tackle the themes. If the team finds it difficult to estimate some stories because they don't fully understand the technical or functional aspects, they do focused research or prototyping in a timeboxed iteration called a *spike*. The planning meeting is also an opportunity to reflect on progress, identify internal fixes and external bottlenecks, understand how well the team is meeting customer needs, and focus on the big picture. The final planning practice is *slack*, which is similar to the concept of spare capacity in Lean thinking. Slack involves adding low-priority stories to the weekly and quarterly cycles; if the team falls behind, they are dropped to prevent overcommitment.

The final two primary XP practices belong in the integration category. The *ten-minute build* practice aims to run an automated build for the whole codebase and run tests in under 10 minutes. The time limit is chosen to encourage teams to run tests and get feedback as often as possible. The other practice is *continuous integration*, where integrating code transitions into the larger code base and integration testing at least every 2 hours. Finding problems before making more significant changes makes them easier to fix. Figure 4-2 shows the XP practices described so far in the XP lifecycle.

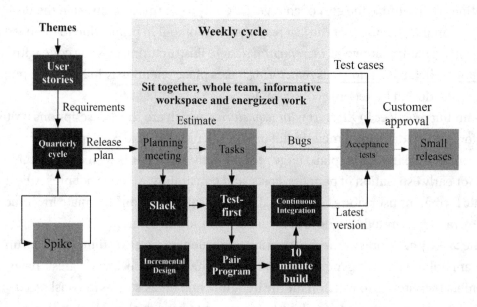

Figure 4-2. *The XP agile lifecycle*

Kanban Method

The Kanban method (usually just referred to as Kanban) is the application of Toyota's visual inventory management system, the theory of constraints, W. Edward Deming's ideas, and the thoughts of others, in knowledge work. While Scrum focuses on managing product development and XP centers on practices to deliver code, Kanban is a framework for process improvement. Teams that use Kanban apply the Lean mindset to eliminate waste from their processes rather than the agile mindset of adaptiveness to change.

Four principles facilitating change management underpin Kanban, namely, *start with what you do now, agree to pursue incremental, evolutionary change,* and *encourage acts of leadership at every level.* Unlike agile frameworks, Kanban does not require you to adopt new processes. There is no Kanban project management method or Kanban software development process. Kanban relies on continuous steady improvement and doesn't prescribe particular roles or cross-functional teams. Kanban has a set of six core practices, namely, *visualize, limit WIP, manage flow, make policies explicit, implement feedback loop,* and *improve collaboratively, evolve experimentally.*

A Kanban board is the most common way to visualize work and processes by teams. Superficially, Kanban boards are very similar to Scrum task boards. However, there are fundamental differences. Kanban is based on continuous flow instead of discrete iterations (sprints) like Scrum. Scrum teams prioritize product backlog ahead of sprint and populate an empty task board with tasks. Once a team has committed to the sprint backlog, a task board collectively belongs to the team, the product owner cannot edit it or add new tasks, and the sprint ends with (hopefully) all tasks in "done" before starting with a clean board again.

Kanban board *work items* are not tasks. They are self-contained units of work that require individuals to perform tasks to move them across the board. So, Kanban board column names often represent a workflow, for example, analysis, development, testing, and release, and the board sometimes include an expedite lane for urgent work. Unlike Scrum, a team does not own the Kanban board as workflows can span multiple teams. Instead, items are assigned to individuals when ready to progress and managers can edit the board. A Kanban board is persistent, so as items complete, teams and individuals have options on which new items to pull across columns.

Both Scrum and Kanban limit work in progress (WIP) to prevent overburdening and unevenness, which we know from Lean thinking slow down the flow of work. Scrum limits WIP through timeboxes and Kanban through limits on the number of work items in a column at any given time. Setting WIP limits on columns restricts options by preventing items from moving to columns at their capacity. The reason for this contradiction within Lean thinking is that it makes teams think carefully about which items to progress next instead of doing everything as quickly as possible. There is no point in doing more development if it overloads development testing. Instead, teams can look elsewhere on the board to find other items to move and keep flow progressing. WIP limits on columns should result in queues no bigger than required to smooth workflow by minimizing the time items are waiting for individuals to work on them or individuals are waiting for items of work.

Teams use the manage flow practice to maximize the flow of items across the board and minimize *lead times*, which is the time between initiation and completion of items or how long items stay in the system. Teams follow the manage flow practice by measuring the total number of items in the workflow and lead times to identify and eliminate bottlenecks and loops where work has to pass back through columns. By understanding the whole workflow, making experimental changes as a team, and measuring the impact, Kanban teams use the scientific method to improve the flow of items and make it more predictable.

Kanban policies explain processes as transparently as possible, so everyone is on the same page and collaboration is effective. Examples of policies include column names that reflect the workflow and WIP limits. Other examples include the rules for items exiting a column or the definition of done.

There are multiple feedback loops in the Kanban method at differing cadences. Kanban teams deliver services to their customers, and *Strategy reviews* take place quarterly to assess the services to provide, while *operations* and *risk reviews* happen monthly to decide the people and resources deployed across services and to manage delivery risk. A biweekly *service delivery review* is similar to a retrospective that focuses on Kanban method improvement. At the work item level, the weekly *replenishment meeting* is a planning meeting to identify items to work on next.

Kanban and Scrum have their advantages and disadvantages. Scrum is prescriptive in nature with defined roles, artifacts, and timeboxed sprints. The rigid guidelines provide discipline and ensure commitment to deliver production-quality code at the end of the sprint. Short sprints reduce risk and provide an opportunity for learning and improvement through regular reviews and retrospectives. On the other hand, Scrum practices do involve sizable overhead. Even short timeboxes require waterfall-like predictive estimation of the sprint backlog, and unexpected issues during the sprint can cause the team stress. Scrum also only works well with experienced cross-functional teams that are capable of operating independently and autonomously.

Kanban is better suited than Scrum for unplanned and hard-to-estimate work as there is no commitment to deliver specific tasks, only to maximize flow. The lack of commitment to delivering at the end of an arbitrary timebox also means a shippable increment can potentially be released earlier or dropped altogether for higher priority items if it is not going to be valuable. However, Kanban does have drawbacks too. Work items are expected to flow only once through the workflow stages as they would on a manufacturing assembly line. In practice, complicated items may have to return to previous stages. Kanban boards can be designed to accommodate complex workflows, but that makes simple visual management more difficult.

Scrumban

Corey Ladas originally introduced Scrumban (a combination of Scrum and Kanban) as a way to help teams transition between Scrum and Kanban, but it has become an approach in its own right.[6] Scrumban is a way to employ continuous improvement and work visualization practices of Kanban to Scrum, but there are no hard and fast rules about its composition. Since Kanban is not prescriptive and starts with what you do now, Scrumban usually involves applying Kanban principles and practices to Scrum.

Scrumban typically includes some of the roles, meetings, and artifacts of Scrum. Work is organized around the development team unit, but like Kanban, other roles are only specified when needed, and the team does not need to be cross-functional. Scrumban doesn't push daily meetings, and timeboxed iterations are optional to facilitate continuous prioritization. However, planning, review, and retrospective meetings are undertaken when needed. Scrumban uses a task board to visualize work but doesn't use sprint backlogs or burndown charts as they do not fit with the Kanban approach of continuous flow.

The Scrumban board differs from a Scrum task board in that it contains buffer columns to improve flow and includes backlog and ready columns with WIP limits. Scrumban teams pull work from the backlog column into the ready column and finally into in-progress columns based on priority when they can take it on. Instead of planning at fixed intervals, urgent tasks and a small backlog are triggers for just-in-time planning and analysis on demand. Scrumban teams do not wait for retrospectives to improve processes. They follow the Kanban spirit of continuous improvement and are continually looking for ways to decrease lead times.

Scaling Agile

The agile frameworks described so far cover the development phase and technical practices for single products. However, work starts before the development phase as part of a product lifecycle. Potential products need identifying, prioritizing, and feasibility assessment during the *concept stage*. Next, active stakeholder participation is required to establish funding, build teams, and create requirements during the *inception stage*. The work does not end with release into production. Product support is necessary for operational activities such as fixing defects and enhancing product design before products are eventually retired from operation and shutdown.

As well as horizontally scaling to oversee the product lifecycle, organizations also have to manage multiple products or teams. The three most popular frameworks for scaling agile beyond a single team or the development phase of a single product are *SAFe*, *Scrum of Scrums*, and *Disciplined Agile Delivery* (DAD).[7] Figure 4-3 compares the coverage of the three agile frameworks across the product lifecycle.

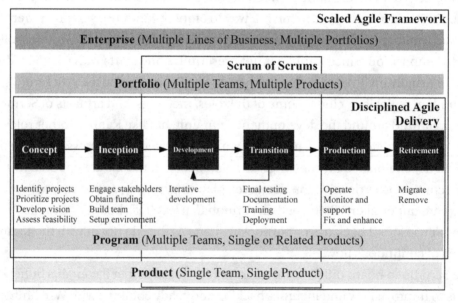

Figure 4-3. *Coverage of Scrums of Scrums, DAD, and SAFe across the product lifecycle and enterprise*

Scrum of Scrums

Scrum of Scrums is a simple mechanism to scale Scrum by moving everything up a level. Instead of creating huge Scrum teams to deal with large or multiple products, teams remain in the ideal size for Scrum of 5 to 10 people. Each team nominates an ambassador to participate in a daily or slightly lower frequency Scrum of Scrums meeting with their counterparts from other teams. The Scrum of Scrums follows a similar pattern to the team daily Scrum meeting with ambassadors sharing team progress, team next steps, and team impediments as well as disclosing developments that may embed obstacles to other team's progress. The purpose of the Scrum of Scrums is not to report to external stakeholders or management, but help teams deliver their commitments. The Scrum of Scrums allows teams to synchronize, align, and problem solve quickly without external interference.

Disciplined Agile Delivery

Disciplined Agile Delivery (DAD) is a nonprescriptive hybrid toolkit of Kanban, Lean software development, and several agile frameworks including Scrum, XP, SAFe, Spotify's agile model, *Agile Modeling* (AM), and *Unified Process* (UP).[8] DAD covers the full delivery lifecycle from concept to retirement and is part of a wider *Disciplined Agile* (DA) framework that also includes *Disciplined DevOps*, *Disciplined Agile IT* (DAIT), and *Disciplined Agile Enterprise* (DAE).

DAD starts with desired organizational outcomes and provides three levels of scaffolding in the form of contextual advice on lifecycles, process goals, and practices to achieve the goals. At the core of DAD are 21 process goals (process outcomes) that all teams need to tackle from forming teams to addressing risk. For each process goal, there is a visual decision tree diagram that depicts the decisions points to consider. DAD recognizes solution delivery is inherently complex, and choices are better than one-size-fits-all prescriptions, so every decision point has options in the form of brief summaries of potential strategies together with their trade-offs.

DAD supports six lifecycles to give teams the flexibility to choose the most appropriate approach. The six lifecycles are *Agile* (Scrum-based for solution delivery projects), *Continuous Delivery: Agile* (Scrum-based for long-standing teams), *Exploratory* (Lean startup-based for running experiments), *Lean* (Kanban-based for solution delivery projects), *Continuous Delivery Lean* (Kanban-based for long-standing teams), and *Program* (for a team of teams). Teams determine the appropriate lifecycle based on a flowchart that takes into account constraints such as team skill level, team and organization culture, the size and frequency of releases, and stakeholder availability and flexibility.

Scaled Agile Framework (SAFe)

SAFe applies Lean and agile principles to all levels of solutions delivery, product, program, portfolio, and enterprise. It also covers the entire product lifecycle from concept to retirement. SAFe is configurable. It can provide small-scale solutions employing 50-125 practitioners utilizing the *essential SAFe* configuration. SAFe can also provide large-scale solutions for complex systems that require thousands of people using *full SAFe* with *portfolio SAFe* or intermediate-scale solutions with *large solution SAFe*.[9]

At the heart of SAFe are long-lived, cross-functional agile teams applying practices from Scrum/XP or Kanban. Teams, not team members, are assigned work, and a team member can belong to only one team. Agile teams are themselves attached to a long-lived virtual group of teams called an *Agile Release Train* (ART). ARTs form around an organization's significant value streams, for example, home loans sales for a bank. ARTs work to a shared vision, roadmap, and program backlog and possess all the skills and technical infrastructure capabilities to deliver solutions independently.

Four significant activities synchronize each ART: *Program Increment* (PI) planning, *system demo*, *Innovation and Planning iteration* (IP), and the *Inspect and Adapt* (I&A) event. The PI planning event brings together all members of the ART physically or virtually over 2 days to establish alignment and collective objectives for the next PI timebox, which is typically 8-12 weeks. At the end of every 2-week iteration, the integrated work for all teams is shown at a system demo to stakeholders who provide feedback to adjust the train's direction. A continuous focus on delivery can squeeze out innovation, so the last iteration in the PI is an IP iteration that allows teams to work on innovation, tools, and learning. The I&A event takes place at the end of the program increment to demonstrate all the features developed by the ART during the PI, review the quantitative metrics the teams agreed to collect at the start of the PI, and undertake a retrospective workshop to identify the biggest impediments using root cause analysis.

SAFe also includes its technical practices (in addition to those used by XP) to execute the program increment. Each ART builds and maintains *release on demand*, which is a continuous delivery pipeline approach to regularly release small increments of value at any time. An *architectural runway* enables continuous delivery by providing the components and technical infrastructure to implement high-priority features during a PI without excessive redesign or delay. As new features are added, ARTs start to run out of runway. They use *emergent design* to extend the runway by adding enablers that support new functionality or fix existing problems such as capacity limits. Emergent design is an incremental and evolutionary approach that works alongside *intentional architecture*, which is a planned architectural initiative that guides interteam design and synchronization. Figure 4-4 shows the essential SAFe lifecycle.

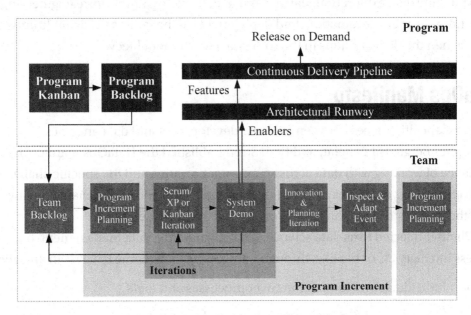

Figure 4-4. *The simplified essential SAFe lifecycle*

The *Portfolio SAFe* configuration adds practices to manage a portfolio of solutions for multiple value streams to essential SAFe. The *large solution SAFe* configuration delivers large complex solutions such as medical, banking, and aerospace systems and is sometimes called systems of systems. The final *Full SAFe* configuration is a combination of portfolio and large solution SAFe.

Agile For DataOps

Like software development, data science is a creative and unpredictable business that requires responsiveness to change. Many of the values and principles of agile software development apply to data science as well as the practices, roles, artifacts, and events of agile frameworks. But, some do not. For example, delivering working software frequently is a crucial principle of agile software development, but it is not software alone that makes better decisions. A good decision is also based on high-quality data and algorithms. A fully functioning dashboard with poor data integrity or a low latency recommendation engine API that gives no better than random predictions is of no use to consumers. Also, the data science development lifecycle does not always lend itself to agile practices such as 2-week sprints. Business understanding, data acquisition, data wrangling data exploration, data cleaning, data exploration feature engineering, model training, model evaluation, and deployment can be far less predictable and more iterative than the delivery steps in the software development lifecycle.

DataOps Manifesto

To address the differences between software development and data analytics, Christopher Bergh, Gil Bengiat, and Eran Strod published the DataOps manifesto.[10] Their experience of working with data across many organizations and the specific challenges of delivering fast cycles times for a wide range of data analytics with reliable quality shape the manifesto. The manifesto is composed of five values:

"Whether referred to as data science, data engineering, data management, big data, business intelligence, or the like, through our work we have come to value in analytics:

- Individuals and interactions over processes and tools

- Working analytics over comprehensive documentation

- Customer collaboration over contract negotiation

- Experimentation, iteration, and feedback over extensive upfront design

- Cross-functional ownership of operations over siloed responsibilities"[10]

Working analytics replaces the agile software value of working software, *iteration and feedback* replace responding to change, and *cross-functional ownership* is a new value to reflect the need for multiple skillsets to develop and maintain data pipelines.

DataOps Principles

The DataOps manifesto also lists 18 principles:

- **Continually satisfy your customer**. Our highest priority is to satisfy the customer through the early and continuous delivery of valuable analytic insights from a couple of minutes to weeks.

- **Value working analytics**. We believe the primary measure of data analytics performance is the degree to which insightful analytics are delivered, incorporating accurate data, atop robust frameworks and systems.

- **Embrace change**. We welcome evolving customer needs, and in fact, we embrace them to generate competitive advantage. We believe that the most efficient, effective, and agile method of communication with customers is face-to-face conversation.

- **It's a team sport**. Analytic teams will always have a variety of roles, skills, favorite tools, and titles.

- **Daily interactions**. Customers, analytic teams, and operations must work together daily throughout the project.

- **Self-organize**. We believe that the best analytic insight, algorithms, architectures, requirements, and designs emerge from self-organizing teams.

- **Reduce heroism**. As the pace and breadth of need for analytic insights ever increases, we believe analytic teams should strive to reduce heroism and create sustainable and scalable data analytic teams and processes.

- **Reflect**. Analytic teams should fine-tune their operational performance by self-reflecting, at regular intervals, on feedback provided by their customers, themselves, and operational statistics.

- **Analytics is code**. Analytic teams use a variety of individual tools to access, integrate, model, and visualize data. Fundamentally, each of these tools generates code and configuration which describes the actions taken upon data to deliver insight.

- **Orchestrate**. The beginning-to-end orchestration of data, tools, code, environments, and the analytic teams work is a key driver of analytic success.

- **Make it reproducible**. Reproducible results are required, and therefore, we version everything: data, low-level hardware and software configurations, and the code and configuration specific to each tool in the toolchain.

- **Disposable environments**. We believe it is important to minimize the cost for analytic team members to experiment by giving them easy to create, isolated, safe, and disposable technical environments that reflect their production environment.

- **Simplicity**. We believe that continuous attention to technical excellence and good design enhances agility; likewise simplicity – the art of maximizing the amount of work not done – is essential.

- **Analytics is manufacturing**. Analytic pipelines are analogous to Lean manufacturing lines. We believe a fundamental concept of DataOps is a focus on process thinking aimed at achieving continuous efficiencies in the manufacture of analytic insight.

- **Quality is paramount**. Analytic pipelines should be built with a foundation capable of automated detection of abnormalities (*jidoka*) and security issues in code, configuration, and data and should provide continuous feedback to operators for error avoidance (*poka yoke*).

- **Monitor quality and performance**. Our goal is to have performance, security, and quality measures that are monitored continuously to detect unexpected variation and generate operational statistics.

- **Reuse**. We believe a foundational aspect of analytic insight manufacturing efficiency is to avoid the repetition of previous work by the individual or team.

- **Improve cycle times**. We should strive to minimize the time and effort to turn a customer need into an analytic idea, create it in development, release it as a repeatable production process, and finally refactor and reuse that product.

As with the values, many DataOps principles overlap those of agile software development. Still, there are some additions to support the *analytics as a Lean manufacturing like process* mindset and analytics as code thinking with delivery through code and automation instead of interactive tools. However, I would argue that some other additions such as disposable environments and monitoring are DataOps practices (things you do) rather than principles (things that guide what you do).

Data Science Lifecycle

DataOps values and principles together with the data science lifecycle help define which agile practices, events, artifacts, and roles are useful. Figure 4-5 shows a typical data science lifecycle.

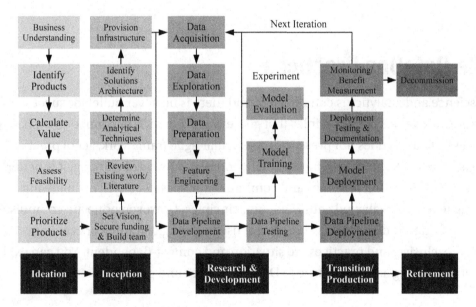

Figure 4-5. *The data science lifecycle*

The *ideation* phase exists to identify and prioritize potential products, and the *inception* phase captures the initiation efforts before product development begins. The *research and development* phase is where the bulk of effort takes place. Compared to a software development lifecycle, there is much more focus on data and experimentation in the data science lifecycle. Data needs must be identified, acquired, and explored to understand its usefulness and identify extra processing requirements where quality and timeliness of data might be improved. Model training is iterative. To achieve an acceptable level of accuracy, data scientists experiment with multiple data sources, data features, algorithms, and algorithm tuning with hyperparameters. The experimentation activity introduces a layer of uncertainty to the product development process.

Research and development analytics are implemented in the *transition/production* phase. Scalable code and data pipelines are deployed in production environments and monitoring setup. Monitoring must measure not only the performance of models but also the distribution of data flowing through the pipelines as poor data quality or shifting data distributions can decay the performance of otherwise good models. Measurement of *Key Performance Indicators* (KPIs) determined during the ideation or inception stages validate model benefits. At some point, it will be necessary for the product to enter the *retirement* phase to decommission the model and pipelines. Perhaps the initial experiment failed or it does not generate the benefit required to justify the maintenance effort.

Agile DataOps Practices

Data science and analytics is complicated, and there is no silver bullet for success. There are only values and principles that guide what you do to maximize your chances of success. DataOps does not prescribe a particular agile framework, set of practices, artifacts, or roles. Nonetheless, instead of inventing new ways of working, it is better to adapt existing proven practices and combining them as needed. The following are useful agile practices aligned with DataOps principles. However, none are compulsory, and if you find they do not add value, do not use them. Agile frameworks are not mutually exclusive, and practices are situation and context-dependent. You can explore alternatives as long as you stay true to DataOps values and principles.

Ideation

Henrik Kniberg produced the famous metaphor of agile and Lean development as a skateboard to a car rather than a partial car to big bang delivery.[11] However, agile is much more than iterative product development. Collaboration between teams is fundamental. The starting point for preventing misalignment between data scientists and the rest of the organization is ideation, which is the very first phase of the project lifecycle.

SAFe practices ensure that portfolio of products aligns to organizational objectives and organization stakeholders receive a constant flow of feedback. While collaboration in agile software development involves business stakeholders and the agile development team, data analytics requires three groups to collaborate including data producers, data consumers, and business stakeholders.

Organizational executives, data analytics management, enterprise architects, and leadership of teams responsible for the supply of data, such as data engineering or IT operations, collaborate to create a virtual *Lean portfolio management* (LPM) team. The LPM agree on *strategic themes* that align organizational strategy to the analytics portfolio via simple statements such as "appeal to a younger demographic" or "ensure compliance."

Strategic themes inspire the *portfolio vision*, which details the gap between the desired future state and current state based on the organization's objectives. Initiatives to close the gaps are called *epics*, which capture the more significant business and (technical) enabler ideas needed to achieve the future state in the form of short statements. An epic represents initiatives large enough to meet the definition of an MVP, need analysis, or require financial approval.

New ideas for epics can come from any source and enter the *ideation* column of an *epic Kanban board*, which is designed to visualize the state on the way to development or rejection as shown in Figure 4-6.

Epic Kanban Board					
Ideation	**Feasibility**	**Analyze**	**Backlog**	**Develop**	**Done**
No limit	WIP limited	WIP limited	No limit	Team WIP limits	No limit
Big Ideas: • New Product & feature creation opportunities • Customer experience enhancements • Business efficiency improvements • Improvements to existing solutions	• Epic hypothesis statement • Rough sizing of effort • Benefit estimation • Prioritization matrix	• Investigate alternative solutions • Refine cost and benefit estimates • Define MVP • Measurement plan developed • Prioritize	• Epics selected for development by Lean portfolio management team • Continuous prioritization of epics	• Epics broken into into work items, stories or tasks. • Teams begin development when they have capacity • Epic tracking	• Benefit measured versus plan • Stop or persist decision made.

Figure 4-6. *The epic Kanban states*

Epics move from ideation to a WIP-limited *feasibility* column based on their potential to deliver the portfolio vision. The feasibility stage is kept as short as possible. Its purpose is to articulate epics and identify relative economic benefits and risks to determine if it is worth proceeding to the *analyze* stage. An *epic hypothesis statement* articulates the problem the epic will solve, how it will be measured, other teams that need to be involved, and its data and *non-functional requirements* (NFRs). NFRs specify the quality attributes of a system such as performance, security, and reliability. Figure 4-7 shows an example template structure for the hypothesis.

Epic Hypothesis Statement		
Structure	**Description**	**Example**
Achieve	[strategic theme objective]	compliance goal
through	[target portfolio vision outcome]	improved anti-money laundering (AML) risk assessment
for	[customers]	Money Laundering Reporting Officer (MLRO)
By	[proposed solution]	applying machine learning to automatically monitor customer transaction data to identify anomalies for investigation
Resulting in	[predicted benefit]	reduced risk of fines
measured by	[metrics]	value of AML penalties relative to peers
Partnering with	[other teams and partners]	Compliance and IT teams;
Integrating	[sources and data types]	financial transaction and customer identity data
and Requiring	[non-functional requirements]	ability to scale and match transaction volumes, and achieve 99.99% availability

Figure 4-7. *An example epic hypothesis statement*

Epic effort and benefits can be estimated in many different ways. However, in the absence of qualitative or quantitative evidence, complex formula-based methods such as financial analysis can lead to false precision and confidence. A more straightforward estimation approach is to use relative points rather than actual money or time units. The agile concept of *story points* used to size the relative effort of work for stories in a Fibonacci sequence format can also apply to epic effort and benefits.

Nevertheless, even relative estimation is hard and should use as much expert input as possible from stakeholders to achieve consensus and buy-in. Epic efforts and benefits help calculate *weighted shortest job first* (WSJF), which is a model to sequence jobs for maximum economic benefit by dividing the *cost of delay* by job effort.[12] Cost of delay is calculated by summing not just the revenue impact of delaying but also the time criticality of delaying and the risk reduction or opportunity enablement value of the epic.

Unlike software development, effort and economic benefit are only two of the major factors required for data science prioritization. Many data science products fail to make it into production, deliver better decisions, or create measurable results because of lack of stakeholder interest or power, poor data quality, deficient solutions architecture, and absence of benefit measurement. These additional factors can also be captured as relative points on an epic prioritization matrix as shown in Figure 4-8.

Theme	Epic	Stakeholder Power/ Interest	Data Availability / Quality / Integration	Current Solutions Architecture Capability	Benefits Measurement Capability	Effort	Cost of Delay
Ensure Compliance	Identify anomalous transactions	20/2	20/20/8	2	13	20	13
	Classify sensitive content	20/5	2/8/1	1	5	20	8
Improve customer retention	Calculate customer churn probabilities	8/20	8/13/8	13	20	5	8
	Compute customer lifetime value	8/13	8/8/8	13	13	8	13
Improve customer service	Prioritise customer complaint messages	5/13	8/5/5	8	13	8	8

Figure 4-8. An example epic prioritization matrix

The epic prioritization matrix provides additional insight into risks, missing capabilities for possible enabler epics, and priorities for stakeholder management. Along with WSJF, the extra elements help the LPM decide which epics make their way to the analyze column when it has free capacity.

Inception

Epics that make it to the analyzing column are assigned an *epic owner*. An epic owner is a data analytics leader who is responsible for managing the progress of an epic through the epic Kanban board. If it is an enabler rather than a business epic, the owner can instead be a technical specialist such as a solutions architect. The epic owner works with stakeholders to undertake a more thorough analysis of effort and cost of delay and risks, explore alternative solutions and architectures using the Lean set-based design principle, identify data sources, define an MVP, and create a monitoring and measurement plan for KPIs. A vision document, which can be a *Lean business case*, *project, charter, business canvas,* or *summary vision statement,* captures the critical information. The LPM reviews the vision document, and, if approved, epics move to the epic *backlog* where they wait for implementation by a team when capacity is available.

Once epics are pulled on to the relevant team backlog, the epic owner helps teams to split the epic into features of the data product that might include visualizations or accurate predictions by an ML model and potentially reusable components such as infrastructure, software libraries, and data pipelines. The features and components are split into further work, items, stories, or tasks depending on which agile framework the team intend to use to deliver the epic. Once this is complete, teams are ready to move on to research and development.

Research and Development

The DataOps principle of "continually satisfying your customer" means we should first deliver the minimum viable product (MVP) to validate the epic hypothesis as quickly as possible. The MVP should consist of a "just good enough" end-to-end skeleton working data pipeline and analytics to get something in front of potential end users and measure how they react. The purpose is not just to learn from customers, the MVP proves out the architecture and data pipelines as early as possible to reduce future risk and reduces the temptation for data scientists to waste time perfecting models that have no customer value.

DataOps teams have a choice of agile framework to apply to the research and development phase to deliver the MVP and future iterations. For example, teams can use Scrum, Scrum/XP, Kanban, or Scrumban. Kanban is the preferred framework for data analytics. Kanban has an advantage over Scrum and Scrum/XP due to its greater ability to cope with the uncertainty of data science and data analytics development as well as the flexibility to deal with different size problems and varying degrees of stakeholder availability.

The limited academic research on data science project management also suggests that Kanban produces better results than Scrum.[13] The findings show that Scrum encourages teams to dive into the analysis and not spend enough time understanding client requirements or the data. Teams using Scrum also found it challenging to estimate tasks with enough accuracy to give them the confidence needed to complete them within a sprint.

Scrumban is also a framework option, but like Scrum is team-based rather than workflow-based like Kanban. Scrumban and Scrum require cross-functional teams that have a mix of data engineering, data science, data analyst, or other skills necessary to self-organize. Cross-functional teams that are self-sufficient enough to span the entire data science lifecycle are highly desirable, but this may not be feasible for all organizations from day one.

Although Scrum and Scrum/XP have challenges as frameworks for delivering data analytics, they include practices that support DataOps principles. The DataOps principle of paramount quality means we should adopt the thinking behind XP's test-first programming practice and add tests to catch bugs in the data before they flow down the pipeline. The DataOps principle of daily interactions is fulfilled through a daily Scrum or *daily Kanban* meeting to help teams coordinate activities for the day. Regular retrospectives ensure team members spend time to reflect on their work and find ways to improve cycle times by addressing bottlenecks sustainably. By involving stakeholders in daily or weekly meetings and retrospectives, data analytics teams increase transparency, get to share the intermediate output, improve synchronization, improve business domain knowledge, and gain feedback on business goals.

Transition/Production

As data pipelines are developed during the research and development phase, they should be built with the transition to production in mind. Monitoring, policy-based governance, security, data lineage tracking, elastic scalability, and automated deployment need to be built into pipelines as early as possible. Analytics environments must also be built with production in mind. For example, separate languages and libraries for research and production should be avoided to prevent recoding.

The DataOps need for continuous delivery to satisfy the customer requires the ability to productionize data pipelines and analytics in the shortest possible time. Historically, this has been a challenge with many manual steps and teams involved, but modern tools and architectures have evolved to the point where the end-to-end process can be delivered via self-service automation.

Once the research and development data pipelines and analytics meet the requirements for the MVP and successfully pass tests, they are ready to be deployed in a production environment as a data product. Often, the data product is a feature of another product or application developed by a different product team. This parallel development creates dependencies between teams. So, to avoid disconnected backlogs, it is essential that data analytics teams collaborate and align on timings by providing updates at the product team's meetings during the transition phase.

The initial deployment is usually only a partial deployment to a subset of users. A partial deployment reduces the operational risk of the rollout and enables the calculation of benefit measurement KPIs comparing users exposed to the MVP and those who are not. When sufficient data is captured, the measurement plan is used to decide whether to initiate another research and development iteration to optimize the pipeline and analytics or abandon it and move onto another epic. However, even if the data product is optimized, production is not a one-and-done process. Continuous monitoring and benefit measurement may trigger further maintenance iterations that can be anything from small investigations into data quality to full-blown model development from scratch.

A focus on continuous flow through agile practices should improve near-term results. But, it is important not to neglect medium- and long-term opportunities that investments in maintenance, new techniques, and technology can facilitate. There are several agile practices to employ that ensure good time management. XP provides practices of slack and spikes. SAFe has its IP iteration and also the concept of *guardrails*. The first guardrail safeguards resource budget allocations across *evaluating, emerging, investing/extracting,* and *retiring* investment horizons. Planning horizons ensure that not all effort goes into the near-term investing/extracting time horizon, which would create long-term risk by neglecting innovation. The second guardrail guarantees that capacity allocation of resources is spread across new development, technical enablers, maintenance, and the reduction of technical debt as fixed percentages.

Summary

Data science can be very iterative and unpredictable because of its many data sources, data features, model algorithms, and architectures to explore before finding an acceptable solution. This uncertainty makes predictive project management hard, but this is not an excuse for the ad hoc delivery approaches adopted by many data science teams. An informal approach to data science project management leads to a lack of alignment or collaboration with organizational stakeholders and other teams and a focus on algorithms and insights over rapidly productionizing products that can add value to the organization every single day.

Agile practices can bring discipline to data science through support for the values and principles of DataOps. However, just as there is no perfect agile framework or set of practices for software development, there is no single set of best agile practices for data science. The right practices to use are context and organization specific and help data analytics teams become more adaptable and collaborative and tighten feedback loops to produce faster (and better) results. The successful application of agile and Lean thinking to data analytics requires observation, constant experimentation, and adjustment. The next chapter introduces measures and feedback that facilitate adjustment and improvements in performance.

Endnotes

1. Russell Jurney, Agile Data Science, 2.0, June 2017.

2. Stack Overflow, Developer Survey Results 2018, January 2018. *https://insights.stackoverflow.com/ survey/2018#development-practices*

3. Agile Manifesto, Agile Alliance, February 2001. *www.agilealliance.org/agile101/the-agile-manifesto/*

4. 12 Principles behind the Agile manifesto, Agile Alliance, 2001 *www.agilealliance.org/agile101/12-principles-behind-the-agile-manifesto/*

5. VersionOne 12th Annual State of Agile Report, April 2018. *https://explore.versionone.com/state-of-agile/ versionone-12th-annual-state-of-agile-report*

6. Corey Ladas, Scrumban – Essays on Kanban Systems for Lean Software Development, January 2009.

7. VersionOne 12th Annual State of Agile Report, April 2018. *https://explore.versionone.com/state-of-agile/ versionone-12th-annual-state-of-agile-report*

8. A hybrid toolkit, Disciplined Agile, *www.disciplinedagiledelivery. com/hybridframework/*

9. Scaled Agile Framework, *www.scaledagileframework.com/#*

10. The DataOps Manifesto, *http://dataopsmanifesto.org/*

11. Henrik Kniberg, Making sense of MVP (Minimum Viable Product) – and why I prefer Earliest Testable/Usable/ Lovable, January 2015. *https://blog.crisp.se/2016/01/25/ henrikkniberg/making-sense-of-mvp*

12. Don Reinertsen, Principles of Product Development Flow: Second Generation Lean Product Development, May 2009.

13. Jeffrey Saltz, Ivan Shamshurin, Kevin Crowston, Comparing Data Science Project Management Methodologies via a Controlled Experiment, Proceedings of the 50th Hawaii International Conference on System Sciences 2017.

CHAPTER 5

Build Feedback and Measurement

No data analytics professional comes into the office every morning and thinks, I'd like to spend a very long time producing nothing of value while costing my employer money. Despite best intentions, many data analytics projects fail or take much longer than expected to generate a positive outcome. There is no point blaming data engineers, data scientists, and data analysts. According to W. Edwards Deming, "every system is perfectly designed to get the results it gets" and "the system that people work in and the interaction with people may account for 90 or 95 percent of performance."[1]

Unfortunately, while there is always pressure to go faster and do more in most organizations, there is little pressure to stop, reflect, and improve effectiveness. Arbitrarily setting increasing targets each year (as if people were not working hard enough last year) is wishful thinking. Sustained increases in productivity and customer benefit only come from monitoring and improving the system within which people work.

Systems Thinking

Most of the time, people think in linear cause-and-effect terms. For instance, you flip a switch and the lightbulb turns on. Linear thinking is very effective at solving simple problems. However, the world mostly consists of complex interrelationships between people and objects, and it is hard to predict the impact of a change due to unanticipated side effects and feedback loops.

The world is an example of a *system*, which is a set of components that connect to form something more complicated. Organizations are a system that includes components such as teams, hierarchical structures, technologies, processes, policies, customers, data, incentives, suppliers, and conventions. Data analytics is also a system that interacts and supports other systems in an organization.

113

© Harvinder Atwal 2020
H. Atwal, *Practical DataOps*, https://doi.org/10.1007/978-1-4842-5104-1_5

Systems thinking focuses on understanding how components of a system interrelate, work over time, interact with other systems to identify patterns, solve problems, and improve performance. Agile and Lean thinking are example subsets of systems thinking. Agile aims to make a system more adaptable to uncertainty, while Lean thinking endeavors to drive waste out of the system.

Continuous Improvement

There are many ways data analytics teams can improve their system of delivering the right thing, in the right way. Systems thinking requires a disciplined approach to examine problems thoroughly and ask the right questions before jumping to conclusions and acting upon them. One of the most common approaches to improvement is through iterative continuous improvement. W. Edward Deming's *Plan-Do-Study-Act* (PDSA) loop is a common approach with teams implementing continuous improvement. The first stage is to identify a potential improvement with clear objectives and create a *plan* to deliver it. The *do* phase involves running an experiment with the improvement change and collecting data. Next, *study* results and compare to expected outcomes. Finally, if the experiment is successful, *act* to implement the improvement and create a higher baseline of performance. With every iteration of the PDSA loop, there are opportunities for continuous improvements in process or gains in knowledge.

The Lean change management cycle is an alternative improvement cycle based on ideas from Eric Ries' Lean startup. The Lean planning cycle starts with *insights*, which is time spent observing the current situation to discover problems. Next comes *options*, which are hypotheses for improvement with associated costs and benefits that turn into *experiments* in the form of *minimum viable changes* (MVCs) to test if the adjustments work. Experiments have a sub-cycle. *Prepare* is the first step, which is the planning stage used to validate assumptions from people affected by the change. The second step is *introduce*, which is when the MVCs are incorporated into processes and allowed to run for long enough to generate sufficient data to decide if the change is successful. The final step is *review, which is when teams can choose to stick with changes that work and drop ones that do not through a process of validated learning.*

Teams using Scrum follow a different path to continuous improvement. Scrum applies *empirical process control theory*, which is the belief that control of undefined and unpredictable systems comes through observation of inputs and outputs, constant experimentation, and adjustment. Application of the theory to Scrum relies on three pillars – transparency, inspection, and adaption. Transparency involves making all information, good or bad, visible to everyone, and in Scrum comes from prioritized backlogs and information radiators. Inspection requires everyone in the team to assess processes, products, and practices to identify opportunities for improvement, and adaption involves making changes that result in improvement. Inspection and adaption typically happen through sprint planning, daily Scrum, sprint review meetings, and sprint retrospectives.

There are several other data-driven improvement cycles that teams can implement. Before producing the PDSA technique, Deming created the *Plan-Do-Check-Act* (PDCA) cycle based on the statistician Walter Shewhart's ideas. Toyota developed *OPDCA* (Observe-Plan-Do-Check-Act) from PDCA by adding an initial step to observe current conditions before the plan stage. US Air Force Colonel John Boyd designed the *Observe-Orientate-Decide-Act* (OODA) loop to aid learning and adaption in ambiguous environments. Another common data-driven improvement cycle is *Define-Measure-Analyze-Improve-Control* (DMAIC), which is popular with organizations using *Six Sigma*. Six Sigma is a set of techniques for process improvement.

Despite their differences, all continuous improvement techniques share the same basic idea that is founded on the scientific method. The idea is that feedback from the system helps identify hypotheses for potential improvement, and effectiveness of the possible enhancement is determined through experimentation and measured against clear outcomes. Successful ideas are implemented and ineffective ones discarded. Figure 5-1 shows how the experimentation loop and scientific method can wrap around a system to deliver continuous improvement.

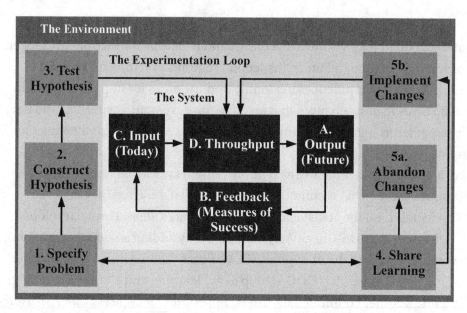

Figure 5-1. *A scientific approach to continuous system improvement*

Several DataOps principles such as continually satisfy your customer, reflect, quality is paramount, monitor quality and performance, and improve cycle times are simpler to achieve by taking a systems thinking viewpoint, gathering feedback, and combining it with the scientific method to deliver continuous improvement.

Feedback Loops

Lean and agile thinking provides the ability to adapt to change and deliver quickly. But, *fitness for purpose* is also needed. Fitness for purpose is the ability to change in the right direction and stay relevant to customers. To ensure the data analytics system is delivering the right thing, in the right way, and moving in the right direction feedback is required on performance. Feedback is an essential element of systems thinking. For example, in linear thinking, adding more workers to a project that is behind schedule may seem a good idea, but systems thinking may demonstrate the opposite. Historical feedback from adding more workers may show it slows projects down as they need to come up to speed, and alternative solutions that do not waste resource should be considered instead.

Reflect is the eighth DataOps principle. It is when analytic teams fine-tune their operational performance by self-reflecting at regular intervals on feedback provided by their customers, themselves, and operational statistics. It is possible to gather many types of feedback and metrics. But, it is essential to cover all the kinds of feedback required to improve the data analytics system.

The organizational coach Matt Philips proposes that knowledge work consists of two dimensions where internal and external viewpoints are on one dimension and product and service delivery are on the other.[2] Philips uses the restaurant metaphor to describe the elements. When eating out, customers care about how the food and drink are delivered (service delivery) as much as the product itself (the food and drink). The staff also care about the service and product. But, from an internal viewpoint, they want the food to be consistently good, ingredients stored correctly, and everyone to work well together as a team. Figure 5-2 shows the two dimensions and the feedback needs in each quadrant.

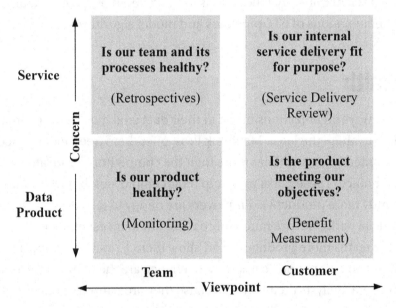

Figure 5-2. *The two dimensions of knowledge work*

Feedback and measurement help us build the right thing and build things right by answering the questions in each quadrant including is our product healthy, is our team healthy, is the product meeting its objectives, and is our service delivery fit for purpose.

Feedback loops for data products are easy to understand. We can gauge metrics such as time taken to process records, data quality errors, model prediction accuracies, or revenue uplifts and then experiment by making changes and observing outcomes. Feedback loops for service are harder to comprehend and implement. However, all knowledge work is a service, and organizations are networks of services. The IT helpdesk provides a service to users of computers. Graphic designers and content teams provide a service to marketing, public relations, and web site development teams. Human resources provide a service to managers and employees. Service delivery consists of two viewpoints. First, an internal viewpoint describes how well the service team thinks they are delivering. Second, customer have an external viewpoint describing the fitness for purpose of the delivery.

Data analytics is not just about the end data product. It is also a service for customers. Data engineers create data pipelines for data analysts and data scientists to develop data products such as dashboards and machine learning models. The data products are further used by internal customers to make decisions, or other teams embed them in their consumer-facing product. Gathering feedback on service encourages data science and analytics teams to think about purpose instead of just technical implementations of ETL pipelines and model algorithms.

Team Health

There are many ways organizations invest in their data analytics teams including incentives like buy them the latest MacBook Pros, offer them free food and beer, send them to conferences, pay them more than the competitors, or locate them in a trendy hipster office. These perks may help retain employees, but won't make the team significantly more productive. Employers are happy to take the easy route and finance superficial perks, but are much more reluctant to invest in the painful changes needed to make teams more productive and allow them to make an impact that garners job satisfaction. The best people to ask what to change are the data scientists, data engineers, and data analysts themselves because they are natural complex problem solvers. However, managers need to develop competency to ask them in the right way at the right time.

Retrospectives

Classical organizational improvement using large programs can take too long and is often inefficient and ineffective. The agile practice of retrospectives allows DataOps teams to reflect on their way of working and become continuously better at what they do. Agile retrospectives are meetings to learn lessons from what has happened recently and identify actions for improvement. The team owns the agile retrospective. The team both agrees upon actions in a retrospective and carries them out. As such, there is no handover of responsibility. The actions from a retrospective are communicated and added to the team's backlog to perform alongside other work.

People do not usually stop to reflect during work, especially when they are busy. Contemplation is not a natural activity, which is why it's so essential to formalize a behavior and make it a ritual. Regular retrospective cadences at different levels of the organization help deliver continuous improvement without creating local optimums and detachment from organizational objectives. Biweekly retrospectives focus on the team's work item delivery, customer-focused metrics, lead time, and quality. Monthly retrospectives have the same focus as biweekly retrospectives, but cover a team of teams with the aim of *optimizing the whole*. Quarterly retrospectives focus on strategic themes and portfolio vision to review and adjust the delivery of epics and ensure we are still doing the right things.

Some rules make retrospectives more effective. Teams must look for actions that can be defined and completed by themselves. The retrospectives must focus on learning and understanding and avoid the inherent inefficiencies of blame and accusation. The number of issues and action items should be limited to the most critical constraints and root cause analysis used to find the causes and not symptoms of problems. Teams should follow up on and evaluate the progress of actions to help them understand why some activities worked and some did not, which is a process known as *double-loop learning*.

Health Check

No single retrospective exercise always gives the best results. So, we should use different activities depending on the issues at hand and the mindset of the team. A way to determine improvement areas to focus on and useful choice of retrospective exercises is to undertake a *health check assessment*. Such an assessment was popularized by Spotify's Squad Health Check model.[3] Team health check assessments are monthly or quarterly workshops that enable teams to discuss and assess their current situation based on many attributes.

A health check workshop is an hour-long facilitated face-to-face conversation structured around no more than ten attributes of a healthy team. For each attribute, the team tries to reach consensus or a majority decision on their state from three levels. *RAG* (red/amber/green) statuses, thumbs up/sideways/down, or smiley/neutral/sad faces are ways to visualize the levels. A red, thumbs down or sad face status indicates that the attribute needs improvement and the team is not healthy. An amber, sideways thumb or neutral face denotes the attribute needs addressing, but it is not a disaster. A green, thumbs up or smiley face status signifies the team is happy with the attribute. Keep discussions brief, but it is essential to understand why everyone chose the rating because no problems have actually been solved as of yet. Figure 5-3 shows an example of the health check assessment.

Team Health Check		
Attribute	**Description**	**State**
Balanced Team	The team is the right size, has the right skills, and everyone knows what is expected of them.	😊
Values & Metrics	Success is clearly defined and measured.	😐
Shared understanding	The team has a shared vision. They know why they are here and where they are going.	😊
Learning	The team learns interesting things all the time.	😊
Teamwork	Team members collaborate, self-organize, share insights to improve effectiveness, and trust each other.	😊
Speed	The team can get work done quickly.	☹
Decisions	Decisions are made at the right level and the team have the appropriate influence.	😐
Support	The team get the right support from others and are also seen as supportive by other teams.	😐
Fun	The team is fulfilled, motivated and proud of their delivery.	😐
Delivery Process	The team are happy with their practices, understand risks, are proud of their quality and ease to get things done.	😐

Figure 5-3. *A health check assessment grid*

A health check is not a method for rating or judging individuals and teams. Rather, it is the basis for focused improvement, feedback to management, and a record of how the team has evolved over time. The team is free to add, remove, or change the questions to cover what they think is most important.

Once each attribute is assigned a status, the team chooses one or two of the attributes requiring improvement as a focal point for retrospective exercises. A quick Internet search should reveal numerous retrospective exercises tailored to solve specific types of problem. To get started, the following are examples of three simple activities that require little preparation, are suitable for any team, and apply to a wide range of problems.

Starfish Retrospective

The starfish exercise starts by drawing a circle with five lines enclosing five words on a flipchart or whiteboard as shown in Figure 5-4.

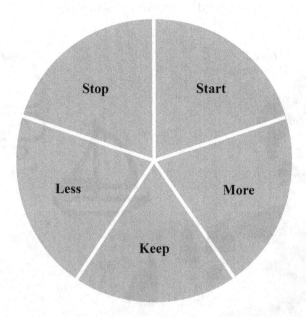

Figure 5-4. *A starfish retrospective diagram*

After drawing the picture, the team starts brainstorming *stop* **ideas and recording them on sticky notes. Stop ideas** are activities that introduce waste into the process and have no value to the team or customers. Once everyone places their ideas on the **corresponding section of the** diagram, the team spends 10 minutes discussing and consolidating the points. Repeat the process for *less* are activities that bring little benefit, but require a high level of effort. Next, the team moves onto *keep,* which are current activities team members want to continue exploring. After keep, the team continues to *more* (activities a team should perform more often) and finally concludes with *start* (actions or ideas that a team wants to begin).

By following this process, a team gains a good overview of what's working, what isn't, and what needs to change. For the final step, the team votes for the single most important initiative in the start section. The initiative is then turned into work items that are added to the team's backlog and delivered alongside other work.

Sailboat Retrospective

The sailboat retrospective is an adaption of the speed boat innovation game designed by Luke Hohmann.[4] The sailboat exercise begins by drawing a sailboat, rocks, clouds, and an island on a flipchart or whiteboard as shown in Figure 5-5.

Island
Goals/Vision

Wind
Helping team

Anchor
Slowing team

Rocks
Risks

Figure 5-5. *The sailboat retrospective drawing*

The sailboat is a metaphor for a team heading toward a goal (represented by an island). Wind symbolizes things that help propel the team, an anchor characterizes impediments that hold the team back, and rocks signify risks that can stop a team from reaching a goal.

The facilitator writes the team's goal on the picture and asks them to think of what might be slowing it down, propelling it forward, and future risks related to the goal they may face. The team records their ideas on sticky notes, which are placed either above or below the boat to indicate if they are wind, anchors, or rocks. Once everyone has a chance to share their thoughts, a team member groups the notes into related categories and assigns labels. The team discusses the grouping and adjusts as necessary. When the team reaches consensus, they consider how they can continue to practice in the wind area. Finally, the team votes on labeled groups that are most critical to address in anchor and rocks so they can move onto root cause analysis of the problems and determine steps to fix them.

Premortem

We often look back on projects that have gone badly wrong and ask ourselves, what happened? We undertake retrospectives and postmortems to try and explain how we failed. But, after a project has failed is the wrong time to discuss solutions. A premortem is a preemptive retrospective exercise developed by Gary Klein that is conducted at the outset of a piece of work to identify causes of failure and mitigate them before they happen.[5] Premortems are a valuable investment in project success, but are criminally underused.

I suggest to aside at least 90 minutes of uninterrupted time for a face-to-face meeting. If that seems like a lot of time, keep in mind how long it took to clean up the mess the last time disaster struck a project. Invite everyone with a significant role to the premortem. If you fail to include the right people, blind spots will inevitabley occur.

During the premortem, imagine your project has failed. Imagine your project failed miserably. Think with regret about what you could have done better and actually feel bad about what happened. This may seem dramatic, but it can really help. During the first 45 minutes, place a sticky note on a whiteboard or wall that includes every problem with even a remote chance of occurring that derailed your project. And, have everyone just concentrate on the sticky note problems. At this stage, no problem is off-limits (even inconvenient truths). The only forbidden topics are proposed solutions. Solutions are strictly forbidden because they draw the team away from getting every single problem out into the open.

After everyone lists the reasons for failure, group the causes into similar themes. The team then votes to establish the top three risks to the project. Voting should focus on the most critical problems that are likely to happen and issues over which the team has control. Spend the final 30 minutes creating proactive solutions or backup plans for the three problems. Finally, assign actions and responsibility for them to team members. Otherwise, risks will not be mitigated resulting in unsolved problems.

Service Delivery

Team health checks and retrospectives are useful for helping analytics teams go faster, but it is equally vital for analytics teams to know whether internal customers believe their service delivery is fit for purpose. Often, trust in the analytics team's responsiveness, ability to deliver, and empathy are as important to stakeholders as the robustness and benefits of the product itself.

Service Delivery Review Meeting

A *service delivery review meeting* should be a regular assembly for the analytics team to discuss with internal customers how well they are meeting their service delivery expectations. Although it originates as part of *Kanban Cadences* (a suggested series of bidirectional communication meetings proposed by David Anderson), it is not restricted to Kanban teams or large organizations.[6] The discussion enables collaborative agreement on speed and trade-offs while minimizing misunderstandings on needs and expectations.

The frequency of meetings can be weekly, biweekly, or monthly, but any more time between meetings increases the risk of failing to meet customer expectations due to lack of feedback. The agenda should be data-driven and include metrics to avoid becoming subjective and allow tracking of improvement over time. However, the meeting is also an opportunity to share relevant qualitative feedback that would otherwise be missed, for example, user research from call centers or other frontline staff.

Quantitative metrics should focus on the analytics team's delivery from the viewpoint of the customer. Typically, customers are interested in how quickly the team delivers, whether it meets deadlines, how informed they are kept, how risks to delivery are mitigated, the mix of work the team undertakes, and the amount of time spent fixing problems relative to new jobs. Corresponding metrics to measure customer concerns include lead times, cycle times, percentage allocation to different work types, due date performance, number of blocked or delayed items, and rework rates due to errors or miscommunication.

These measures form the basis for discussing shortfalls, if any, against customer expectations. Based on measures, analyze gaps with root cause analysis and make changes to the way the analytics team works to improve their capability in the eyes of the customer. It's important to remember the discussion is bidirectional. As such, not all customer expectations may be reasonable. The meeting is also an opportunity to request support from a customer, for example, asking the customer to respond more quickly to questions or provide backing to escalate and resolve blockers elsewhere in the organization. Ultimately, a service delivery review should build trust and improve relationships between analytics teams and their customers.

It may seem that retrospectives and service delivery meetings add time to an environment where everyone is busy. However, these aren't traditional inefficient business meetings. They have a clear agenda, require active participation, and end with value-added actions. Although these meetings take time, service delivery review meetings and acting on the feedback should save hours inevitably wasted on poor processes and misunderstandings. To reduce overhead and resistance, I recommend merging the practices into meetings already taking place before adding new timeslots in calendars. As with all methods for continuous improvement, frequency, duration, and attendance should be adjusted over time to make things work with the objective of becoming a habit for everyone involved.

Improving Service Delivery

Successful service delivery reviews require data to inform the discussion and track improvement. I suggest to start by tracking simple metrics such as total work in process (WIP), *blockers* that halt the progress of items, throughput, lead time, and due date performance.

Total WIP is the count of all tasks that have been started (by anyone) but not finished. As a gut check, divide total WIP by the number of team members to get an average per person and assess if this feels right. This measure is usually an eye-opener as people realize they have far more work on their plate than they imagined. You will start seeing this top-line number decrease as you better manage WIP. A blocked item cannot progress forward. Maybe this happens because you're waiting on information from an external source and cannot proceed without it. It is a good idea to record how often items are blocked, how long they stay blocked, and where in the process they get stuck. Group blockers into external and internal causes, and then further group into similar subgroups such as waiting for system access, waiting for review, waiting for testing, and so on. Prioritize the subgroups for root cause analysis and solution implementation.

Lead time is how long it takes to complete work from the moment of request or addition to the team's backlog. So, record the start date of any new work item and calculate the average lead time of every item that finishes that week. Reduce the size of queues in your system to decrease average lead time. For items with deadlines, record how well those dates are met and the cost of any misses and compare with an acceptable success rate. Throughput is the number of items completed per period. At the end of each week, record the number of finished items. Track this number weekly to see how changes you make affect how much work gets done.

Service delivery review metrics track measures that teams do not usually discuss and increase transparency. You might find out that customers are not aware of the number of blockers the analytics teams face. Or maybe the analytics team is trying to do too many things and customers would rather that they prioritize hitting deadlines on high-priority items instead. These are just some of the important things that service delivery metrics might uncover.

Product Health

Deploying data products including data pipelines in production is not the end of the journey but the start of a process. Data products are a combination of data and code. Data feeding the product can stop, or change suddenly or slowly over time. And, changes in code such as updates to a machine learning model or ETL pipelines can also unintentionally worsen performance. Over time, changes in the underlying relationships in the data, known as *concept drift*, may degrade the performance of predictive models or render dashboards less and less useful. So, monitoring checks that data products are fit for purpose so updates and rollbacks can correct issues.

KPIs for Data Product Monitoring

The production system for a data product can be broken down into components. Data is first captured and ingested into storage or streaming processing. Next, data pipelines transform the data and supply it to the data product which further processes it before consumption by users or other systems. The health of each of these components impacts the ability of the data product's consumers to make decisions, so KPIs need to monitor them.

The most important KPI is the *correctness* of the data ingestion and data pipeline. The logic of the data product can be correct, yet bugs in data can corrupt its output and cause it to return the wrong answers. The correctness of data ingestion is the number of correct records ingested as a proportion of all records ingested. Correctness of the data pipeline is the number of records with correct values coming out of the pipeline as a proportion of those going in.

The *timeliness* of data and *end-to-end latency* of data pipelines are significant KPIs. The speed at which the organization can get value from data matters a lot, so unexpected bottlenecks need to be identified. Timeliness of data is the proportion of data accessed by consumers that has been updated more recently than a specified time threshold. Timeliness matters, for example, in ML model predictions or dashboard metrics. The end-to-end latency of data pipelines is the proportion of records that entered and exited the pipeline faster than a stipulated time threshold. A related KPI is *coverage*. For batch processing, coverage is the proportion of records successfully processed out of all records that should have been processed. For stream processing, coverage is the proportion of records entering the stream successfully processed within a stated time window.

Data product consumers are also interested in KPIs for *availability* and *latency*. Latency is the proportion of responses to requests from the data product faster than a particular threshold. There is the availability of the data product itself, for which the KPI is the proportion of requests that received a successful response. For example, a machine learning model API may be expected to return a prediction response within 100 milliseconds and return a response for 99.99% of prediction requests each day. Availability of correctly ingested data also matters to data consumers. Data that is not available for further processing in data pipelines, for example, today's operational records waiting for overnight batch processing or records in cold storage that cannot be retrieved easily, might as well not exist. The availability KPI for data ingestion is the proportion of correctly captured records that can be processed by data pipelines.

It is possible to consider many other KPIs, but it is best to start with a few that matter most and only add more if there is a benefit in doing so. For example, correctness always matters, but in a properly running pipeline, all processing will eventually get done. So, if it does break but is fixable without too much user pain, timeliness may not matter so much.

KPIs and targets for data product monitoring need to be approved by all stakeholders including the analytics teams responsible for meeting them. Avoid mean or median average measures as they can hide problems if there is highly skewed performance. For instance, an average response time for the latency KPI may look fine across the week but hide outages during peak usage times. This is a worse outcome than if the average had been the same with no outages even if some users had slightly slower responses. Instead, base KPI targets on the ratio of *good events* (events meeting an acceptable performance threshold) divided by total events over an appropriate period.

One hundred percent is not a feasible target for KPIs. Despite best efforts, systems will fail and data will get corrupted. Set thresholds for KPIs at a level that matters to data consumers or at a point they start to notice such as 100 milliseconds for a prediction API to return a response. The effort to improve performance above the threshold level may go unnoticed or not bring many benefits.

As you increase KPI performance targets, it also starts to become exponentially more expensive to achieve them. Teams have to grow in size so they have the capacity to proactively respond to impending problems, and redundant components have to be on standby ready to take over if systems fail. At some point, the costs outweigh the benefits. Excessively high KPI targets also discourage new development because any change introduces the potential risk of jeopardizing performance. By avoiding any change, the risk of falling below a very high-reliability KPI decreases, but this comes at the opportunity cost of adding new benefit.

Monitoring

The Fifteenth Data Ops principle is *quality is paramount*, which states that analytic pipelines should be built with a foundation capable of automated detection of abnormalities (jidoka) and security issues in code, configuration, and data and should provide continuous feedback to operators for error avoidance (poka yoke). The production system for data products can contain many components, each with many processing steps and different monitoring code.

Monitoring starts at the ingestion stage. The correctness of data ingestion is not straightforward to measure. There can be many reasons to reject incorrect data such as missing values, truncated values, data type mismatches, duplicates, or values that do not conform to the field type. One approach is to write as many tests as possible and continually add checks with every potential defect discovered to prevent bad data entering pipelines. The tests help diagnose why problems are occurring and help inform discussions with upstream data suppliers to avoid reoccurrence. The ratio of correct records ingested to total records gives the correctness KPI for data ingestion.

The correctness of data pipelines is also not straightforward to measure. In addition to adding tests, an additional method is to store a representative sample of test input data with known validated output and put it through the data pipeline after every change. The ratio of records with correct values coming out of the pipeline as a proportion of those going in provides the correctness KPI for data pipelines.

Calculate timeliness of data and end-to-end latency of data pipeline by adding watermarks with timestamps of major processing steps to the data. For the timeliness KPI, every time a data product consumer interacts with the product, the time of the request can be compared to the time the data was last updated. For example, from an app on his tablet, an engineer requests a maintenance time prediction for a machine that is provided by an API. The API can log not only the time of the request but also when the prediction for the machine was last updated. The proportion of times the data accessed by consumers has been updated more recently than a specified time threshold is the timeliness KPI. The end-to-end latency KPI of the data pipeline is easy to compute by taking the differences between start and end processing timestamps and calculating the proportion of elapsed times under the agreed threshold.

Calculation of the data coverage KPI is straightforward. The data pipeline exports a count of the number of records entering the pipeline and the number of records processed successfully. Computation of the availability and latency KPIs for data products depends very much on the application. Ideally, the data may already exist in server logs or existing application monitoring dashboards. Otherwise, we must instrument from scratch.

Manually monitoring KPIs is not an option. The process for detecting anomalies **must** be automated to free people up for more critical areas of focus. The best way to provide feedback to the operators of the production system is through dashboards and alerts fed from monitoring code. The purpose of the monitoring code, dashboards, and alerts is to identify problems and their causes as early as possible before they impact KPI targets and, hence, consumers of the data product.

Keeping a buffer between the external consumer KPI target and team target for internal alerting creates a warning zone that allows you to respond before the problem becomes acute. In some cases, changes can be sudden, and if the KPI target is not met, it is necessary to stop the production line as the cost of downstream data corruption and future reprocessing is greater than fixing the problem immediately. Monitoring also has the benefit of generating feedback on bottlenecks, so the most significant constraints, whether infrastructure architecture and capacity, manual processes, or slow code, can be removed or refactored.

Concept Drift

Machine learning and deep learning models learn rules from historical input and output data to make predictions from new input data. The relationship between new input and output data is assumed to remain the same as historical input and output data, so the machine learning model is expected to make useful predictions for new unseen data. The relationship may hold in some cases, for instance, those fixed by laws of nature such as image recognition algorithms for cats. However, other relationships like customer purchasing behavior, spam email detection, or product quality with machinery wear will eventually evolve in a process known as concept drift.

A passive strategy to solve the problem of concept drift is to retrain models using a window of recent data periodically. However, this is not an option in some circumstances due to negative feedback loops. Imagine a recommender system where specific customers see recommendations for product X based on previous purchasing relationships. The data for these customers is now biased because they are now even more likely to buy product X. A model trained on this data will boost the recommendation for product X further, even if in the outside world the original relationship has changed and customers prefer product Y to product X.

One solution to the negative feedback problem is to randomly hold out some instances from model predictions to create a baseline to measure model performance and generate an unbiased dataset for model training. Another strategy is to use a trigger to initiate a model update. Concept drift can be challenging to discover, and there are multiple algorithms for detection. Some of the commonly used algorithms are *Drift detection method* (DDM), *Early drift detection method* (EDDM), *Geometric moving average detection method* (GMADM), and *Exponentially weighted moving average chart detection method*. These algorithms can be built into continuous diagnostic monitoring of performance and alert when a model requires retraining. Predictions can then be turned off for some or all instances to generate unbiased data for retraining to avoid negative feedback loops. The retraining only happens when the model is not performing well so the cost of training and opportunity cost of prediction benefit is lower than the other two methods.

Product Benefit

A healthy data product is not sufficient on its own for success. Ultimately, the aim of data science and data analytics is to make better decisions and improve product creation, customer experience, and organizational efficiency. The primary measure of data analytics and data science performance is the benefit those improved decisions bring to the organization. Continuous real-world feedback measures if data products are meeting their benefit objectives.

Benefit Measurement

The first step in benefit measurement should take place while a data product is still in inception phase with the creation of a monitoring and benefit measurement plan for KPIs such as cost savings, revenue increases, or improvements in customer experience metrics. The second step should occur during the research and development (R&D) phase of the data science lifecycle while creating the MVP. Data scientists and data analysts should gather feedback from technical and subject matter experts to gauge the performance of their early iterations of the data product. The initial feedback provides a guide to whether the data product is likely to be fit for purpose and helps in the design of monitoring in ongoing use.

Offline feedback during the inception and R&D phases while very useful has limits. There are several significant differences between offline development and online production with live data. For instance, in real-world production, hardware and data may not be as reliable as the development setup. For example, a sensor may fail to provide data. Consumer behavior may change as a result of the data product creating a reinforcing feedback loop that generates new data influenced by the data product outputs. In some use cases, adversaries such as fraudsters, spammers, hackers, and competitors will change their behavior to circumvent predictive models. The solution is to create a reporting framework capable of providing feedback on MVPs and ongoing iterations in production by measuring the benefits.

The cleanest solution is to create the ability to partially deploy the data product to a random subset of consumers and use *A/B testing* experiments also known as *random assignment*. In A/B testing, the benefit measurement KPIs are calculated by comparing consumers randomly exposed to the data product with either those who are not (known as a *holdout control group*) or the current best approach (known as a *champion/ challenger experiment*). Statistical hypothesis testing validates how likely the difference in benefit measurement KPIs between groups is due to our *treatment* of the different groups or due to chance. A/B testing can be extended to include more than two groups or variants. However, the more variants that are concurrently measured, the more time it takes for the statistical hypothesis tests as one of their inputs is the number of observations measured. Most web testing and marketing automation platforms such as Google Optimize, Optimizely, Adobe Target, Mixpanel, and Salesforce Marketing Cloud can facilitate A/B testing. Open-source alternative A/B testing tools include Alephbet for front-end applications and Wasabi and Proctor for server-side implementation.

Once A/B testing of the MVP is complete, the benefit measurement plan for the data product should be used to decide whether the cost-benefit outcome warrants another research and development iteration to optimize the pipeline and analytics or abandon it and move on to another epic. However, unless the data product is retired, benefit measurement persists. The measurement baseline continues to be a holdout or previous champion control group. However, the proportion of consumers in these groups can be reduced compared to the initial A/B test as fast learning is not as important now as maximizing benefit.

Sometimes, it is not possible to use an off-the-shelf tool for monitoring benefits. This usually happens because the KPI data is not available in the tool or the logic for selecting treatment groups is complex and needs to be handled outside the tool. As with data product monitoring KPIs, manual monitoring of benefit KPIs soon becomes unmanageable and needs to be automated and ideally presented in a dashboard with a simple *user interface* (UI).

The dashboard needs to calculate statistics such as p-values, confidence intervals, and significance in addition to measurement KPIs. The data stores and data pipelines to feed the dashboard need to keep track of which consumers are in which bucket of an experiment or treatment group, when they enter and exit groups, and which metrics to track for each data product. The benefit measurement framework can be extended beyond data products if data analytics teams are responsible for measurements of experiments run by other parts of the organization.

Benefit measurement reporting frameworks can become complex data products in their own right, but the investment in them is critical for long-term success. Figure 5-6 shows the feedback loops from benefit measurement.

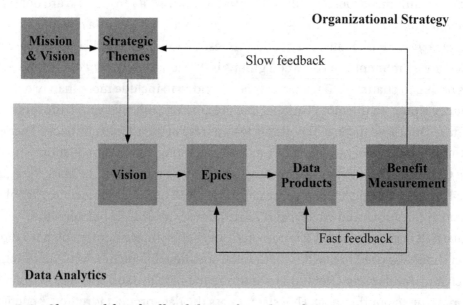

Figure 5-6. *Slow and fast feedback loops from benefit measurement*

Fast feedback from benefit measurement helps optimization of current data products, learning and prioritization of future data products due to better estimation of the cost of delay, and justifies the investment in data analytics to senior stakeholders. Slow feedback over a more extended period helps the organization understand how well its strategy is working.

Benefit Measurement Challenges

There are technical, practical, and cultural challenges to measuring product benefit correctly. A/B testing and measurement have many pitfalls. It is much harder than it sounds to ensure complete randomization of treatment between groups because bias can creep in from many sources. I once discovered an email service provider was sending the champion group emails before the challenger group. Although both groups were representative of each other, the timing of emails meant that differences between the groups were not due to treatment effects alone.

Once the integration of the benefit measurement framework is complete, it is recommended to validate it by running A/A tests to confirm the measurement is correct. An A/A test treats both the randomized control and test groups the same. If the testing and measurement framework is functioning correctly, there should be no significant difference in outcomes measured between the groups. However, if there are significant differences, the process needs investigating.

Many organizations don't measure the benefit of their initiatives beyond simple correlations such as we performed an action and revenue went up at the same time, so it must be due to our action. There can be many reasons why revenue increased that have nothing to do with the action. As anyone who has seen charts from Tyler Vigen's spurious correlations web site knows, correlation doesn't imply causation.[7] Without a *counterfactual* (a measure of what would have happened if the action had not occurred), it is difficult to determine cause and effect.

Counterfactuals are the reason A/B testing is the gold standard for measurement. However, in certain circumstances for regulatory, ethical, or trust reasons, it is not possible to treat customers differently by assigning them to random treatment groups. Sometimes, there are also not enough consumers or observations of usage of the data product to calculate robust output from statistical hypothesis test. In this case, direct feedback from consumers can help estimate benefit.

Some organizations are reluctant to measure benefit because they operate in a culture that rewards outputs and not outcomes. The substantial process changes from JFDI (Just Freakin' Do It (polite form)) execute and move on mode to run experiments and wait for results before iterating is a significant barrier to benefit measurement. Many managers also lack statistical knowledge or fear statistics and do not want their decisions guided by something they do not understand. There is a common but misguided fear among revenue generating departments like marketing that measurement reduces income due to the opportunity cost of holdout groups. This behavior is like placing all your chips on red at the casino roulette table because you're worried that holding back chips will reduce your winnings.

It can be hard to break an organizational culture that does not routinely measure benefit. One option is to find the thin end of the wedge (a low-risk area of the organization) to run experiments and demonstrate the benefits achievable before slowly expanding to other areas. Another option is to reduce the cost of experimentation and benefit measurement by automating as much of the process as possible or using alternative measurement approaches. There are alternatives to randomized A/B testing and measurement, but there are no magical free lunches in statistics, only shortcuts that come with trade-offs.

Alternatives to A/B Testing and Measurement

The social sciences and especially *econometrics* (the branch of economics that applies statistical techniques to data) have developed a set of techniques to determine cause and effect when A/B testing is not an option. The simplest method is *regression analysis*, which is a way to measure the relationship of multiple variables to an outcome). For example, a taxi company introduces an ML model to forecast demand for its service so it can flex capacity and increase gross bookings. By using data from before and after implementation of a model, a regression of gross bookings on ML model usage controlling for all other factors that influence it (i.e., day of week, time of day, weather, and events) isolates the contribution of the ML model. The pitfall of regression analysis is that we may not have data on all the factors to control for in the model, which overstates the contribution of the treatment.

Differences-in-differences (DID) is another commonly used econometric technique. DID relies on a comparison of pre and post outcomes between the treated group and a control group that is not identical but displays parallel trends. Imagine our taxi company uses the ML model in Washington but not yet in Baltimore where it also operates and shows very similar patterns. Without the model, the same trend in gross bookings is expected between Washington and Baltimore. Hence, a comparison of the change in the delta of gross bookings between cities, before and after implementation of the model, provides an estimate of the model's effectiveness. The drawback of DID is that if something other than the treatment changes trends during the post period in one group but not the other, it violates the parallel trends assumption.

Multiarmed bandit algorithms are an example of an approach that some people claim is superior to A/B testing. In standard A/B testing, you usually split users 50:50 between two versions of your data product. One of the versions will perform worse than the other, so there is an opportunity cost of exposing users to this variant. With multiarmed bandit algorithms, you also start with an equal split during an *exploration phase* (typically 10% of the total time the experiment is expected to last). However, in the following *exploitation phase,* users are split based on the relative performance of the variants with more users exposed to the better-performing variant. This split reduces the opportunity cost of testing, but because the lower-performing variant is exposed to fewer users, it is harder to tell if it is worse or if the difference is due to chance. It takes much longer to reach statistically significant results than if users are split equally between variants. If the difference in performance between variants is small, even the opportunity cost-benefit is negligible over A/B testing.

Metric Challenges

The benefit measurement plan contains the KPIs to measure the success of the data product, which ultimately aims to deliver the organization's strategic objectives. However, some metrics may not be readily available in systems or only available in the long-term such as market share, customer retention, or net present value (NPV). Ideally, the measurement should wait until the long-term metrics are available. But in reality, there is pressure to approximate from short-term measures.

There are two challenges. First, long-term measures, especially accounting metrics, can encourage failure since they incentivize managers to come up with hyperbolic scenarios to justify investment in the competition for funding. If they gain funding, managers have to pursue a "go big or go home" plan to hit their fantasy forecasts. The second challenge is that readily available short-term success metrics may not positively correlate with long-term or even midterm metrics.

The solution is to find leading indicators of success by analyzing historical correlations and not rely on assumptions. It is unlikely you will see perfectly correlated short-term and long-term metrics, but statistical or machine learning models are likely to find metrics directionally associated with each. For example, customer feedback, per customer revenue, repeat purchase, and retention rates tend to move together.

Avoid the temptation to cover all bases and measure everything. When there are too many measures, it becomes difficult to optimize and make trade-offs. The solution is to raise the measurement one level and reduce the number of measures. Find the one thing that matters that will drive the right results for the lower-level metrics and facilitate trade-offs. For example, when measuring metrics for a web site, instead of trying to increase average session duration, page views, return visitor conversion, new visitor conversion, and interactions per session while reducing bounce rate, you should target higher revenue per visit.

Summary

The quote "insanity is repeating the same mistakes and expecting different results" is misattributed to Albert Einstein but originally appeared in a 1981 Narcotics Anonymous publication.[8] Nevertheless, an addiction to keep delivering work, in the same way, every time cannot lead to improvement.

Escape from the prison of mediocrity is possible. Knowledge workers in the 21st century have two jobs. First, perform their daily work and continuously seek to improve their work. DataOps leaders continually look for new ways to cultivate a culture of continuous improvement in productivity and customer benefit. Sustained continuous improvement needs constant investment of time and effort to develop a systems thinking mindset, collect feedback from teams and customers, and apply the scientific method to deliver faster, better, and cheaper. Second, for measurement-based improvement to be successful, data must be dependable. The next chapter describes how to increase trust in data and trust in users of data.

Endnotes

1. W. Edwards Deming, W. Edwards Deming Quotes, The
    W. Edwards Deming Insitute. *https://quotes.deming.org/*

2. Matt Philips, Service-Delivery Review: The Missing Agile
    Feedback Loop? May 2017. *https://mattphilip.wordpress.
    com/2017/05/24/service-delivery-review-the-missing-
    agile-feedback-loop/*

3. Henrik Kniberg, Squad Health Check model – visualizing
    what to improve, September 2014. *https://labs.spotify.
    com/2014/09/16/squad-health-check-model/*

4. Luke Hohmann, Innovation Games: Creating Breakthrough
    Products Through Collaborative Play: Creating Breakthrough
    Products and Services, Aug 2006.

5. Gary Klein, Performing a Project Premortem, Harvard Business
    Review, September 2007. *https://hbr.org/2007/09/
    performing-a-project-premortem*

6. David Anderson, Kanban Cadences, April 2015. *www.djaa.com/
    kanban-cadences*

7. Tyler Vigen, Spurious correlations. *www.tylervigen.com/
    spurious-correlations*

8. Narcotics Anonymous Pamphlet, (Basic Text Approval Form,
    Unpublished Literary Work), Chapter Four: How It Works, Step
    Two, Page 11, Printed November 1981. *https://web.archive.
    org/web/20121202030403/http://www.amonymifoundation.org/
    uploads/NA_Approval_Form_Scan.pdf*

PART III

Further Steps

CHAPTER 6

Building Trust

Cars have brakes not to stop, but to travel fast. If cars had no brakes, people would still drive but just slowly enough so they could use a nearby tree or lamp post to stop safely in an emergency. The better the brakes, the faster you can safely go. The introduction of carbon/carbon brakes by the Brabham formula one racing team in the early 1980s allowed the team to win their first championship in 14 years and dominate the competition until other teams copied them.

Carbon/carbon brakes allowed Brabham's drivers to drive faster into corners than competitors because drivers knew they could slow quicker. To go more quickly, however, you need more safety features. Wearing a seat belt is mandatory when driving a standard vehicle in most jurisdictions. However, vehicle racing needs a racing harness, roll cage, fire extinguishing equipment, helmet, fuel cut-off switch, head and neck restraints, and fire-retardant suits. So, speed and safety features go hand in hand.

Unfortunately, many IT departments believe the route to reducing risk is not to introduce safety features but metaphorically remove the tires from the vehicle and make it as hard as possible to drive. It is indeed one strategy to prevent accidents, but it also guarantees you will not go anywhere quickly. This approach leads data analytics teams to view data governance as a barrier to their work. As such, they create a parallel shadow IT operation that makes analytics less safe.

For data analytics to go faster, it needs brakes in the form of rules and constraints to build trust. Two types of trust are required, the organization needs to trust people with data and systems access, and users of data need to trust the data they are using is correct. With trust in people, the organization can ensure its data professionals can easily access the data and systems they need, while keeping data secure, meeting regulatory requirements, and efficiently utilizing resources. With trust in data, data professionals work quickly with less fear of things going wrong.

© Harvinder Atwal 2020
H. Atwal, *Practical DataOps*, https://doi.org/10.1007/978-1-4842-5104-1_6

Trust People with Data and Systems

With traditional approaches to making data and systems available to consumers, a multitude of IT professionals create well-governed data warehouses and data marts through slow, labor-intensive processes. Unfortunately, accessing data, adding new data, or making changes to data in the warehouses and marts takes too much time for effective DataOps.

DataOps requires that data scientists, data analysts, and data engineers have quick access to data, tools, and infrastructure to eliminate bottlenecks. That is, they need to be able to access, add, or modify data quickly by themselves. We term this availability to data self-service. Through self-service, data analytics professionals can create data products in far less time than with traditional approaches.

The challenge with self-service is getting data security, data governance, and resource utilization right. In many regulated industries, prescribed data security and data protection policies must be followed. Even in nonregulated sectors, commercially sensitive and *personally identifiable information* (PII) must be safeguarded. Self-service data must be made available without contravening internal rules and external compliance regulations. Self-service is also not an excuse to resource binge and rack up significant costs.

Accessing and Provisioning Data

Traditionally, an IT or data team sits between users and data while performing the role of gatekeepers. Users request access to data by raising tickets. The gatekeeping team then manually decides, based on security and governance considerations, whether the data is released. However, this approach does not scale well to the large volumes and varieties of data organizations currently capture nor does it support the self-service model. This method also does not promote collaboration.

Typically, users who have been with the organization for the longest time or worked on a wide variety of projects end up with more access to data than recent recruits. Such activity creates a bottleneck for collaboration as well as causing some people to wait for data access.

The traditional approach is also a blocker to innovation. Users may need to explore new data sources to understand their value but might find it difficult to access such data because of gatekeeping team obstacles.

One solution to the problem of data access is to grant everyone full access. However, this is not an option where sensitive data is concerned or where industry regulations restrict who has access to information. Laws also change over time. That is, data legitimately stored and accessed today may not be the same tomorrow.

An alternative route is to tie user identities to roles and access policies for data through *Identity and Access Management* (IAM). IAM is a framework of technologies and policies that ensure an identity has access to the right resources such as applications, services, databases, data, and networks. IAM relies on a central directory of users, roles, and predefined permissions to authenticate users and grant them access rights, which are typically based on *role-based access control* (RBAC).

RBAC uses predefined job roles and associated policies to control access to individual systems and authorize the operations a job role can perform within the context of a specific system. For example, RBAC can define several roles that go beyond merely blocking or allowing access to all data. One role may have read-only access to the entire dataset in a system, while another may allow full access only to specific fields within the dataset, with all other fields masked. A third role may allow full access to some systems but not others. A fourth may allow all operations on a system except the ability to export, share, and download (and so on).

The alternative to RBAC is user-based access with permissions created at the individual level. User-based access control allows permissions that are more granular for individuals but comes with additional management overhead, so it is only warranted if the extra control is needed.

There are many ways and tools to implement IAM to define how roles access data based on an organization's systems and needs. The most critical requirement is that IAM delivers data access through centralized technology that integrates with existing access and sign-on systems. When IAM frameworks manage data access, it becomes much easier to map users to data access policies as well as collect audit logs of all interactions and build intelligent monitoring for security and governance.

Data Security and Privacy

Creating a self-service data culture requires robust security and compliance controls. Data security and privacy laws and regulations exist at the industry, region, national, and international level. For example, the *General Data Protection Regulation* (GDPR) has robust standards for data protection, security, and compliance across the *European*

Economic Area (EEA), while the *Health Insurance Portability and Accountability Act* (HIPAA) sets standards for protecting sensitive patient data in the United States.

A data classification policy is the foundation for data security and protection of sensitive data. The organization's risk appetite and regulatory environment inform the data classification policy, while a separate security policy defines the requirements for safeguarding storage, processing, transmission, and access rights for each category of classification.

The first step in creating a data classification policy is to define the goals such as comply with industry and national regulations and mitigate the risk of unauthorized access to personal data. Ideally, an organization should create only three or four data classification levels after establishing goals such as *sensitive, confidential*, and *public*. The sensitive category includes personally identifiable data, payment card information, health records, authentication information, or highly commercially sensitive information. The confidential level may contain internal or personal information not intended for public consumption. The public classification level includes information freely disclosable outside the organization.

Data owners should be responsible for classifying data they own according to the classification policy. However, manual classification and labeling of data may not be feasible due to the volume and variety of data. Thankfully, automated data classification solutions exist including *Macie* on Amazon Web Services (AWS) and *Data Loss Prevention* on Google Cloud. Together with the IT department or Information Security office, data owners develop the access, storage, transmission, and processing policy for each data classification label.

Restricting access to sensitive data is not the only option to keep it secure. Often, sensitive data is useful for analytics either for testing, joining datasets on identifiers, or as a feature for analysis. For example, geographical analysis requires address information. *Data masking, secure hashing, bucketing,* and *format-preserving encryption* are common ways to de-identify or anonymize such data.

Data masking or data obfuscation involves substituting similar data such as names or addresses, random shuffling of data, or applying random variation to values to keep the data meaningful in a process known as *pseudonymization*. In other cases, data masking is more extreme and includes nulling out or deleting data fields or masking out characters and digits such as all but the last digits of a phone number or credit card.

Secure hashing differs from encryption in that it is a one-way process to turn a string of text into a fixed-length string of text or numbers with a mathematical function.

The function returns the same hash every time for the same input, but even if the hash function is known, it is virtually impossible to reverse the process and find the original value. Sometimes, additional random text known as a *salt* is added to data to make the process more secure.

Bucketing replaces individual values with grouped values, for example, replacing dates with months or years, salaries with salary ranges, or job titles with occupation groupings.

Format preserving encryption encrypts data while keeping its form, so an encrypted telephone number still looks like a telephone number. Format preserving is essential to pass validation tests later in data pipelines that check data formats are as expected.

Securing sensitive data centrally and early in the ingestion process before making it available for development and testing minimizes security risks and prevents later delays from needing to protect data each time it is accessed.

IAM controls which users can access resources, but it is also essential to block visibility of data for users who accidentally or maliciously gain access to it. Data encryption achieves protection of *data at rest* (or data in storage) and *data in motion* (or data moving from one location to another). Encrypting data when storing and decrypting (when it is accessed) protects data at rest. The data may be encrypted client-side before transmission by the system sending data or server-side by the system storing the data.

Encrypted connection protocols such as HyperText Transfer Protocol Secure (HTTPS), Secure Socket Layer (SSL), and Transport Layer Security (TLS) secure data as it moves across networks. In addition to encryption, network firewalls and network access controls provide further security against unauthorized access.

In a self-service DataOps world, teams need access to data and the infrastructure to process the data. The infrastructure is likely to be *multitenant*, which means that many teams are sharing the same system resources and data assets. Data also needs protecting from users and applications accidentally deleting or corrupting data.

Data versioning is a method to protect data in multitenant scenarios. When updating data, copies of previous versions are kept and can be reverted to if needed. For further protection against accidental loss, multiple zones or regions can store data in the cloud.

Unfortunately, many countries and economic areas erect data localization policy barriers as a form of data protectionism. It is thereby crucial that rules and governance be in place to ensure data is only transferred, stored, and processed in geographies where local law allows.

To ensure compliance with laws, regulations, and internal data governance policies, auditing and monitoring are essential. Log files capture data access, data processing operations, and user activity events. Regulations may require that those log files are retained for a defined period to provide as an audit trail. Alerts are created by analyzing log files in real-time to detect abnormal behavior and raise the alarm or flag for further investigation. There are several solutions to capture and analyze log data and proactively identify issues such as AWS CloudTrail and Elastic Stack.

Resource Utilization Monitoring

Multitenancy requires users to share infrastructure fairly between them. Otherwise, users are stuck waiting in queues for their queries or processes to run, or end consumers notice latency of the data product. While modern cloud platforms allow for almost infinite scaling of resources, it is nevertheless necessary to have constraints in place. An organization still needs to maximize the return on its data infrastructure costs, and resource constraints are a way to discourage wasteful processes.

Setting hard or soft quotas for budgets, computing resource or query workload in databases through defined contracts between the data infrastructure team and users is a suitable way to ensure fairness. Short-term feedback on infrastructure usage and costs back to users allows them to trade-off the value of their work against the cost of producing it. With longer-term measurement of benefits, KPIs assist in adjusting quotas so that the most valuable or time-sensitive workloads gain priority over other usages. Unfortunately, workloads can spike and break quotas for a variety of reasons such as seasonal demand variation or expensive exploratory analysis.

Sometimes, quotas are broken accidentally. For instance, every inexperienced data analyst or data scientist has inadvertently run a Cartesian join query that joins every row in one table of a database to every row in another table. Cartesian joins are computationally expensive because the output can result in billions of returned rows. Unanticipated inefficient processing of data or rogue queries consumes resources or budget at the expense of other users.

There are several ways to safeguard against unexpected resource utilization affecting budgets or other workloads. A common approach is to isolate workloads in a separate infrastructure so that ad hoc analysis cannot affect more critical work. Monitoring tools such as AppDynamics, New Relic, DataDog, Amazon Cloudwatch, Azure Monitor, and Google Stackdriver track metrics for resources and applications in data centers or the cloud.

With such tools, you can view visualizations and statistics, store logs, set alerts, and monitor real-time performance to isolate and resolve issues quickly. Many databases feature workload management tools to optimize performance for users and applications by dynamically assigning tasks based on process priorities, resource availability, and perform actions if a query violates monitoring rules.

Budgets in cloud platforms can be set to monitor spending over time and alert on exceeding thresholds to manage costs proactively. Cloud platforms also provide granular cost and usage reporting that help pinpoint opportunities for optimization and improvements in ROI of data products.

Figure 6-1 shows the pillars to establish trust in users of data.

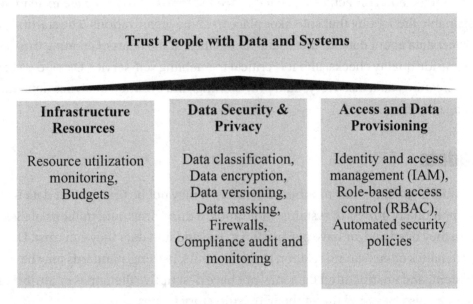

Figure 6-1. *The pillars for trust in users of data*

People Can Trust Data

Earlier in my career, I often had to spend days and sometimes weeks investigating if a sudden change in a business metric was real or a data quality glitch. It nearly always turned out to be a data quality issue that was not detected early enough to be corrected in the data pipelines and embarrassingly traveled all the way to stakeholders. Garbage in leads to garbage out. That is, a simple algorithm using clean data will outperform a fancy algorithm using dirty data. Yet, sexy uses of data such as AI receive far more focus and resource than data quality.

Veracity is the accuracy of data. It is the fourth V of big data after volume, variety, and velocity and arguably the most important. Without veracity, big data offers the opportunity to make bad decisions much faster, at bigger scales than before.

Data quality continues to be a significant source of wasted effort in data analytics. A Harvard business review study by Tadhg Nagle, Thomas Redman, and David Sammon found that only 3% of 75 participating companies had a data quality score rated as acceptable (97 or more correct data records out of 100).[1] A total of 47% of newly created records had at least one critical work-impacting error.

When data is bad, it stops being an asset and becomes a liability as a single bad data item can impact multiple reports and machine learning models for months or years if undetected. A proactive approach is needed for users to trust data instead of the unsustainable firefighting that still takes place in many organizations. The starting point is to collect data about data, or metadata. Metadata is at the heart of creating trust in data alongside quality checks, and it is critical to enabling self-service DataOps. Much of the data cleaning, data discovery, data provisioning, and eventual analytics depends on collecting metadata.

Metadata

Organizations contain a vast number of datasets. It may not be practical for data users to trawl potentially dozens of systems, thousands of directories, and millions of files to find data they need and/or have permission to use and find data they can trust. Dataset and field names often bear no relation to the contents, naming standards may be inconsistent, and unstructured data may not have descriptive filenames or attributes. Datasets can also be stored under the wrong directory names.

It can be virtually impossible to understand what datasets represent even if you could inspect them all. Before using data, there has to be a way to discover it, know where it came from, what it means, who owns it, and what part of it can be used by whom. *Metadata*, data about data, helps users understand what the data represents. The National Information Standards Organization (NISO) in the United States defines three main types of metadata, *descriptive metadata, structural metadata,* and *administrative metadata.*[2]

Descriptive metadata describes data for identification and discovery. Descriptive data includes the subcategories of *business metadata* and *operational metadata.* Business metadata consists of user-friendly names, labels, tags, ownership information, and masking rules for the data that make it much easier for people to browse, search, and decide if it is the right dataset for them. Operational metadata captures useful information such as the source of the data, who ingested it, usage of data, and results of processing operations on the data. Operational metadata encapsulates the provenance, lineage, versioning, quality information, data lifecycle stage, and profile of data. Descriptive data helps users and data discovery tools find, catalog, explore, and understand datasets.

Structural metadata is data about the organization of information and its relationship to other data. Structural metadata describes the data structures such as system names, table names, field names, indexes, and partitions so that it is possible to know a particular data asset's place in a hierarchy or collection of data. Beyond organization, structural metadata documents the relationship between data items. For example, structural metadata logs that one version of a file is the raw, unprocessed version of another file or documents the foreign key relationships between two datasets.

Administrative metadata contains three subtypes of metadata including *technical metadata, preservation metadata,* and *rights metadata.* Technical metadata assists in decoding and using files by providing information such as file types, file sizes creation times, allowed values, data types, and compression schemes. Preservation metadata such as *checksums* (or the output of running a cryptographic hash function on a piece of data) allows for verification of data integrity after transfers, format migration, or other processing. Rights metadata holds the policy information associated with the data. This type of metadata captures policies related to data access, data processing rights, and lifecycle policies specifying data retention periods.

Metadata helps users trust data by making it faster for them to identify the data they want and can use. Metadata is essential to self-service data analytics. Without it, even if users have access to the self-service infrastructure, they still have the bottleneck of needing expert IT help to use datasets. Metadata also helps increase trust in users of data by facilitating data governance, which dictates policy standards for management, quality, access, and use of data. Critical capability metadata rests on a robust, scalable framework that captures and manages metadata.

Tagging

There are challenges in delivering a framework to manage metadata. Different applications, teams, and even suppliers may describe and structure similar data in very different ways. Without standards, metadata can become inconsistent thereby defeating its purpose.

The traditional approach to solve the problem is to centralize metadata management. Data warehouse and data mart teams produce and adhere to metadata standards and handle changes in data using metadata management tools. Centralized metadata management synchronizes data and metadata with no inconsistency in metadata management. However, with increasing volumes and varieties of data captured by organizations, change management processes employed for centralized manual metadata management can quickly become a bottleneck. The wait for metadata creation slows down the ingestion and availability for new or updated data sources if it is manually created or if the data is converted to fit the organization's metadata standards.

An alternative to centralized metadata management is, you guessed it, decentralized metadata management. Since there is not a single person or team in the organization that understands every data item, decentralized metadata must be crowdsourced. Subject matter experts and data users associate descriptive metadata to fields and datasets in a process known as *tagging*.

For consistency, business metadata tags should be harmonized with existing *business glossaries, taxonomies,* or *ontologies*. These restraints are critical for making metadata taggers adhere to a strategic vision rather than their own. Business glossaries contain standard definitions of business terms and synonyms used by the organization. Business taxonomies classify objects in a hierarchical structure such as department, location, topic, or document type. Business ontologies describe individual instances or objects, sets or collections of objects as classes, attributes of those objects and classes, relationships between classes and objects, and rules and restrictions.

Ontologies have a much more flexible structure than taxonomies. For example, the Financial Industry Business Ontology (FIBO) describes terms, facts, and relationships with associated business entities, securities, loans, derivatives, market data, corporate actions, and business processes in the financial industry. FIBO helps firms integrate technical systems, share data, and automate processes using a common language.[3]

The disadvantage of decentralized metadata approach is that it requires a large number of committed users to maintain the metadata. Another drawback is that while users document popular datasets and fields thoroughly, a large pool of untagged dark data may remain.

A final solution is to combine decentralized metadata management with software automation. Subject matter experts and data users tag data, and then advanced data catalog tools use machine learning to learn the rules for tagging further data. Feedback on the accuracy of automated tagging helps improve the machine learning models.

Unstructured data does not even need tagging as cloud services from Amazon Web Services, Google Cloud Platform, and Microsoft Azure extract metadata from images, videos, voice, and text.

Trust During Ingestion

Building trust in data starts as soon as batch processes or real-time streams from source systems ingest data. File validation and data integrity checks safeguards against loss of data integrity or duplicate data loads during ingestion. *File duplication checks* incrementally examine filenames, schemas, and checksums of incoming file contents against existing files and delete any duplicate files.

Errors in transmission can corrupt data. So, *file integrity tests* look to see if the file ingested is the same as the transmitted file. A hash function in the source system converts the contents of the file into a message digest and sends it with the file contents. Applying the hash function on the received file contents verifies the integrity of the file if the output matches the message digest.

File size checks are another type of file validation check. They are similar to file integrity tests but compare the sizes rather than hashes of files transferred. *File periodicity checks* monitor file counts at regular intervals and send alerts if the expected number of files are not received during the appropriate period.

Data integrity checks during ingestion assure the accuracy and consistency of data received. The most straightforward data integrity check is a comparison of total record counts between the source system and the ingested data. Other data integrity checks involve comparing the schema or column counts of ingested data with the data source to detect structural changes in the data.

The earliest opportunity to capture metadata is upon ingestion. At the ingestion stage, vital information is obtained on the ingestion timestamp, the source of the data, who initiated the intake, the file schema, and the retention policy. Business, operational, and administrative metadata tags are also applied at this stage as are data classification rules according to the data classification policy. In addition to metadata capture, data *watermarking* of ingested data enables lineage tracking as data moves through the data pipeline and across the lifecycle all the way to deletion. Unlike metadata, watermarking alters original data by adding a unique identifier to a file or record.

Data Quality Assessment

After ingestion, data is ready for direct consumption or *data integration*. Data integration is the process of combining data from multiple sources. Integrating multiple data sources maximizes the value of data.

Unlike traditional warehouses, which only integrate structured data, most organizations today need to integrate structured data sources with semi-structured machine-generated data and even unstructured data such as customer review text in on-premise data lakes or the cloud. However, combining inaccurate, incomplete, and inconsistent data dilutes the benefit of data integration and in some cases is counterproductive because it joins good data to bad. Low-quality data must be detected and transformed or flagged before integration.

Files can pass validation checks, and data integrity checks can accept poor-quality data because the quality problem is created in the source systems that generate data. The incoming data should be inspected to ensure it fits the formats and range of values expected.

Data profiling is the process of statistics and summary information collection from an existing file or data source to generate metadata. Data profiling tools or code can produce descriptive summary statistics such as frequencies, aggregates (count and sum), ranges (minimum, maximum, percentiles, and standard deviation), and averages (mean, mode, median).

Data profiling is a way to detect poor data quality and create metadata for data cleansing. In practice, data profiling metadata should be captured and monitored not just once. It should be captured along the entire data pipeline every time data is transformed, on new data pipeline creation, and during pipeline updates.

For data quality purposes, additional profiling values are captured. It is essential to know how *complete* the data is, how *correct* the data is in comparison to business rules, and how *consistent* the data is across datasets. For data completeness, data profiling captures metadata such as the occurrence of null values, missing values, unknown or irrelevant values, and duplicates. For data correctness, useful profiling includes metadata on:

- **Outliers**. Values above and below the range of valid values, or atypical string lengths and values.

- **Data types**. The data types for fields should be the expected data type, for example, integer, date/time, Boolean, and so on.

- **Cardinality**. Some values may need to be unique across the data field.

- **Set memberships**. Values in specific fields must come from a discrete set, such as countries, states, or genders.

- **Format frequencies**. Some values, such as phone numbers, must fit a regular expression pattern.

- **Cross-field validation**. Precise conditions should hold across fields; for example, end dates should not be before start dates.

Data consistency metadata captures information on the coherence of data relative to other data such as violation of referential integrity rules. For example, if one dataset references a value such as a customer ID, the referenced value must exist in another dataset like a customer details table.

Beyond profiling, data quality also includes detecting anomalies in *accuracy* and *uniformity*. Accurate data conforms to standard measures and values such as verified addresses. Uniformity of data ensures equal measures of data use the same units. Standardization is especially crucial when integrating US data with world data, where distance, volume, and weight measures are in different units.

Data Cleansing

As noted in Chapter 1, data scientists regularly cite poor-quality data as their biggest challenge in surveys. Tackling the problem is one of the most efficient ways to eliminate waste in the data science process and improve the quality of decisions making:

> *More data beats clever algorithms, but better data beats more data.*
>
> —*Peter Norvig, Director of Research at Google Inc.*

Once the data quality metadata provides a clear understanding of the data quality issues, there are some choices for correcting problems. The preferable option is to fix data quality issues in source systems before data ingestion, for example, preventing record creation unless it matches predefined formats or does not contain missing values. Other options are to cleanse the data or accept the data quality issues and allow users to decide based on the data quality metadata tags whether, or how, to use the data. Data cleansing involves removing or correcting data and collecting operational metadata to record these cleansing operations.

The traditional approach to dealing with data correctness or data completeness problems is to delete the data or impute values, so problem data does not pass down the pipeline. Any deleted data is archived in a separate file for audit purposes. Imputation fills missing, null, or incorrect values with new values using statistical methods. New values can be based on averages (mean, mode, or median) for the field or in more sophisticated approaches imputed by prediction models. The deletion or imputation approach was acceptable when the main analytics use case was descriptive analytics using summarized and aggregated data. However, it is problematic with machine learning which typically makes predictions at the observational level.

The problem with dropping records with missing or null data is that the process drops information. Imputing missing values also does not add new information. It merely embeds existing patterns into the data.

In the real-world, machine learning predictions often need to be made even if some data is missing, so models benefit from seeing examples during training. So, a better approach over deletion or imputation is to adopt the monitoring method outlined in the previous chapter, which is a KPI threshold.

A KPI threshold can be set for data quality. For example, we can accept that at least 99.9% of values in an age field should fall between the allowed values of 0 and 125. If monitoring shows that data quality exceeds the KPI, the data is accepted and passed down the pipeline. If the KPI starts to get close to the threshold warning, alerts are triggered for investigation. If quality falls below the threshold, brakes are applied to prevent bad data from going further. If the problem is fixable, the missing data is backfilled and made available again.

Data quality metadata tags store the proportion of records or fields meeting the data quality thresholds. The metadata informs users of the data quality and actions they need to take. Data scientists create a feature (or categorical label) for missing values allowing machine learning algorithm to learn an optimal way to treat missing values. Business Intelligence developers may decide to delete the data or impute values based on the same metadata.

Entity resolution (or fuzzy matching) can sometimes resolve data consistency problems. The same data or entity may appear inconsistently in the data because of a typo, mislabeling, or erratic capitalization. Entity resolution and fuzzy matching techniques attempt to identify where the record is likely to be the same.

Data accuracy correction can be hard to achieve through data cleansing alone as the true value is not known. Often, the only way to correct for accuracy is if an external data source contains the real value. For example, zip/postal codes can be matched to external address databases to ensure that address details are correct. Nonuniform data can be cleansed easily by applying an arithmetic transformation to make the data a single measure.

Data Lineage

Data quality metadata tells data engineers, data analysts, and data scientists how good the data is. It is also useful to know its lineage, where the data came from, where it has moved, and what has happened to it. Often, data users are building on the work of others rather than reinventing the wheel or working with raw data for the first time. Answers to questions on lineage such as "I'm not sure where that data comes from" or "The guy who built that pipeline left months ago" do not inspire confidence in the data.

An understanding of data lineage (or data provenance) aids trust as some sources of data and processes may be more reliable than others for similar data items. Data lineage also helps track back sources of error, allows reproduction of transformations, and provides attribution of data sources. In some industries, especially financial services, regulatory compliance requires lineage documentation of data used for financial reporting.

Many commercial BI and ETL tools automatically capture lineage information as they process data. However, capturing data lineage is not a trivial process if multiple systems, tools, and languages are involved in the pipeline, especially if they are open source.

Some ETL processes may use SQL queries, others a *graphical user interface* (GUI)-based tool, and some a programming language such as Java, Scala, or Python. This mix of languages and tools makes it challenging to standardize the representation of processes or sometimes even identify if the tools and code are extracting data from the same or different systems as each other.

The most straightforward tactic is to document business-level lineage to describe data lineage in business terms and simple language. The issue with business-level lineage is that it is a manual process to create and maintain it.

The alternative to business-level lineage is to create technical lineage showing the specific code used to perform transformations on data. As data lineage is only useful when traced back to the source, and many systems may be involved, lineage information is stitched together from multiple sources to build a complete picture. Within the Hadoop ecosystem, the governance and metadata tools Apache Atlas and

Cloudera Navigator provide the ability to visualize data lineage. Other tools such as IBM Infosphere Discovery, Waterline data, Manta, and Alation can extract data processing logic from multiple sources and platforms to generate lineage reports.

Data Discovery

Data consumers need to understand data, its structure, content, trustworthiness, and lineage to find relevant data and make efficient use of it. Data discovery guides people to pertinent datasets in a two-step process. The first step is to make data discoverable, and the second step is performing the discovery.

Metadata makes data discoverable without having to search for and access the data directly. Just as libraries use metadata such as subject, author, and title to organize and catalog their data, so organizations need to organize and catalog their datasets. However, without a query-able interface to search for data using metadata or the data content, data users will struggle to find what they need. Without searchable catalogs, data users fall back on *tribal knowledge* (or unwritten information in the organization), which is a time-consuming approach.

Data catalog software to make metadata and data searchable can be purchased off-the-shelf from vendors such as IBM, Collibra, Alation, Informatica, Waterline Data, and others. However, it also possible to construct a data catalog using open-source software and cloud services. For example, a data catalog for all data stored in a data lake's S3 buckets can be constructed using AWS Lambda to extract metadata and save it to Amazon DynamoDB for objects on creation. Amazon Elasticsearch can then be used to search the metadata by users.

More advanced data catalog solutions offer capabilities beyond search for data discovery. Some data catalogs automatically tag data and allow users to rate data sources, add comments, and provide additional context on business meaning and relationships between data. Other features include the ability to integrate with a wide range of tools to link with business glossaries, tag data owners and stewards, pull in data lineage data, mask sensitive data, and share tags with access control tools to limit data access and provision only to authorized users.

Figure 6-2 summarizes the workflow to deliver trust in data and people as data passes through various stages from acquisition to use.

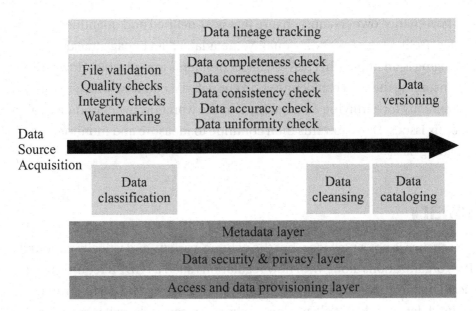

Figure 6-2. *The workflow to deliver trust in data*

Data Governance

Many of the activities described so far are a subset of data governance. Data governance aims to ensure the quality, security, availability, and usability of data in the organization. Many traditional data governance approaches struggle due to the command and control approach taken, which creates an *us vs. them* mentality. Data governance efforts are seen as onerous and thereby ignored. Instead, a Lean/agile data governance program promotes a collaborative process between data producers and data consumers.

Trust in data comes from developing a data quality culture across many teams in the organization. Developers and other data producers must be educated on why trust in data and access to data is essential and the benefits it brings the organization. Data consumers must work collaboratively with data producers to implement data quality checks and monitoring, which provide feedback for continuous improvement. Clear guidance and automation reduce the cost of data governance and reduce risk by embedding processes into day-to-day work rather than separate compliance activities.

Data governance must still have owners, or it will die in the face of competing attention for resources and time. The best people to own data governance are business stakeholders as they are the group that benefits the most from it and can balance the risks. IT and data consumers tend to take a technology or data-centric view on governance instead of a business-driven approach.

Data governance owners must ensure that well-defined and quantifiable goals are in place. Delivering perfect data quality, metadata, data lineage tracking, and data cataloging is an impossible task as not all problems are solvable. However, the people consuming the data can define good enough data quality, which in turn sets the requirements for certifying data quality and the workflow to check data quality and cleanse or fix issues. Data stewards then continue to measure and monitor data quality on an ongoing basis.

Summary

Data governance is not a new idea, but the volume, variety, and velocity captured by today's organizations along with new regulations such as GDPR require a new approach. Organizations capture huge repositories of structured, semi-structured, and unstructured data but do not always know what they have, where it is stored, or how accurate and sensitive the data is. The lack of such information creates compliance, commercial, and reputational risk. Traditional solutions rely on manual management or even blocking of access to data and systems outside carefully curated data warehouses or marts to reduce risk. However, this approach severely impedes the ability of data professionals to create new data products that help the organization and its customers.

The solution is to create trust in users of data and trust in data by users by automating the identification, categorization, security, provision, quality assessment, and cleansing of data. IT moves from being gatekeepers to shopkeepers. Instead of spending energy keeping customers out of the store and starving the business, the shopkeeper invites customers to browse and encourages them to serve themselves. Just as underage people are not allowed to purchase restricted items, so polices ensure those without the correct credentials do not access sensitive data items.

Fostering trust in people to access data and systems safely and creating user trust in data quality eliminate two of the most significant sources of waste in the data science process. Trust in data and systems enables self-service access to data and infrastructure by removing the bottleneck of endless IT requests and negotiation for resources and permissions. Trust in data enables data scientists, data analysts, and data engineers to spend less time cleaning data, tracing its meaning and provenance, worrying about drawing incorrect inferences, and more time developing data products and making decisions.

The next chapter focuses on DevOps practices to speed up data cycles and the time to data use. Data scientists, data engineers, and data analysts need to continually ingest new data sources, construct and improve data pipelines, and create new data products at lightning speed while still maintaining quality.

Endnotes

1. Tadhg Nagle, Thomas C. Redman, and David Sammon, Only 3% of Companies' Data Meets Basic Quality Standards, Harvard Business Review, September 2017. *https://hbr.org/2017/09/only-3-of-companies-data-meets-basic-quality-standards*

2. Jenn Riley, Understanding metadata, what is metadata, and what is it for? 2017. *https://groups.niso.org/apps/group_public/download.php/17446/Understanding%20Metadata.pdf*

3. About FIBO, The open semantic standard for the financial industry. *https://edmcouncil.org/page/aboutfiboreview*

CHAPTER 7

DevOps for DataOps

Creating trust in data and trust in users of data minimizes risks. Trust safeguards regulatory compliance, reduces commercial risk, and protects the reputation of the organization. Trust in data also ensures the integrity of data and makes it easier for users to identify and safely consume it. Leandro DalleMule and Thomas Davenport describe this aspect of data strategy as *data defense* in their famous Harvard Business Review article.[1] Data defense is vital, but so too is *data offense* for a balanced data strategy. Data offense centers on data use to make decisions that increase organizational efficiency, enhance customer experience, and improve product creation.

Like any sports team, all organizations need a balance of defense and offense to thrive. DalleMulle and Davenport believe the optimal trade-off varies and depends on the organization's strategy, regulatory environment, competitive landscape, data maturity, and budgets. For example, heavily regulated industries will place more weight on data defense than data offense. However, all organizations need at least some offensive initiatives to avoid wasting opportunities. Data offense initiatives require different methods than data defense. Data offense uses approaches that go beyond data governance, data management, and risk reduction.

For data offense to succeed, an organization needs *speed*, processes in place to develop and release new data products as rapidly as possible, and *scale*. Scale is the ability to grow data products quickly to match increased demand. Software development and IT Operations have developed a set of cultural philosophies, practices, and automation technologies to improve the velocity of application delivery and iteration known as *DevOps*. The process innovations introduced by DevOps can improve the speed and scale of data analytics delivery.

161

© Harvinder Atwal 2020
H. Atwal, *Practical DataOps*, https://doi.org/10.1007/978-1-4842-5104-1_7

Development and Operations

DevOps is revolutionizing the speed and scale of software deployment. The pace of new development and feature releases that was acceptable in the 1980s, 1990s, and even 2000s is unacceptable today. Historically, the latest features and versions of software took millions of dollars and several years to develop and release.

Microsoft Windows was a canonical example of the old way of releasing software. Each new release was a major global event and took several years to develop. There was nearly a 6-year gap between Windows XP and Windows Vista. Today, Windows is updated frequently, and very few people know or care which version of Windows 10 they use (I am writing this book on version 1903). Even fewer people know which version of popular applications such as Google Chrome or Facebook they use because the pace of updates is genuinely staggering. DevOps makes it possible for Facebook to release tens to hundreds of updates every few hours.[2]

The Conflict

Most organizations still struggle to deploy software changes in production every week or month let alone hundreds of times a day. Often, those production deployments are high-stress affairs involving outages, firefighting, rollbacks, and occasionally much worse. In August 2012, a trading algorithm deployment error by the financial services firm Knight Capital led to a $440 million loss in the 45 minutes it took to fix the problem.[3]

A significant contribution to the slow release of products and features to market are the conflicting goals between software development and IT Operations teams. Software development teams want to deploy new features and respond to market changes by making changes in production code as quickly as possible. IT Operations teams like customers to have a stable, reliable, and secure service. They also want it to be impossible for anyone to make changes that jeopardize this goal. Consequently, development and IT Operations teams have opposing goals and incentives. This conflict results in a downward spiral resulting in ever slower time to market for new products, worse quality, increased technical debt, and daily firefighting.

The authors and IT gurus Gene Kim, Jez Humble, Patrick Debois, and John Willis describe the downward spiral in three acts.[4] In the first act, IT Operations have the task of running complex applications and infrastructure that are poorly documented and burdened with technical debt. Unable to find time to clear the technical debt, constant workarounds are required to maintain systems prone to failure. When production changes fail, they impact availability to customers, revenue, or security.

In the second act, the development team is tasked with another urgent project to make up for the problems caused by previous failures. As such, the development team cuts corners that adds to the technical debt to meet deadlines. In the final act, everything takes longer to complete due to increasing complexity, more dependent work, slower coordination and approvals, and long queues.

As the downward death spiral takes hold, production code deployments take longer and longer to complete. *Tight coupling* (software components that are highly dependent on each other) caused by adding new features to old development rather than loosely separating components instigates significant failures on even small changes. Each new deployment adds complexity and results in further firefighting by IT Operations to hold everything together, which reduces the time available to pay down technical debt, separate components, and provide feedback to developers. The cost of the conflict is not just economic. For the employees involved, it creates stress and decreased quality of life through working evenings and weekends to keep the ship afloat.

Breaking the Spiral

DevOps breaks the death spiral caused by the conflict between development and IT Operations. DevOps practices seek to achieve the aims of multiple IT functions, development, QA, security, and IT Operations while improving the organization's performance.

In the DevOps model, development and IT Operations teams are not separate silos. Small, long-standing project or product-focused development teams independently work across the entire application lifecycle from development to operations. The teams develop their features, peer review, and test their code in *environments* with an operating system, libraries, packages, databases, or tools that match the final production environment where it will eventually run.

Small updates and fast feedback allow problems to be detected early and reduce risk. As soon as new code is committed into *version control* (software for managing changes to files), automated tests are triggered to determine if the code will run as planned in production. Rapid feedback enables developers to find and fix mistakes in minutes instead of weeks later during integration testing. Immediate problem fixing reduces the buildup of technical debt and increases learning with every bug found to prevent a similar recurrence.

A central component of DevOps is the *configuration management* process, which is the practice of handling changes in a system so that it maintains its integrity over time. In software engineering, configuration management encompasses every item that must be configured for the success of the project including, operating systems, source code, servers, binaries, tools, and property files. These items are collectively known as *configuration items*.

Once identified, configuration items are controlled and managed in *version control*, *artifact repositories*, databases for storing binary files, and *configuration management databases* (CMDB). CMDB are repositories that store the inventory and relationships between infrastructure, applications, databases, and services. Typically, version control software manages human-readable code such as configuration files, source code, test, build, and deployment scripts. Artifact repositories handle machine-readable files such as compiled binaries, test data, and libraries. A CMDB assists with impact analysis during change management of applications, databases, or infrastructure as it stores dependency relationships between them. The CMDB can also act as a source of truth for other configuration management tools to provision environments.

The standardized architecture and self-service tools used by DevOps teams allow them to work independently of other teams through high levels of automation. As soon as teams produce a small batch of development, they can deploy it quickly with few dependencies on other teams allowing for much faster customer benefit. Code that passes automated testing is speedily and securely deployed into production environments making deployment a routine process rather than a major event. Once in production, automated telemetry in the code and environments monitors deployments to ensure everything is running as intended. Release of new features through A/B tests or dark launches that are progressively rolled out to users or rolled back quickly with configuration changes further reduces risk and negative consequences.

Systems thinking and the scientific method are fundamental to DevOps. Hypothesis testing, experimentation, and measurement are critical to process improvement. Transparent communication and blameless culture allow teams to thrive and improve customer satisfaction. DevOps teams use postmortems and retrospectives to identify the causes of failure to prevent repetition. Ultimately, DevOps culture and practices give teams the confidence to evolve products at high velocity and rapidly deliver their organization's goals without the stress and fatigue associated with traditional development and operations processes.

Fast Flow from Continuous Delivery

It is useful to understand more details of DevOps for software development before applying the philosophy and approaches to data analytics. To sustain the fast flow of new features across the application lifecycle from development to operations, DevOps has specialist architecture and practices. The technical practices are needed to reduce the risk of deployments and releases in production and allow software professionals to work faster. The most important of DevOps technical practices is *continuous delivery*. Continuous delivery consists of a foundational deployment pipeline, continuous integration of new development, and automated testing leaving the code in a state ready for release into production at *any* time. Continuous delivery is the opposite of the traditional big bang release process, which defers the integration and testing of big batches of work to the end of the project.

Reproducible Environments

To safely deploy development into operation, the preproduction environments used to develop and test code must be as close to production environments as possible. Otherwise, there is a real risk that the application will not run as expected and result in avoidable negative feedback from customers. Historically, IT Operations have manually provisioned test environments. Long lead times and potential misconfiguration mean lack of time for testing or differences in environments, which leads to problems in production.

With DevOps, developers use scripts and configuration information for a stable and secure production environment and a standard build process to ensure the development and test environments are identical. Self-service automation of the process removes the error-prone manual effort required by IT Operations. There are multiple approaches and tools for automatically building environments that are often used in combination with each other. Here are some examples:

- **Configuration orchestration**. Tools such as Terraform or AWS CloudFormation allow infrastructure to be created, modified, or destroyed with configuration files.

- **Operating system configuration**. Automated installers such as Debian Preseed and Red Hat Kickstarter enable multiple individual computers to install the same version of the operating system from a single file that contains all the answers to questions asked during the process.

- **Virtual machine (VM) environments**. Virtualized environments containing software along with an entire operating system are constructible in various ways including shell scripts or with products such as Vagrant. Existing VM images can be copied to a *hypervisor*, which is software that runs virtual machines as guests on a host machine.

- **Application container platforms**. Container platforms such as Docker and CoreOS rkt allow code and all its dependencies to be packaged as isolated lightweight containers that run the same way in different environments.

- **Configuration management**. Tools such as Puppet, Chef, and Ansible install and manage software on already provisioned infrastructure. However, there is an increasing capability overlap between configuration orchestration and configuration management tools.

- **Package management**. Software such as Anaconda Distribution manages Python/R data science and machine learning libraries, dependencies, and environments.

Version control (synonymous with *source control* and *revision control*) has been used by software engineers since the 1970s to track changes to application code. Git, created by Linux inventor Linus Torvalds, is currently the most popular version control system for software development. Version control allows developers to compare, restore, and merge changes to files while concurrently working on them. Modifications are committed to repositories along with metadata on the user making the change and an associated timestamp. In the case of Git, entire snapshots of files are committed to repositories.

Version control repositories are the single repository of truth and allow developers to track each other's changes and reproduce the state of the code at any point in time. Reproducibility is another significant benefit of version control. Instead of wasting time repairing code when things go wrong, reproducibility offers a straightforward way to revert file changes to a known good state in the case of mistakes.

To reliably reproduce not just code but identical environments to run it, the scripts and configuration information for building environments must also live in version control. All infrastructure provisioning scripts (including networking), operating system configuration files, files for creating VMs and containers, application code and dependencies, application reference data, code to create database schemas, automated test scripts, project documentation, and so on must be committed to version control.

The list of configuration items required for reproducibility can become very long, but it must include everything. Changes to production environments must be applied to preproduction environments to maintain consistency. Putting modifications into version control allows the tools used for building environments and managing configuration to replicate the updates everywhere automatically rather than through fallible manual alternatives.

Deployment Pipelines

Once production-like environments are instantiable on demand, developers can not only check that specific functionality works in their development environment but that their application will run as intended integrated in production long before the first production deployment or end of the project. Developers can even verify that the application copes with production workloads by using the same monitoring and logging tools used in production.

However, if a separate QA team is responsible for tests in a later phase, it will take longer to fix errors and provide feedback to developers. Requiring developers to write and test small code iterations themselves helps detect problems early and drastically reduces development risk. Manual testing will not scale to the frequency of testing required. Only automated testing solves the problem.

To facilitate high-frequency automated testing of code, DevOps has the concept of a *deployment pipeline*. Deployment pipelines eliminate waste in the software development process by providing quick feedback to teams without running excessive tasks. Software deployment is split into stages with tasks running sequentially or in parallel within each stage. Only when all tasks in a stage successfully pass does the next stage starts. There are numerous tools for automating deployment pipelines including Jenkins, Travis CI, TeamCity, Bamboo, and Gitlab CI. Figure 7-1 shows an example deployment pipeline.

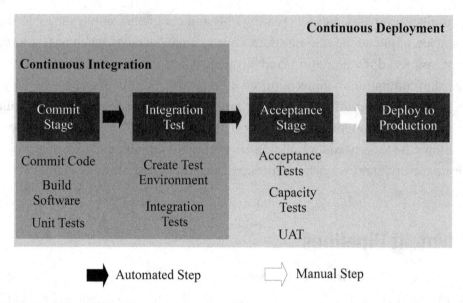

Figure 7-1. *A simplified deployment pipeline*

The deployment pipeline starts when the code is committed to version control by developers in the commit stage initiating an automated *build process*, which includes the steps required to create a standalone software application from the code. The build process compiles the code (including the test source code), runs automated unit tests, performs code analysis, and creates software packages such as JAR files for Java code.

Unit testing validates the smallest testable part of the software such as whether a class or function works as designed, while code analysis detects problems without executing programs. Passing these tests triggers the automated deployment of the software packages into a production-like test environment to run *integration tests*, which expose defects in the interaction between the newly integrated units of code and its interfacing code as a combined group. Developers merge their code commits and build as often as possible in small batches, which is why these stages are known as *continuous integration* (CI).

The passing of integration tests triggers the acceptance stage to verify that the application meets high-level user requirements without introducing *regression errors* (i.e., without breaking previous functionality). *Acceptance tests* run during the acceptance stage, and if passed, the application is made available for manual QA testing and *user acceptance testing* (UAT) by actual software users. These further stages, when combined with continuous integration, are called *continuous delivery* (CD). At the end of the CD process, the application is ready to deploy to production at any time.

Continuous Integration

Version control allows developers to create personal *development branches* and work on different parts of the system in parallel. Development branches are duplicates of the master object(s) under version control. Otherwise, individuals would all be working on the master version, potentially introducing many errors. However, the longer developers work in isolation, and the larger the batch size of changes they make, the more potential problems they add when merging changes back into the master branch. Integration bug hell and test failures involving sporadic merges by multiple developers can take a long time to fix, which is why we end up with the downward spiral DevOps try to solve.

CI resolves the integration problem by optimizing the branching strategy for team productivity over individual developer productivity. CI avoids issues caused by multiple independent developers merging code late and creating integration problems for each other. Everyone works off the master branch and minimizes the size of individual development branches. Developers commit and merge their code at least once per day. This practice moves us closer to Lean thinking ideals of small batch sizes of work and delivers faster deployment lead times. However, because any commit can break the deployment pipeline, CI is heavily reliant on automated tests to provide brakes and feedback to fix problems.

Automated Testing

The deployment pipeline needs to provide rapid feedback to fix glitches immediately. Otherwise, problems are stored up to snowball later or developers see the practice as a hindrance to hitting deadlines. Fast running unit tests execute first to find bugs as early as possible, followed by slower running integration and acceptance tests, and finally manual QA or UAT. A unit test is created to find similar bugs earlier next time when discovering an error in later stages. In this way, the bulk of testing effort takes place early. Google suggests that 70% of tests should be unit tests, 20% integration tests, and only 10% end-to-end tests.[5]

Tightly coupled architecture makes unit testing difficult because the functionality is not well separated in the code. Instead, DevOps encourages loosely coupled systems with minimum dependencies between components so that functions, classes, and modules are independently testable. Tests also need to run fast in the deployment pipeline. One way to achieve this is to run tests in parallel either by running the same type of tests across different servers or different categories of tests at the same time.

DevOps teams frequently use test-driven development (TDD) and *acceptance test-driven development* (ATDD). By writing tests that fail first before writing code that passes the tests, testing becomes part of daily work. In addition to the *functional testing* covered so far, which verifies that the code meets requirements and specifications, there is a need for *non-functional testing*. *Non-functional requirements* (NFRs) cover the operation or quality attributes of the system and include performance, reliability, usability, and security.

The automated tests are all committed to version control to create a comprehensive test suite. With automated testing in place, there is a high degree of confidence that code will operate as designed when deployed in production. No new commits are permitted to enter the pipeline whenever a build or automated test fails to keep the application code in a deployable state at all times. This practice is analogous to pulling the *Andon cord* or stop cord in the Toyota Production System. Highly visible indicators act as information radiators and alert team members to either rollback the commit or fix the problem immediately.

Deployment and Release Processes

The continuous delivery deployment pipeline described so far ensures that application code is in a deployable state for *manual* promotion to production. Higher levels of competency in DevOps require more automation and self-service. To release tens to hundreds of updates like Facebook requires a highly automated process to deploy code to production. Extending the deployment pipeline to cover the last mile reduces the friction related to production deployments.

Self-Service Deployment

It is common practice for the operations team to deploy code in production instead of development teams due to the separation of duties concept. Separation of duties is a popular control mechanism in organizations to reduce the risk of error and fraud by splitting tasks among at least two individuals. However, separation of duties introduces delays, and making deployment someone else's problem disincentivizes developers from investing in changes that make deployment more manageable. DevOps eliminates this problem by using different control mechanisms to minimize risks such as automated testing, automated deployment, and peer reviews.

Fast flow occurs when anyone in a development or operations team can deploy to production through an automated process in seconds or minutes at the push of a button. For the push-button approach to work, three things must be in place. The first is a shared build mechanism that synchronizes the development, test, and production environments. The second is that deployment pipelines create tested packages from version control that are deployable in any environment. The final requirement is that the automated deployment mechanism from test to production is the same for development to test environments to rehearse deployments well.

An automated scripted deployment process can replace many conventional steps when moving code between environments. The scripts build and package code and files into a reusable artifact, run tests, configure VMs or containers, copy files to production servers, migrate databases, undertake *smoke tests*, require a minimal test of functionality, and so on. Anybody with access to the production environment can deploy packages into it by executing deployment scripts in version control.

Automated scripts have their limits because without constant maintenance to keep up with changes in environments they will break. An extension of the script approach is to use one of the many CI/CD tools that can extend the deployment pipeline, so after acceptance tests pass, they trigger scripts to deploy the application. More advanced tools take a *model-driven approach* to deployment. Instead of writing scripts, users specify the desired end state, and the tool orchestrates the deployment process across systems to bring the deployment into line with the model. Finally, the extreme form of deployment is *continuous deployment* where all changes in development deploy immediately into production after successful testing.

Release Processes

The terms deployment and *release* are often considered the same. However, they are different activities. Deployment is the process of installing or updating software in a specific environment. In contrast, a release happens when features of the software are made available to some or all users. Deployments can trigger immediate release, but this is a scary process if things do not go to plan and customers start complaining. To reduce risk, decouple releases from deployments. The deployment pipeline ensures new development is deployed to production rapidly and frequently at low risk. A separate release process safeguards against the risk of the new deployments not achieving their desired objectives.

Several different release processes dramatically reduce risk. A general and straightforward pattern is *blue-green deployment*. This pattern consists of two identical production environments labeled blue and green. At any time, only one live environment is serving customers while new development deploys and tests into the other. During the release, the environments switch and the development environment becomes live while the previously live environment becomes staging for new development. If anything goes wrong, it is simple to revert traffic to the original environment.

Blue-green releases are still similar in some ways to traditional processes where a new version of software completely replaces the previous version in a big bang. A more complicated alternative involves a gradual rollout where new development deploys to a subset of servers in the production environment. *Load balancers* are devices that distribute network traffic. They steer a small segment of initial users to the new deployment servers. If all goes well, coverage rises to expose 100% of users to the new version. This approach is called a *canary release*.

A canary release is named after the small birds used by miners as an early-warning mechanism of toxic gases in mines. When poisonous gases overcame the birds and they stopped singing, it was time for miners to evacuate. The new development is the canary, and if it worsens business KPIs or fails to meet non-functional requirements, it is relatively easy to roll back to the old version while fixing problems with the new. Exposing the new functionality to customers at random allows for A/B testing of old vs. new applications.

Blue-green and canary releases are examples of environment-based release patterns. An alternative route to decouple releases from deployments is to keep the environments and servers constant but manage the release of new features through the application code. *Feature toggles* are a powerful way of modifying the behavior of an application without maintaining a separate version of it. Feature toggles selectively enable and disable new functionality without having to change the production code.

There are different ways to manage and switch feature toggles. A common approach is to wrap the new feature inside a conditional statement, which toggles it on or off based on conditional statements that reference an application configuration file or database. The toggle can turn on features for internal users or segments of external users to test functionality similar to canary releases. If the feature performs as expected, it rolls out to all users. Otherwise, the toggle is turned off. Feature toggles also enable *dark launches* by stealthily releasing features to a small set of users to get feedback before a broader rollout. Google, Amazon, and Facebook who incorporate dark launching into their feature feedback tool Gatekeeper commonly use this release approach.[6]

DevOps Measurement

Measurement and feedback are necessary to understand if applications and systems are running as expected, whether goals are achieved, to fix problems, and innovate fast. At the deployment pipeline level, example metrics include *deployment frequency*, *change lead time*, the time it takes for a new feature or bug fix to go from inception to production, *failure rate* for production deployments, and *mean time to recovery* (MTTR). MTTR is the average time to recover from production failure.

At the application and infrastructure level, it is useful to measure KPIs such as transaction and response times, service availability, CPU and disk load, and application errors. Finally, the business-level measurement must be in place to know if the application is meeting its business goals such as revenue, cost savings, or operational efficiency. With comprehensive and highly visible telemetry in place, it is easier to identify bottlenecks, detect problems earlier, fix production issues while they are small, and improve the flow of releases.

Review Processes

DevOps methods to reduce the risk of production changes before deployment and release rely on peer reviews and inspection. Ironically, traditional change controls can increase the risk of change. Requiring senior management or multiple stakeholder approvals, long lead times for evaluation, and excessive documentation create an overhead. The high friction either discourages change and continuous improvement or causes developers to aggregate changes into fewer big deployments. The more significant the change, the riskier it is. The less frequent the release, the less feedback developers receive. The further the approvers are from work, the less likely they are to understand it and the more likely they are to approve breaking changes.

Instead of external approval, DevOps culture encourages peer reviews of changes and applies to modifications of environments as well as application code. Those closest to work are more likely to find errors. Although for high-risk changes, other subject matter experts from the organization should be invited to review. The process also encourages higher quality through peer learning because few people want to waste their colleagues' time assessing substandard work. The best time for review is before the code is committed to the master development branch. In the process of CI, changes committed to the master branch are in small batches making review relatively easy as review difficulty increases exponentially with the size of the change.[7]

Traditional peer review processes rely on developers inspecting changes over the shoulder, walkthrough meetings, or via email systems. However, a more elegant approach is to use specialized tools or functionality. For example, the popular web hosting service for version control *GitHub* has built-in lightweight code review tools. A developer commits code to their local branch and regularly pushes the changes to the same branch on GitHub. When the changes are ready to merge into the master branch, the developer opens a *pull request* to tell others about the changes, adds a summary, and @mentions users to notify them of a pull review request. Reviewers can submit feedback and approve the merging of proposed changes, request further changes by offering feedback, or comment on the pull request without approving it.

DevOps for Data Analytics

In contrast to the rapid pace of software deployment and releases the leading organizations are achieving, the speed of new data product development and release is typically painfully slow. Data analytics is several years behind software development in adopting DevOps culture and practices but can benefit from them to create a fast flow of data product releases.

In part, slow adoption of data analytics is because it is a far more exploratory process than software development. However, it is easy to overstate the bottleneck caused by the extra loops of exploratory analysis when compared to application development. As highlighted in the previous chapters, data scientists cite data acquisition and cleaning as their biggest bottlenecks. Excessive exploratory analysis is caused by the inability or unwillingness to release a minimum viable data product. Accomplishing continuous delivery for data analytics is instead complicated for two reasons. First, data results in an extra dimension of complexity in addition to the code. Second, data pipeline environments are more complicated to reproduce than software application environments.

The Data Conflict

Traditional application architecture is *monolithic* consisting of a single codebase or *layer architecture* with monolithic layers that separate concerns such as a presentation layer, persistence layer, and database layer. Monolithic layered application architecture is simple, but as the application or development team grows, it becomes difficult to change and scale. The entire application or layer must be built and deployed on every change increasing build and test execution time and limiting parallel development. Tight coupling of code means if anything goes wrong, it breaks the entire product.

DevOps encourages the use of *microservices* architecture, which is a type of *service-orientated architecture* (SOA) where applications are a modular set of small services that communicate with each other over a network. Example microservices for an e-commerce site can include a search feature, user registration, and product reviews. Each service component is simple, reusable, and isolated making it easy to deploy independently without affecting other services. Microservices are loosely coupled, which means they are not dependent upon each other. Consequently, communication between services is either *orchestrated* through a central brain or *choreographed* with each service subscribed to events emitted by other relevant services.

The development and architectural paradigms for data analytics are different from software applications and center on data pipelines that feed data products. Data pipelines are analogous to operations on a factory floor. Raw data from source systems is processed in a series of steps such as cleansing, transformation, and enrichment and delivered to a data product which can be BI software, an ML model, or another analytics application. Traditional data pipelines are optimized for slowly changing data warehouses and reporting. Figure 7-2 shows a typical data pipeline.

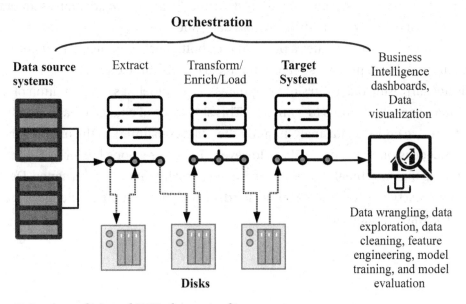

Figure 7-2. *A traditional ETL data pipeline*

In traditional data pipeline development for data analytics, processing steps are highly focused on ETL and performed sequentially. Data is extracted from source systems, transformed and enriched, and then loaded into target systems. The target systems can include data warehouses, *online analytical processing* (OLAP) products that summarize data by important dimensions such as time periods, geographies or customer groups, or other specialized analytical data marts. Target systems provision data to consumers for BI or advanced analytical purposes.

Traditional ETL data pipelines have many of the downsides of monolithic and layered application architecture. These downsides make fast flow development, handling the transition from development to production, and management of production operations extremely challenging. Tightly coupled interdependencies and brittle connections may trigger unpredictable consequences even with small changes. For example, a simple alteration in field name from segment to segment_membership or a schema change to add or remove fields from a file can cause major downstream problems. Failure of one step may require the whole ETL process to be rerun rather than just the affected parts.

There are further challenges, numerous data sources, languages, tools, and technologies involved in the data pipeline making end-to-end orchestration and testing extremely difficult. Many ETL tools are optimized for structured data only making it problematic to use semi-structured and unstructured data. There are many sequential batch steps that read data from disk, process data, and write to disk before the next step can start. Slow processing creates a performance bottleneck with high data volumes and makes it impossible to process streams and integrate real-time data.

It is not surprising that even simple updates to ETL pipelines or integration of new data sources can take months to complete. This slow pace of change creates a genuine conflict. Data scientists, data analysts, and other data consumers in the organization want to meet customer needs quickly. However, IT teams responsible for ETL don't like anything that may break processes and need to maintain data governance. DevOps culture and practices resolve this conflict for data analytics, but the challenge is greater than for software development.

Data Pipeline Environments

Every organization needs to create new or improve existing data products, which all depend on data pipelines. Contemporary data pipelines now extend beyond ETL for data warehouses, data marts, and OLAP to include machine learning models, data visualization, and more. There may be a requirement for hundreds or even thousands of new data pipelines, but traditional methods of creating and modifying pipelines are not fast enough to meet needs. The end-to-end creation of data pipelines from source to data product and updates to production data pipelines needs to be as fast and automated as possible.

Analogous to software development, new DataOps development is undertaken and tested in clones of the production data pipeline. Use of the same tools and languages before deployment facilitates automation and rapid development. However, it is not as easy to reproduce and build on-demand production data pipelines, data pipeline orchestration, and source datasets as it is a software application environment. For example, there may be multiple heterogeneous data sources, many data extractions, transformation, load jobs and tools, several stream processing stages, various compute clusters including VMs, containers and distributed compute, a variety of ETLs, data preparation, data science and BI tools, and petabytes of data in distributed file systems involved.

DataOps platforms are in their infancy, but attempt to solve the problem of creating and rapidly deploying data pipelines in complex big data environments. Platforms such as Infoworks, Nexla, and StreamSets aim to dramatically reduce the time it takes to build batch and streaming pipelines. The solutions create the ability to integrate diverse data sources, version control changes, monitor performance, enforce data security, track data lineage, manage metadata, deploy and orchestrate pipelines efficiently in production, and more within one platform. These platforms provide self-service *graphical user interfaces* (GUIs), which can remove the bottleneck caused by the lack of data engineering resources.

An alternative to the GUI-based platform approach is to treat pipeline tasks as code comparable to a software application and combine with DevOps principles of configuration-as-code and infrastructure-as-code for managing changes to the environment in which they run. This method allows DevOps tools and practices to develop, build, test, deploy, and release data pipelines and is the method favored by DataOps platforms and tools such as DataKitchen and dbt.

Ultimately, even when using a GUI-based DataOps platform, there will be a requirement for code-based development that does not fit within the confines of the platform. There are several requirements to deliver automated and self-service DevOps for DataOps:

- Monitoring and testing of data in the pipeline exist.

- The infrastructure, data pipeline tools, and pipeline orchestration configuration are in a configuration management tool and under version control.

- The data pipeline and pipeline orchestration code are in version control.

- Reusable deployment patterns for data pipelines and pipeline orchestration are in place.

- Teams use CI.

- The technology stack is simplified.

Data pipeline developers, usually data engineers, data scientists, and data analysts, need isolated preproduction environments to develop and update data pipelines. Manual creation of individual environments is error-prone and hard to audit and does not guarantee consistency with the eventual production environment. Shared environments also pose a challenge. Changes made by one user can break the environment for others, and it is not easy to know if tests fail because the code, data, or environment has changed.

Configuration orchestration and configuration management tools can replace multiple custom Shell, Perl, or Python scripts and graphical interfaces used to create production pipelines and their environments. The tools typically use human-readable *YAML* (YAML Ain't Markup Language) or a *domain-specific language* (DSL) to deploy infrastructure and applications, install packages, and configure operating systems.

It is also essential to configure access to systems and data in development to reflect the production environment. Otherwise, there is a risk that different security levels mean development data pipelines rely on systems they cannot access in production. Infrastructure-as-code and configuration-as-code combined with version control ensure that production and development environments stay in sync because they are built from the same code.

Some complexity in reproducing data pipelines can be further abstracted away through the use of virtual machines and containers. Vagrant is a tool that simplifies building and sharing of VMs through its package format Boxes. When combined with configuration management tools to install software and alter configurations, bringing up a Box creates an identical environment for any user on any machine.

Increasingly, containers are replacing VMs as they are simpler to configure, faster to launch, and easier to combine to create end-to-end pipelines. Docker is the most popular application container platform, and docker images are snapshots of self-contained containers that include everything required to run an application including its environment, code, and dependencies. Unlike VMs, containers share the host operating system making them a very lightweight solution for creating applications that are easily transportable across many environments.

Containers will run in the same way anywhere a corresponding container runtime such as Docker Engine runs. As with SOA and microservices, breaking out the data pipeline into loosely coupled, simple, reusable, and isolated tasks running in separate containers makes it easier to test changes to the data pipeline. Data pipeline developers only need to know how to interface with other containers without having to worry about their inner workings.

Data Pipeline Orchestration

There is an additional orchestration requirement beyond the automated deployment of infrastructure, software, and application code. The data pipeline from raw data to data product typically but not always follows a *directed acyclic graph* (DAG) data structure with nodes representing tasks where data is stored or processed and edges denoting data flow. Connections between nodes are directed. Data cannot go in the opposite direction. The output of an intermediate task is the input to another. The DAG is acyclic (noncircular) because moving from node to node can never take you back to a previous node.

A DAG usually requires orchestration because the sequence of steps occurs in a specific order with dependencies between different components. However, choreographed DAGs are becoming more commonplace with the rise in real-time streaming architectures. Such architectures are often based on Apache Kafka or other publish-subscribe systems where tasks are triggered by subscription to event data emitted by other tasks and services.

Apache Airflow is the most common open-source platform to create, schedule, and monitor DAG workflows for non-streaming data pipelines. Airflow workflows orchestrate *operators* and their dependencies in the DAG or *sensors*. Operators are single task definitions, while sensors check the state of a data structure or process.

Airflow provides many operators and sensors for everyday data engineering tasks such as executing shell commands, processing SQL queries, running commands inside Docker containers, and pausing execution of dependent tasks until criteria such as file availability are met. Workflows are configurable Python code, which makes them easily scalable, testable, reproducible, and dynamic through user-defined parameters, macros, and templates. As Airflow workflows are configuration-as-code, it is easy to treat the orchestration of production data pipelines as another configuration item in version control to reproduce, develop, and test in preproduction environments.

Data Pipeline Continuous Integration

The data pipeline has many orchestrated tasks that may use multiple tools and languages such as SQL, Python, and Java to extract, clean, enrich, integrate, and transform data. However, all the tasks ultimately involve applying logic in the code to data, and the code should be in version control along with the accompanying configuration-as-code for orchestration. Figure 7-3 shows an example of a machine learning training pipeline broken into tasks with the corresponding code placed in version control.

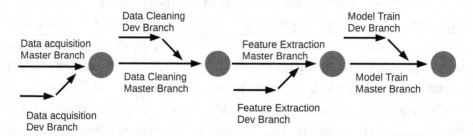

Figure 7-3. *Version control branches for a machine learning training pipeline*

Version control for data pipeline tasks has multiple benefits. It facilitates reproducibility, allows numerous team members to work in parallel on data pipelines, encourages sharing of best practice, provides visibility of changes, has easier bug discovery, and enables CI. With the code for data pipeline tasks in version control, pipeline developers can make smaller changes to development branches, submit pull requests, review code, and test changes before deploying to production.

In DataOps, data pipeline developers are responsible for adding tests and monitoring to their code. The scope for monitoring and testing can be the entire data pipeline, multiple tasks, single tasks in the DAG, or even units within a task. Data pipeline tasks are functional as the output only depends on the input data and code, which makes it ideal to start with *black box testing*. In black box testing, it is not necessary to know the inner working of the tasks, only the inputs and outputs. The checks described in Chapter 6 for data completeness, data correctness, data consistency, data accuracy, and data uniformity can be applied to component test single tasks, integration test sequential tasks, or end-to-end test the entire pipeline. For example, black box testing can validate output metadata such as the number of records, data points outside a range of values, average and standard deviation values, average string lengths, and the number of records rejected.

White box testing of internal task structures is also valuable and requires inspection of task code inner workings. For example, unit tests to check if field names are right, bad data is removed, or the missing rate of a field is above a threshold can be added to tasks to check for correct implementation of pipeline code changes. After making changes, *regression testing* should be run to make sure any new changes have not introduced new bugs elsewhere.

Tests are added to version control so they can run as part of an automated CI process every time a change is made to data pipeline code. Many non-functional tests such as latency KPIs, security tests for password creation and authentication, access control policies, scans for open ports, exposure of cloud storage or sensitive data, code analysis for vulnerabilities, and more can all be automated.

The fact that there are two moving parts in the data pipeline – the data and the code – complicates testing. Data in production databases, data lakes, analytical databases, and data warehouses continually changes as new data is captured, updated, transformed, and deleted. Without fixed test datasets, it is hard to know if variances between the development and production pipeline outputs are due to code changes or data differences. There is also no guarantee that the monitoring and checking code that alerts for problems with data flowing through production pipeline code today is comprehensive enough to detect problems with the data tomorrow. New tests added during development and testing to find code defects should also be appended to existing monitoring and checks of the production data pipeline. Over time, the number and granularity of tests increase to catch errors in both development code and production data earlier.

Historically, IT departments populate environments with test data to support application development. The process is often manual, slow, and error-prone resulting in infrequent updates and delivers a small sample of data. Developers lose time during the wait for data provisioning or from rework when unsuitable stale test data fails to prevent defects in production. *Test data management* (TDM) is the process of managing data for application testing. TDM is more critical for data analytics than software development. There is often more complexity in data than the analytics code. In this case of ML and AI, the model code itself is a function of the data. So, a different dataset will lead to different model code.

Automated testing of development data pipelines requires the rapid and secure provision of fit-for-purpose test data. Test data must reflect the state at the point the data will be processed based on timestamps and not as it is now. Data can arrive late or be further updated and cleaned after processing, so its current state may not reflect the condition of data that will be processed in future.

Ideally, test data should be a full copy of the production data, subject to the data classification policy. If it is not possible to load a large copy into preproduction environments, a large sample is the next best option. Care must be taken to ensure that the sample is a representative distribution of production data, and the code developed will scale to production dataset sizes. An alternative to data samples are scripts that generate fake test data that aims to simulate production data. However, fake data is not ideal except for sensitive data obfuscation and masking or when reproduction of the complexity and bugs of real data is not needed.

Commercial test data management tools, such as Informatica, Delphyix, and CA Test Data Manager, can also rapidly provision test datasets. The software can deliver dataset snapshots at a specific point in time to compare development to known production outputs and enforce security policies, so sensitive data is masked before delivery while maintaining referential integrity. Self-service automated TDM can provision data from heterogeneous sources that mirror production in minutes.

Simplify and Reuse

The final stage of DevOps for DataOps is to automate the build of pipeline environments and give data pipeline developers self-serve ability to create, test, and deploy changes. However, a mixture of diverse services in the data pipeline such as Hadoop, Amazon S3, SQL Server, and Amazon DynamoDB can be a barrier to reproduction and automation. If the entire production data pipeline is impossible to reproduce, the next best solution is to subset the production data pipeline into reproducible sub-DAGs and tasks for unit and integration testing. Nonetheless, end-to-end and regression testing becomes painful to execute unless orchestration of the sub-DAGs is automated. Simplification must come before automation.

DevOps effectiveness increases when there is less heterogeneity in the technology stack. Complexity increases the probability of errors and slows down the flow of deployment because teams find it hard to scale their expertise and apply consistent patterns across data pipelines. The focus of data analytics teams after adopting version control should be to standardize and simplify the set of technologies they use from languages, libraries, and databases to data engineering tools. Figure 7-4 shows an example of how Apache Spark can be used to reduce and simplify the number of technologies required to build a data pipeline.

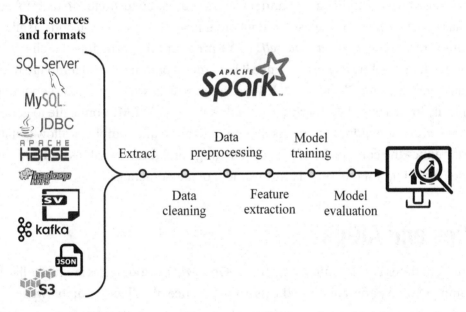

Figure 7-4. *A model training pipeline in Apache Spark*

Spark can handle batch and stream data processing, ingest multiple file formats from numerous data sources, run standalone on a laptop or a cluster of machines, and produce many types of outputs from simple summary tables to machine learning models.

Many other architectures can simplify and standardize the technology stack including containers, managed cloud infrastructure, and nascent DataOps platforms that provide a standard automated workflow on top of multiple big data technologies.

However, the simplification process is not an excuse for data analysts, data scientists, and data engineers to choose their favorite tools in isolation. Operations teams should be consulted to determine what works best in production.

With standardized technology, it is easier to create flexible and reusable data pipelines. Modern data pipelines are not just ETL silos tightly coupled to a data warehouse or a report. Data pipelines may just move data from one system to another, or they can perform *ELT* where source data is extracted and loaded into a target system for later transformation. Data pipelines can handle streaming as well as batch data, and the destination does not have to be database or storage. It could be an event consumer that triggers another process. The flexibility of contemporary data pipelines allows them to be loosely coupled together to make more complex data pipelines. Loosely coupled pipelines are easier to develop, test, deploy, and reuse.

Standardization, simplification, and reuse should not be restricted to technology and data pipelines, but encompass the data pipeline and orchestration code itself by conforming to the *Don't Repeat Yourself* (DRY) programming principle. Much of the code in the data pipeline is reusable once it becomes a parameterized template that reads an external config file at runtime. For example, Airflow DAGs can be generated dynamically from a templated script that reads an external YAML config file to generate workflows with the required operators. Parameterization and templates allow DataOps teams to reduce the complexity of jobs to changing configuration values and focus on rapid delivery of new incremental improvement of data pipelines.

MLOps and AIOps

Despite sometimes being confused with DataOps, *MLOps* and *AIOps* are two adjacent and complementary approaches. MLOps is the practice of collaboration between data scientists and operations teams to manage ML models across the ML lifecycle. Gartner coined the term AIOps, and it stands for *artificial intelligence for operations*.[8] AIOps uses data and machine learning to enhance IT Operations functions through the provision of continuous insight.

Ironically, many IT organizations build sophisticated big data and data science systems for their stakeholders, but fail to use data and advanced analytics to monitor and improve their own IT Operations. The complexity and multitude of IT environments and systems are exploding making it very difficult to create reliable manual monitoring for performance monitoring. AIOps applies machine learning to existing IT data sources such as log events, application alerts, and network performance monitoring data. The ML models identify real-time anomalies in the performance data and perform automated root cause analysis. Predictive analytics proactively recognizes issues earlier, and anomaly detection reduces the false alarms associated with manual thresholds. AIOps enables IT Operations teams to focus on the most critical problems and minimize downtime or MTTR as a result of operational incidents. AIOps is complementary to DataOps and is easily extended to monitor data pipeline operations.

ML Model Development

MLOps combines elements of DataOps and DevOps to the process of automating and productionizing machine learning algorithms. Machine learning adds an extra dimension to code, environments, and data for configuration management and reproducibility in the form of a model. Machine learning consists of two components, namely, *training* and *inference*.

Model training pipelines are a particular type of data pipelines and include data acquisition, data wrangling, data exploration, data cleaning, feature engineering through data transformation, model training, and model evaluation. Models and associated code generated in the training process are released in production and used in the inference stage to make predictions for new observations such as real-time fraud detection or product recommendations.

There are two critical differences between models and most other data products. The first is that the development pipeline for model training does not go into production. Only the code and artifacts required for inference go into production. The other difference is that eventually concept drift will necessitate reoptimization of the model to create new code and artifacts through retraining even if the objective, labels, and features used remain the same. Hence, the ability to easily update production models is incredibly important.

The process of machine learning training in development and inference in production sounds simple but is challenging to put into practice. Until recently, many organizations could take months to deploy models, and once deployed, models were often never retrained. The difficulties of deploying models in production to make inferences are not dissimilar to the conflict between developers and operations teams.

ML Model Production

As with data analytics and software releases, the faster models are released and retrained, the quicker the feedback the organization receives and the better it can achieve its goals. However, there are some significant barriers to fast flow from development to production in machine learning.

Machine learning models are typically trained offline by data scientists who run experiments on local machines using libraries and packages that come with languages such as R or Python. Data scientists will iterate the model training pipeline experimenting with new data sources, data preprocessing techniques, features, and algorithms. Once they are happy with the accuracy of a trained model, it is ready to make inferences in a production environment.

The output of the model training pipeline is model code (the logic that transforms inputs into outputs based on the ML algorithm training data) along with any code required to preprocess the inputs and engineer features. The exploratory and iterative nature of the model training pipeline that creates many training datasets and models combined with a lack of software development skills among data scientists can make the transition to production much harder than it needs to be.

Reproducing the model and associated code in production is dependent on version control of configuration items as the model code often relies on the frameworks that created it to run. The model code itself is also a configuration item as it is not necessarily the final training experiment that yields the most accurate model, so previous iterations must be reproducible. Data scientists may overlook version control and configuration management or use development tools such as notebooks that do not lend themselves easily to version control.

Deployment to production requires engineers to refactor the ad hoc exploratory code to make it run efficiently in the production environment or sometimes rewrite the model code entirely in a language better suited to fast and reliable production operation such as Java. The production inference model outputs must be tested against the outputs of the trained model to make sure it predicts as expected using the same test dataset. Without versioning of datasets, there is no way of knowing if the test dataset is the same version used for model training.

Offline testing is not enough when evaluating ML models as live data will always differ from training data. To validate expected results, models should be released in the same way as new features in software development through blue-green deployments or canary releases. Production model performance must be monitored against a baseline treatment, which can be the previous production model or no model at all. When performance degrades, models need retraining.

Retraining of models requires the model training pipeline to be iterated using new data sometimes resulting purely in changes of the model *parameters* (variables learned from the data) and *hyperparameters* (values that tune the model). Updates to parameters and hyperparameters of a production inference model are relatively simple to make. However, more significant changes such as new data preprocessing steps, new input data, or even a new algorithm such as replacing logistic regression with random forest require considerable modification to the production inference model and its integrated applications. If there is too much reliance on manual steps to deploy, release, and retrain a model, it slows down delivery and reduces the value machine learning can add to the organization.

The value gained from allowing data scientists to train, deploy, and operate their machine learning model has led to some companies such as Uber to develop in-house self-service infrastructure.[9] Fortunately, MLOps is an active area of development, and many vendors are creating services and tools to make the ML lifecycle management simpler.

The simplest solution to the challenge of speeding up the loop between training and inference is to use one or more MLOps services or software solutions that enable data scientists to self-serve the model development, test, deployment, release, and retrain workflow. Examples of solutions include Amazon Sagemaker, Google Cloud AI Platform, and Microsoft Azure Machine Learning service, MLflow, Seldon, MLeap, and Kubeflow to manage the ML lifecycle from training to deployment. Data science platforms such as Domino Data Lab and Dataiku also include functionality for model management. Version control of models and data is a less mature field, but DVC, ModelDB, Pachyderm, and Quilt Data are promising open-source libraries.

Summary

DevOps culture and practices are a major contributory factor for making Facebook, Google, LinkedIn, Amazon, and others what they are today. Without DevOps, adoption of agile practices would have resulted in an ever-increasing backlog of work waiting for deployment and release to customers while operations teams fought daily fires. Instead, the leading organizations can release improvements multiple times a day with customers exposed to fewer software defects than ever before.

Many organizations have the same problem with data teams as they had with turning software development into reliable applications in production at speed. Competitive advantage relies on fast time to market and continuous experimentation. Organizations that cannot develop and deploy data pipelines and data products at high velocity will eventually lose out to competitors who can because they will be slower to make effective decisions. DevOps mindsets and practices are critical to improving the innovation and success rate of data analytics although the challenges are more significant than for software development.

DevOps is more than continuous integration or infrastructure as code as captured by the conceptual *CALMS* (Culture, Automation, Lean, Measurement, and Sharing) model for assessing readiness to adopt DevOps. The model considers an organization's collaboration culture, levels of automation, the ability for continuous improvement and rapid flow of work, performance measurement, and shared responsibility and communication when assessing maturity. Similarly, DataOps is more than DevOps for data analytics because the deployment of a data pipeline is not a use case by itself. DataOps helps organizations make better decisions through more efficient data analytics. DataOps benefits from DevOps, but also requires Lean thinking, agile adaptability to change, trust in data, and the right people culture and organization for success. Without these supporting foundations in place, DevOps for data science and analytics will fail to bring many benefits. The next chapter explores the people aspect of DataOps.

Endnotes

1. Leandro DalleMule and Thomas H.Davenport, What's Your Data Strategy?, Harvard Business Review, June 2017. *https://hbr.org/2017/05/whats-your-data-strategy*

2. Chuck Rossi, Rapid release at massive scale, Facebook Code, August 2017. *https://code.fb.com/web/rapid-release-at-massive-scale/*

3. Nathanial Popper, Knight Capital Says Trading Glitch Cost It $440 Million, New York Times, August 2012. *https://dealbook.nytimes.com/2012/08/02/knight-capital-says-trading-mishap-cost-it-440-million/*

4. Gene Kim, Jez Humble, Patrick Debois, and John Willis, The
    DevOps Handbook: How to Create World-Class Agility, Reliability,
    and Security in Technology Organizations, October 2016.

5. Mike Wacker, Just Say No to More End-to-End Tests, Google
    Testing Blog, April 2015. *https://testing.googleblog.
    com/2015/04/just-say-no-to-more-end-to-end-tests.html*

6. Chuck Rossi, Rapid release at massive scale, Facebook Code,
    August 2017. *https://code.fb.com/web/rapid-release-at-
    massive-scale/*

7. Jason Cohen, 11 proven practices for more effective, efficient
    peer code review, IBM Developer, January 2011. *www.ibm.com/
    developerworks/rational/library/11-proven-practices-for-
    peer-review/index.html*

8. Andrew Lerner, AIOps Platforms, August 2017. *https://blogs.
    gartner.com/andrew-lerner/2017/08/09/aiops-platforms/*

9. Jeremy Hermann and Mike Del Balso, Scaling Machine Learning
    at Uber with Michelangelo, November 2018. *https://eng.uber.
    com/scaling-michelangelo/*

CHAPTER 8

Organizing for DataOps

Organizational structure has an enormous impact not only on output velocity but also on what teams produce and the quality of such. As anyone who has worked within a rigid hierarchical structure knows, the organizational chart often has more influence on what is or is not produced than any technology decision.

For example, with a traditional layered architecture, the simple addition of a new data source to a report requires coordination from every separate functional team responsible for a layer. Cutting vertically across layers requires source system owners, ETL developers, database architects, database modelers, database administrators, BI developers, and front-end developers to communicate, agree, and coordinate changes. The process is slow and painful because responsibility for the outcome splits across teams with their individual priorities and schedules.

The Navy has a saying that convoys move at the speed of the slowest ship. However, data analytics must move at the speed organizations demand to meet their goals rather than the speed of the slowest department. It is difficult to be agile when the organizational structure and culture inadvertently work to slow everything to a trickle. DataOps requires teams to be organized around shared data-centric goals and shared pains to eliminate barriers and work as fast as possible.

Team Structure

Dr. Melvin Conway was one of the first people to study the impact of team organization on knowledge work output. In his 1968 paper "How Do Committees Invent," Conway observed that any organization that designs a system produces a design structure that is a copy of the organization's communication structure.[1] Conway's conclusion is codified as Conway's Law and quoted in various forms. One of the most famous is Eric S. Raymond's summarization that "If you have four groups working on a compiler, you'll get a 4-pass compiler."[2] Since the publication of Conway's paper, many researchers

191

© Harvinder Atwal 2020
H. Atwal, *Practical DataOps*, https://doi.org/10.1007/978-1-4842-5104-1_8

including those from Harvard Business School[3] and Microsoft[4] have found evidence that organizational structure is deeply interrelated with system design, architecture, and outcomes.

Function-Orientated Teams

There are two main models for team member alignment – functional and domain. Functionally orientated teams organize around technical expertise, and domain-orientated teams organize around a market, value stream, customer, service, or product.

Functional orientation is the traditional method for dividing labor in organizations, especially highly skilled professions. Expertise is centralized in teams based on tools or skillsets. For example, data scientists, BI analysts, data engineers, and database administrators will all be in separate teams. There is no duplication of resources across teams, and specialized talent is allocated to projects as soon as they are available, or a new project is prioritized ahead of others currently in progress. This type of structure is optimized to maximize resource utilization of scarce talent and hence minimize cost.

The advantage of functional orientation is that similar individuals group together, which helps deepen without necessarily broadening skills within a specific unit. Many organizations start by creating a centralized team for their data science and data engineering teams, but soon run into problems delivering the change the organization hired them to make.

Centralized teams or consultancy models can work when analytics teams are small, and the value of data analytics comes from reporting and *decision science* to help stakeholders answer specific questions through one-off analysis. However, value comes from the ability to create automated data products such as ML models at speed and scale for many parts of the organization. The complexity and variety of data sources, infrastructure, and skills needed to develop data products require a rethink of the siloed functional team model.

An understanding of Lean thinking and waterfall project management should make the downside of resource-maximizing functional orientation clear. Individuals have little knowledge of how they are contributing to overall organizational goals, which leads to proactive work stakeholders are not interested in, significant rework from misunderstanding, inability to optimize the whole, and lack of motivation. Figure 8-1 shows how work flows through centralized function-orientated teams.

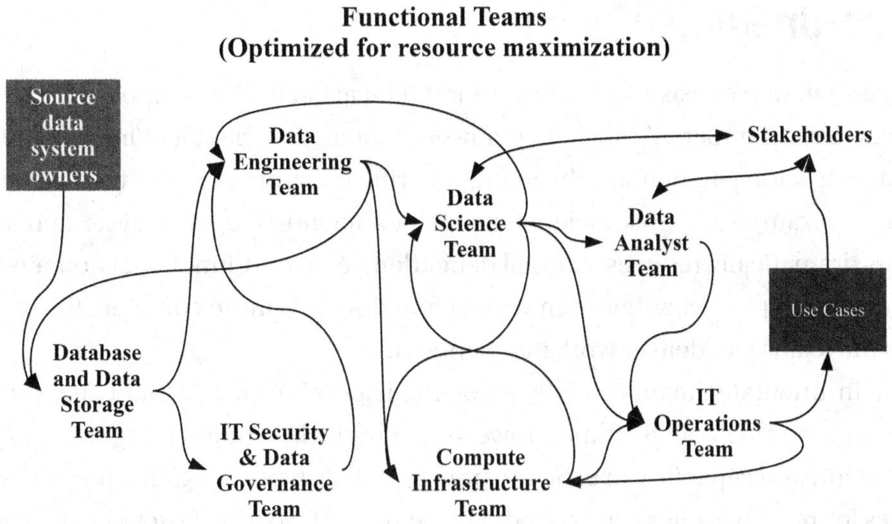

**Functional Teams
(Optimized for resource maximization)**

Figure 8-1. *Workflows through centralized functional teams involve complex coordination and many handoffs*

Every functional team is busy, but very little value is produced at the end because ownership is fragmented. Work must be coordinated and continually handed off to other teams leading to long queues and delays, especially if unanticipated iterations are needed. Constant reactive demand on specialized teams from multiple areas of the organization requires escalation of prioritization requests up and down a hierarchical structure slowing decision-making and disrupting planning. Any saving from local resource utilization maximization is usually more than wiped out from introducing a cost of delay along the entire data product manufacturing line.

It is possible for functional-orientated teams to deliver quickly, but it requires considerable effort and investment to make it work. Every functional team involved in the data product manufacturing line must share the same organizational objectives and goals. Resource utilization efficiency should not be the objective. There needs to be sufficient slack so excessive queues do not form between teams and they can expedite priority work. Functional teams must deliver automated self-service solutions to other teams so they can access data, platforms, environments, monitoring, and so on on-demand to avoid becoming a bottleneck.

Domain-Orientated Teams

Domain orientation consists of many nonhierarchical flat teams composed of cross-functional team members. A single domain-orientated team has all or most of the skills required to develop and manage the manufacturing line from raw data to finished data product. For example, a self-sufficient team of data scientists, data analysts, and data engineers dramatically reduces external dependencies. Cross-functional domain teams no longer have to pass work between several functional teams to complete the work because the teams can deliver work independently.

Domain-orientated teams initially seem inefficient since they cannot guarantee to exploit everyone's skills all the time. However, some slack is a good thing as it allows time for innovation and capability to expedite priorities. This type of organizational structure optimizes for responsiveness and speed. The benefits of working faster outweigh any resource utilization inefficiency, especially once the cost of all the waiting and blocked work in functional organizations is taken into account.

DataOps outcomes are easier to achieve when teams are domain-orientated for speed. Individual team members use their unique and diverse skills to own and deliver shared goals. Teams have greater ownership of outcomes than functional teams and can see how their effort contributes to an end goal.

At the extreme, domain-orientated teams are responsible for the development, testing, security, production deployment, monitoring, defect fixes, iterative improvement, and experiments across the entire lifecycle of a data product. The teams are capable of delivering without manual dependencies on other teams.

Most agile software development teams are small, cross-functional, and domain-orientated to align self-contained output with self-contained teams. Amazon was one of the first companies to move from monolithic to microservice architecture, but they recognized that organizational change had to come first. Just as microservices are loosely coupled, Amazon created teams that can build and own the services with few dependencies on each other. They flipped convention on its head and designed their organizational structure based on the architecture they wanted instead of letting the organizational structure drive the architecture.

It is no coincidence that most technology unicorns are also considered leaders in data analytics. Most successful technology companies have domain-orientated data science and engineering teams, integrate data scientists and data engineers into cross-functional business teams, or provide data platforms to domain-orientated product engineering teams.

For example, Netflix's data science and engineering teams are aligned to its vertical teams, content, finance, marketing, product, and business development and are responsible for analytics, reporting, modeling, and engineering.[5] In Facebook's infrastructure teams, data scientists and infrastructure engineers work in unified teams such as network engineering, storage infrastructure, and release management.[6]

Cross-functional domain-orientated teams have their downsides too. Domain orientation creates challenges for career development, knowledge sharing, and consistent hiring. Even with self-sufficient cross-functional teams, there is value in reusing code and development patterns for data pipelines. When each team reinvents the wheel, it introduces waste through duplication.

There are two chief approaches to reduce the cost of domain orientation without reintroducing excessive communication overhead and coordination problems. The first option is to connect teams loosely through informal coordination roles. The second option is to link teams and team members through a formal hub and spoke model.

The Spotify model is an example approach to loosely connect teams by assigning team members to *Chapters* and *Guilds*.[7] Chapters are people with similar skills. For example, data engineers that work in similar domains meet regularly to discuss their area of expertise and challenges. Guilds are *communities of interest* or *communities of practice* that want to share knowledge, tools, code, and practices. An alternative is to create specific coordination roles outside teams, for example, a data solutions architect who advises on best practice and prevents fragmentation of solutions.

A hub and spoke model maintains connectivity between domain-orientated teams through a central team such as a *center of excellence*, which is a team responsible for harmonizing best practices and consistency across other teams. Unlike self-contained agile software development teams, DataOps teams need more than access to on-demand environments, tools, services, and monitoring to be self-sufficient. DataOps teams also need self-service access to data. Otherwise, they cannot develop data pipelines or data products. Since this requirement is shared across all DataOps teams, it makes sense for data platform capability to sit in a centralized but not siloed team.

Interaction between the central data platform and domain teams is a two-way process. The data platform team provides self-service access to data and infrastructure. In return, the domain teams help the data platform team understand what functionality they should build and what data they should make available for reuse.

Figure 8-2 shows how domain-orientated teams align with specific organizational domains and not job function.

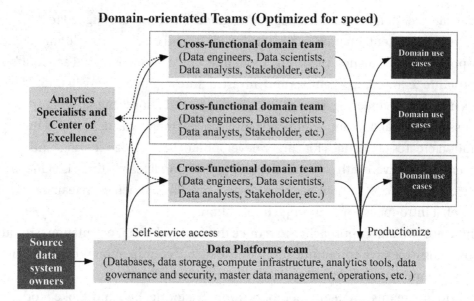

Figure 8-2. *A hub and spoke model for domain-orientated teams*

The New Skills Matrix

Building data analytics capability is not as simple as hiring a dozen PhD data scientists and waiting for the magic to happen. Data analytics is a team sport where DataOps roles fall into two categories – core personas that are usually critical to the success of a DataOps team and supporting personas that appear as required.

Personas are role profiles since this is the easiest way to describe job roles and skills. Organizations have many people who use various job titles for similar responsibilities or specializations of the same position that cluster into personas. For example, data analysts, business intelligence analysts, marketing analysts, and product analysts may undertake comparable activities using similar tools and techniques but for different fields and stakeholders.

Core Personas

The primary personas are *data platform administrator, data analyst, data scientist, data engineer, DataOps engineer, team lead, solutions expert,* and *organizational stakeholder.*

Data platform administrators own the data infrastructure that supplies data engineers with the data sources for their data pipelines and at least some of the infrastructure that operationalizes production outputs. These data platform specialists are responsible for data lakes, data warehouses, application databases, data marts, stream processing, and more. Data platform administrators also take responsibility for other components that make up the data analytics ecosystem.

The administrators ensure the infrastructure and components are performing to their potential by managing capacity and workloads. They are also responsible for data management administration including data integration from source systems, master data management, data governance, data security, data sharing on the platforms, and access control.

Data analysts understand and analyze data to influence business decisions. There are many different types of data analysts including marketing analysts, financial analysts, product analysts, sales analysts, and operations analysts. Data analysts query, clean, explore, interpret, and visualize structured data to report insights and recommendations. They are expected to be numerate and be able to work with databases and other data source systems such as business intelligence tools, Excel and R. However, they are not usually expected to work with big data technology or machine learning because they focus on descriptive and diagnostic analytics.

Data scientists cover a broad multidisciplinary field, which makes the persona harder to define than others. Not unlike data analysts, data scientists help organizations make decisions using data, but use more advanced analytics techniques and applied research for predictive and prescriptive analytics. Data scientists may use inferential statistical analysis, for example, by testing hypotheses to inform human decision-makers or use machine learning to build algorithms that help automated systems make decisions.

Generalist data scientists usually have a solid understanding of statistics and machine learning coding languages such as Python and R (along with their libraries) as well as proficiency in data visualization. They also typically have good knowledge of how to extract data from distributed storage, relational, and NoSQL databases and work with structured, semi-structured, and unstructured data on big data frameworks like Apache Spark. It is almost impossible to be an expert in every domain and competence in data science, hence the reference to unicorns when describing such people. The majority of data scientists specialize in a subfield of data science such as natural language processing or computer vision.

Data engineers build data pipelines and manage datasets on data infrastructure platforms using their software engineering know-how. They are responsible for getting data into the platform and also ensuring it appears in the right format and systems for data scientists, data analysts, and their tools to use. Historically, data engineers have been database-centric with a focus on ETL for populating data warehouses. However, data

197

engineers are now more likely to be pipeline-centric by building use case–specific data pipelines from distributed storage or streaming data sources.

Data engineers are expected to be familiar with big data technologies and programming languages such as SQL, Java, Python, and Scala. Some data engineers are also capable of architecting data stores and distributed systems.

If a centralized or functionally orientated team handles operations, it potentially becomes a source of friction when data engineers want to deploy new data pipelines or data scientists want to deploy new data products. It is better to remove the barrier and integrate Ops competencies into DataOps teams through the DataOps engineer persona.

A DataOps engineer works with the rest of the team to make frequent and rapid releases of data pipelines and data products into production possible. The DataOps engineer knows how to manage and automate the provision of environments and data on data platforms, deployment, testing, release, security and monitoring processes. They have the necessary soft and hard skills to work with multiple teams and personas to proactively recommend improvements in architecture, processes, and tools.

The team lead is a servant leader for a self-organizing team of data analysts, data engineers, DataOps engineers, and data scientists. The team lead is responsible for keeping the team focused on its objectives, removing impediments by interacting with the broader organization, management reporting, organizing meetings and retrospectives, maintaining open communication within the team, and coaching the team on DataOps practices.

A solutions expert has a solid technical background and guides the rest of the team on algorithm, design, and architecture decisions in addition to their daily work. Their hands-on role sets them apart from traditional solutions or technical architects. They are usually a senior data engineer or senior data scientist who spends part of their time guiding, mentoring, and coaching team members on best practices. They contribute to the development of organizational architecture, frameworks, and patterns while ensuring their team uses them where appropriate. They make sure the team adheres to standards, development lifecycles, and QA processes.

An organizational stakeholder is someone impacted by the work of the team. The persona can represent many different types of people depending on the team or organization. A stakeholder can be various individuals such as an end user of the team's output, a senior leader, a program manager, a product manager, the budget holder for the team, or a representative of customers. Occasionally, the stakeholder will want direct access to the data platform so they can undertake some of the data analyst and data scientist tasks themselves.

Core personas are not people or job titles. Not all DataOps teams include the same mix of personas because it depends on the requirements to meet the team's goals. In some teams, a single person may cover multiple personas such as both data engineer and DataOps engineer. In another team, there may be numerous data engineers and DataOps engineers.

Supporting Personas

It is unlikely that the core personas will be sufficient for all types of DataOps teams to function entirely independently. It will be common for teams to need complementary skills to join the team on a permanent or temporary basis. Typical supporting personas include data product owners, domain experts, analytics specialists (such as researchers or specialized data scientists), and technical specialists (e.g., data architects, software engineers, ML engineers, security experts, testers, designers).

A *data product owner* is an individual responsible for the success of the team's data products. In a team without a data product owner, the team lead may also take on some of their responsibility as the stakeholder's go-between. The data product owner represents the stakeholder within the team, owns the backlog, prioritizes work, educates the team about the organizational domain, educates stakeholders about the team's capabilities, demonstrates the team's output, and is the public face of the team.

The data product owner also takes responsibility for the last mile of the data journey and ensures that the team output leads to action through data storytelling and visualization. If the team lead guarantees that the team builds the data product fast and the solutions expert ensures they build the data product right, the data product owner ensures the team builds the right data product.

Domain experts are subject matter experts who help the team when there are gaps in their knowledge. *Analytics specialists* have deep technical expertise in different areas such as Hadoop or recommendation systems that core personas may lack.

Software engineers help integrate models and other data products into applications. *ML Engineers* are software engineers who apply software development best practice to the creation and monitoring of models in production.

Security experts ensure processes are in place to protect systems and sensitive data from unauthorized access, modification, and destruction. The core DataOps personas should undertake most testing, but sometimes, it may be necessary for regulatory or separation of concerns principles to engage specialist testers.

Data architects are responsible for managing the full lifecycle of a database or big data solution to capture, store, integrate, and process data. A data architect is responsible for gathering requirements, solution design, data modeling, testing, and deployment of solution systems. The role requires an understanding of existing and new technology and the big picture of the organization's data architecture.

Every specialist role creates the potential for a functional bottleneck that slows down the flow of work. The benefit of specialists only outweighs the costs in the largest or most complex organization. Otherwise, every effort should be made to reduce specialist roles that do not justify permanent inclusion in a team by investing in cross-skilling and automation technology.

There Is No I in Team

If team orientation has a significant influence on the flow of work across teams, the orientation of individuals within teams has a significant impact on the flow of work within teams. Moving specialists out of functional teams into cross-functional teams reduces the tax on the fast flow of work. Individuals can more easily understand their contribution to an end goal, prioritization is quicker, and unexpected work requests are fewer than with functional teams. While the tax is lower in cross-functional teams, it is not however eliminated simply by moving people with different skills into a new team.

Bill Buxton coined the term I-shaped people to describe specialists with narrow but deep domain skills in one area.[8] Specialists create silos within teams. Although the work they do may only take hours or days to complete, there can be much longer wait times before they are available to work on something new. Even when they have the capacity, specialists are less capable of helping other team members. Instead, they usually enter the zone of diminishing returns by overoptimizing their work such as further tuning machine learning models instead of looking for different ways to help the organization achieve its goals.

The I-shaped metaphor was conceived in response to a much earlier metaphor, which is called the T-shaped person. This metaphor was coined by Tim Brown, the CEO of the IDEO design consultancy.

T-shaped skills people (also known as generalized specialists in Agile terminology) have deep expertise in one area such as data engineering. But, they also tend to have broad skills across many fields such as machine learning and data visualization.

Generalized specialists do not have the fixed mindset of many specialists and are willing to pick up knowledge and skills from others. They can more easily see the impact of their work on others. They can also more easily empathize and look for ways to help the team. For example, a data engineer may integrate useful new data sources that data scientists were not aware of without being asked. T-shaped people can step across functional borders to remove bottlenecks faced by the team and keep work flowing smoothly.

Few people are naturally T-shaped, and they tend to be hard to find since data analytics typically rewards people for specialist skills. It is more usual to start with a team of curious and growth mindset specialists and then cross-train them by having them work alongside other specialists. Over several months, they pick up enough knowledge to be productive outside their expert area.

Team members also come in other skills shapes. Pi-shaped people have a wide breadth of knowledge of many disciplines and depth of skills in two areas. M-shaped people are poly-skilled; they combine the breadth of knowledge of T-shaped individuals with deep knowledge of three or more specialisms.

Pi- and M-shaped people increase team productivity by magnitudes through increased flow of work and ability to cross-train and grow others. E-shaped people have a combination of four Es – experience, expertise, exploration, and execution.

Many analytics teams neglect to include E-shaped members. These teams have plenty of people with experience and expertise who can explore ideas but cannot execute. These teams can flounder and fail to reliably produce what organizations need despite great ideas and technical expertise, which only delivers frustration for everyone.

Dash-shaped people is the final skill shape. They are also known as generalists because they have a breadth of skills, but not the depth of technical expertise. Figure 8-3 shows the different skills shapes for team members.

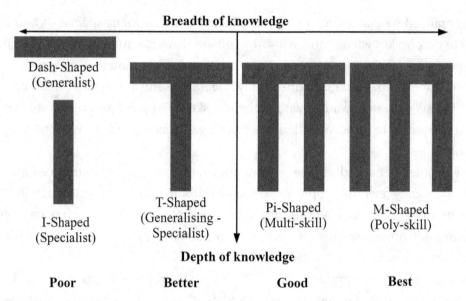

Figure 8-3. *Breadth and depth of knowledge for different people skill shapes*

Historically, teams of specialists have often been led by generalists who have strategic vision, excellent communication, stakeholder management, leadership, and people management skills. However, it is better to train and coach specialists to develop generalist skills or train generalists to add specializations to become T-shaped rather than employ generalists who cannot improve the flow of the team's work. Once team members become T-shaped, the ambition is to add further skills and become pi-shaped, M-shaped or E-shaped.

Creating a team of generalized specialists and multiskilled people requires a change in recruitment policy along with substantial investment in mentoring, coaching, and training. Instead of looking for mythical unicorns with the perfect combination of attributes, recruitment should focus on people with the aptitude and desire to learn skills outside their specialization. Data engineers are often hungrier to learn machine learning than data scientists are to learn to build pipelines or appreciate the need to operationalize and maintain their output.

Optimized Teams

The people and how they are organized are the primary factors behind the success of a team. However, there are other factors to consider including team size, location, and stability.

Communication Lines and Team Size

Many organizations find that large teams do not function well. The late Harvard psychologist J Richard Hackman believed the problems with large teams is not their size but the almost exponential increase in the number of links between people with every person added.[9] The formula for the increase in links with the number in people is

Number of links = n(n-1)/2

where n is the number of people in the team. Figure 8-4 shows how the number of communication links increases with the number of team members.

The number of unique connections between nodes = n(n-1)/2

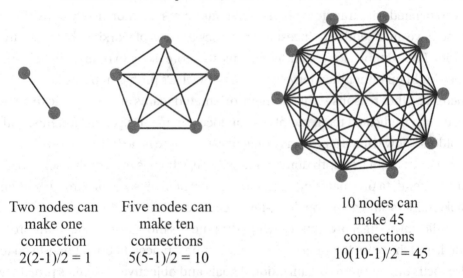

| Two nodes can make one connection $2(2-1)/2 = 1$ | Five nodes can make ten connections $5(5-1)/2 = 10$ | 10 nodes can make 45 connections $10(10-1)/2 = 45$ |

Figure 8-4. *The number of connections for two, five, and ten team members*

For example, a team of 5 has ten connections to maintain between members, but a team of 50 has 1,225 connections. So, a team of 50 has over 100 times as many connections as a team of 5 despite being only ten times bigger.

The increase in links leads to coordination problems as there is a higher chance for miscommunication, misinterpretation, and disengagement. The increase in links also leads to much higher communication overhead costs. Adding too many people to a team leads to diminishing returns and can reduce total productivity by slowing everything down.

It is no coincidence that team size for the most popular team sports in the world varies from 5 for basketball to 15 for rugby union with an average of 9. Smaller teams function better because it is easier to build strong bonds, get support from subject matter experts, and feel social pressure to contribute.

Amazon famously applies the two-pizza rule to team size. The idea is that a team should be no larger than the number of people that can be fed by two pizzas. Amazonians don't state what size pizza they eat, but conventional wisdom expects that two large pizzas feed six or seven people. The motivation is that Jeff Bezos wants decentralized autonomous teams that counterintuitively need to communicate less, not more.[10]

Products Not Projects

Long-lived and stable teams are more efficient than ad hoc or project-based teams. Stable teams avoid the painful and time-consuming forming, storming, and norming phases associated with transient teams. Team members are more likely to trust each other and have an incentive to invest in processes or ways of working that make their jobs easier. For example, long-standing teams are more likely to reduce the technical debt they build up rather than leave it as someone else's problem to solve.

There are other reasons stable domain-orientated teams are preferable to ad hoc project teams. Dedicated team members can focus on meeting commitments, and stakeholders know what everyone is doing because there is no hidden work.

Stable teams gain in-depth domain knowledge, which is incredibly useful for building better data products and decision support analytics, create strong relationships with stakeholders, and gain from long-term feedback. Data products, especially models, are not build-and-forget projects. Concept drift means models must be monitored and refreshed, and the team that makes the models is best placed to do it. Long-lived teams can also focus on long-term organizational goals and objectives, whereas project teams are usually judged on the budget and deadline targets they hit.

Location

When Eric Schmidt, ex-chairman and CEO of Google, published his ten golden rules for getting the most out of knowledge workers, number three was *"Pack them in."* Google believes the best way to make communication easy is to put team members within a few feet of each other.[11] Google is not alone. Most leading technology companies including Apple, Facebook, Microsoft, and Tencent house the majority of their technical employees together in large offices and campuses. Ironically, these companies build large, expensive offices despite having access to some of the advanced remote communication technology in the world.

Humans are hard-wired for face-to-face social interactions and perform less well in their absence. In her book *The Village Effect*, psychologist Susan Parker cites an experimental study of 25,000 call center agents. Half were asked to take breaks alone, while the others took breaks with coworkers. Those who socialized with coworkers showed a 20% performance increase.[12]

Colocation, teams working in a shared physical area, is the most effective way for knowledge workers to collaborate and be successful. The more complicated the task, the more workers benefit from the efficiency of face-to-face conversation and the ability to gather around information radiators or whiteboards.

The reality is that most teams operate on a continuum of face-to-face interaction combined with remote collaboration. Even Google has distributed teams. Multiple research studies show that the virtual distance between team members creates challenges.

A study of 115 project teams found that the greater the virtual distance measured by factors such as geography, time zone, culture, social contact, and face-to-face interaction, the lower the level of trust, goal clarity, and innovation.[13] Another study of 1,100 remote workers published in the Harvard Business Review found remote employees were more likely to worry that coworkers said bad things behind their back, made changes without telling them, didn't fight for their priorities, and lobbied against them.[14]

Distributed teams and remote working for individuals are not without upsides. Distributed teams and remote working allows recruitment from a much bigger talent pool than a single office, makes employment packages more attractive for talented individuals who value flexibility, and increases diversity.

There are strategies to make remote working effective. Conway's law suggests that teams should not be split across sites. Instead, multisite teams should be whole teams with each team self-contained within each location. To avoid a them-and-us attitude, at least some members from each team need to spend time at each other's site to build personal relationships and social bonds.

Google's research recommends further tactics for improving distributed work.[15] For example, team members should use video calls instead of audio calls so they can see each other. Team members should set norms for answering messages out of hours or organizing meetings across time zones. Also, group chat facilitates social interaction as well as work-related questions.

Reporting Lines

There are different options for where the core and supporting DataOps roles sit in the organization. It makes sense for data platform administration and specialist roles to report to centralized teams, enforce governance, maintain standards, and promote tool, pattern, and data reuse. Remaining cross-functional DataOps personas, typically data engineers, data scientists, and data analysts, can be centralized, decentralized, or a hybrid of the two.

In a centralized structure, the cross-functional roles report to a specialist data department that serves the whole organization. In a decentralized structure, the cross-functional roles are fully integrated and report to line functions in the organization such as product engineering, supply chain, or marketing. In the hybrid structure, cross-functional DataOps roles report to a central data team or center of excellence but embed with line function or domain teams.

Data Platform Administration

In most traditional organizations, the data product manufacturing line divides between IT data teams, data analytics teams, and data analytics professionals hired by functional teams. Data platform administration and data engineering are silos that typically report to centralized IT data teams. The consumers of data, data scientists, and data analysts report to data analytics teams or functional teams in the organization.

The IT data teams sit between consumers and the data in the organization. They control data capture, access, and the infrastructure required to process it. Unfortunately, IT data teams do not always recognize that data is an asset that belongs to the entire organization and focus on data defense instead. The problem is significant. In Kaggle's 2017 The State of Data & Machine Learning Survey of 16,000 respondents, "data unavailable or difficult to access" was mentioned by 30.2% of respondents.[16]

The IT barrier is a result of functional organization and misunderstanding of how to safely implement the data offense aspects of data strategy. IT data teams are rarely the consumer of data products, so do not have a data-centric view of the production line. Instead, teams are usually functionally organized by skill or technology and are thereby not incentivized to optimize the whole. However, they do worry about security and compliance issues. Allowing self-service access to data, tools, and infrastructure is the stuff of nightmares for most IT teams and is a reason for them to control data access through carefully curated data warehouses.

Nonetheless, as described in Chapter 6, it is possible to securely provision data, enforce security and privacy policies, and monitor or audit data usage and resource utilization even for big data. It is also possible to address another concern that IT data teams often raise that data analytics teams do not follow development best practice. However, data analytics teams can follow the DevOps practices in Chapter 7 and avoid problems such as development of brittle, hard-to-change data products in production.

Nevertheless, traditional centralized IT data teams are reluctant to hand control of data and infrastructure to data consumers in the organization. The problem is less to do with technology and standards, but more to do with profoundly ingrained culture and psychology. While roles and responsibilities for the data product manufacturing line predominantly live with IT data teams, there is always the risk of unnecessary roadblocks.

If data analytics is vitally important to the organization, it makes sense for data platform administration roles to belong in a culture that understands data analytics processes and has a stake in its outcomes. Grouping data platform administration and specialist roles in a department under a CDO or *Chief Analytics Officer* (CAO) reporting to the CEO is the ideal reporting structure. The CDO or CAO is a technical expert and visionary who can realize the full potential of data to the organization by taking a data-centric view.

Cross-functional Roles

Cross-functional DataOps roles such as team leads, data scientists, data analysts, and data engineers can be grouped into centralized, decentralized, or hybrid teams. Centralized teams make sense in smaller organizations because they do not have the scale to create multiple domain-orientated teams. Centralized teams can report to technical functions such as engineering, CDOs, CAOs, or even directly to the CEO. The teams consult or work on projects wherever their value is highest. Centralized teams facilitate career growth and development of best practice.

The downside of centralized teams is that they can take a long time to build domain knowledge of the organization and develop relationships with functional teams. Centralized teams risk marginalization at the edge of the organization as a reactive support function that fails to contribute to its full potential.

Since organizational goals are the drivers for data products, decentralized cross-functional DataOps roles integrate and report to line function or domain teams such as product or marketing to create full alignment. The head of the functional team has visibility into the integrated DataOps team members' activities and can prioritize their work based on the whole team's objectives.

Integrated DataOps roles ensure close collaboration with the functional team but can lead to the isolation of team members from their peers causing problems for career progression, consistent hiring, and knowledge sharing. Leaders of functional teams may not know how to use DataOps talent best, which creates an opportunity cost and risk of demotivation.

Another challenge with integrated cross-functional DataOps roles is that data platform administration will continue to report to a different part of the organization. This separation brings challenges as it is unlikely that functional team leaders will have much interest in data platforms and architecture making improvements harder. Typically, only organizations with extensive data analytics teams such as Netflix have highly decentralized roles. Netflix calls its culture *highly aligned, loosely coupled* with teams aligning on objectives and strategy while minimizing cross-functional meetings.

Hybrid centralized/decentralized team structures combine elements of centralized and decentralized teams. DataOps roles report to a central department or center of excellence, but embed in cross-functional teams closely aligned to organizational domains or functional teams. Unlike decentralized integrated teams, hybrid team members find it easier to learn from each other and manage careers through a central reporting structure. At the same time, embedded teams can build partnerships and rapport with the teams they work alongside.

If the hybrid team reports to the same leader (e.g., CDO or CAO) as the data platform administration and specialist roles, they create a specialized data function on a par with marketing, product, engineering, and other functions. The ideal data journey from raw data to data product along with the supporting tools, infrastructure, and governance sits under a single reporting line with one person ultimately responsible. The specialized function is the hardest solution to implement, but also the model that offers the most significant potential to eliminate most of the friction data teams face. It is the model my organization moved to with very positive results.

Summary

Every organizational model has benefits and trade-offs. For DataOps, the priority is to optimize for speed of new data product development and reduce risk by making frequent iterative changes instead of large and infrequent ones. Traditional functional orientation of teams leads to slow progress and lost opportunity. Knowledge of Conway's Law and organizational research studies help design organizational structures to optimize for the results we want instead of compromising the outcome to fit the organization we have.

DataOps does not require hiring more or different people but organizes employees around data-centric goals rather than tools, skills, or vertical reporting lines. DataOps teams organize around the most efficient communication pathways, eliminate organizational bottlenecks, and improve collaboration along the entire data product manufacturing production line.

DataOps encourages small, self-organizing, multiskilled, and cross-functional domain-orientated teams that are colocated and long-standing. Centralized functions provide self-service access to data, infrastructure, and services through data platforms. A center of excellence, guilds, or coordinating roles ensure domain-orientated teams do not become silos but benefit from cross-fertilization of best practice and career progression opportunities.

It is important to be pragmatic. Every organization is different, and there are multiple ways to organize for speed. However, whichever route is taken to create a DataOps organization, the objective should always be to facilitate velocity goals and not resource utilization.

The appropriate technology, when implemented well, can reinforce the benefits of the right organizational structure. The next chapter outlines the technologies to support DataOps collaboration.

Endnotes

1. Melvin E. Conway, How do committees invent?, Datamation, April 1968. *www.melconway.com/Home/pdf/committees.pdf*

2. Eric S Raymond, The New Hacker's Dictionary – 3rd Edition, October 1996.

3. Alan MacCormack, John Rusnak, and Carliss Baldwin, Exploring the Duality between Product and Organizational Architectures: A Test of the "Mirroring" Hypothesis, Harvard Business School, 2011. www.hbs.edu/faculty/Publication%20Files/08-039_1861e507-1dc1-4602-85b8-90d71559d85b.pdf

4. Nachiappan Nagappan, Brendan Murphy, and Victor R. Basili, The influence of organizational structure on software quality: an empirical case study, Microsoft Research, January 2008. www.microsoft.com/en-us/research/wp-content/uploads/2016/02/tr-2008-11.pdf

5. Blake Irvine, Netflix – Enabling a Culture of Analytics, May 2015 www.slideshare.net/BlakeIrvine/netflix-enabling-a-culture-of-analytics/8-Team_Structure_Specialization AnalyticsReportingModelingEngineeringAnalystEngineer VizEngineer

6. Rajiv Krishnamurthy and Ashish Kelkar, Building data science teams to have an impact at scale, facebook Code, June 2018. https://code.fb.com/core-data/building-data-science-teams-to-have-an-impact-at-scale/

7. Henrik Kniberg & Anders Ivarsson, Scaling Agile @ Spotify with Tribes, Squads, Chapters & Guilds, October 2012. https://blog.crisp.se/wp-content/uploads/2012/11/SpotifyScaling.pdf

8. Bill Buxton, Innovation Calls For I-Shaped People, Bloomberg, July 2009. www.bloomberg.com/news/articles/2009-07-13/innovation-calls-for-i-shaped-people

9. Diane Coutu, Why Teams Don't Work, Harvard Business Review, May 2009. https://hbr.org/2009/05/why-teams-dont-work

10. Brad Stone, The Everything Store: Jeff Bezos and the Age of Amazon, July 2014

11. Eric Schmidt and Hal Varia, Google: Ten Golden Rules, Newsweek, December 2005.

12. Susan Pinker, The Village Effect: How Face-To-Face Contact Can Make Us Healthier, Happier, and Smarter, August 2014.

13. Karen Lojeski, Richard Reilly, and Peter Dominick, The Role of Virtual Distance in Innovation and Success, Proceedings of the 39th Hawaii International Conference on System Sciences, February 2006. *www.researchgate.net/publication/4216008_ The_Role_of_Virtual_Distance_in_Innovation_and_Success*

14. Joseph Grenny and David Maxfield, A Study of 1,100 Employees Found That Remote Workers Feel Shunned and Left Out, Harvard Business Review, November 2017. *https://hbr.org/2017/11/a-study-of-1100-employees-found-that-remote-workers-feel-shunned-and-left-out*

15. Distributed Work Playbooks, Google. *http://services.google.com/fh/files/blogs/distributedworkplaybooks.pdf*

16. The State of Data Science & Machine Learning, Kaggle, 2017 *www.kaggle.com/surveys/2017*

PART IV

The Self-Service Organization

CHAPTER 9

DataOps Technology

Technology is deliberately left until the final chapter because while it is essential, it is less critical than people, culture, and processes. If tools were all it took to be successful, then Silicon Valley giants would not open-source their crown jewels such as Kubernetes, TensorFlow, Apache Kafka, and Apache Airflow.

Many organizations assume writing a check to a technology vendor or embracing the latest open-source software is an easy solution to their problems. Technology vendors and sponsors are happy to oblige and perpetuate the myth of silver bullets, and managers are willing to accept it because they can always blame the technology or vendor if things go wrong. However, a study of 680 executives in the Harvard Business Review reports that legacy technology is only the fifth most significant barrier to digital transformation.[1] The ability to experiment quickly, change processes, work across silos, and create a risk-taking culture are all more critical enablers of digital transformation. Nevertheless, DataOps is more successful with the right technology to eliminate the friction in data consumption that exists today.

Choosing Tools Based on DataOps Values and Principles

Just as chemistry is not about the tubes but the experimentation, DataOps does not rely on a particular architecture or technology in the form of hardware, platform, framework, tool, application, software library, service, or programming language. However, some architectures and technologies are better at supporting DataOps than others.

215

© Harvinder Atwal 2020
H. Atwal, *Practical DataOps*, https://doi.org/10.1007/978-1-4842-5104-1_9

Align Your Spine

Whenever choosing technology, it is best to never start with the tools themselves. A DataOps technology stack is a means to an end not an end in itself. Applying the spine model by Trethewey and Roux helps make sense of which tools are best to use.[2] Figure 9-1 shows the spine model.

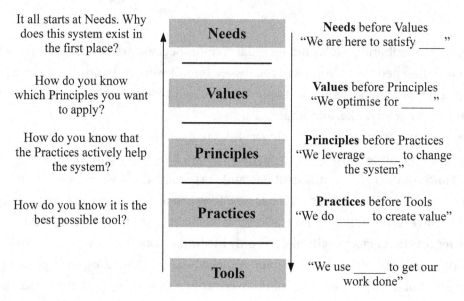

Figure 9-1. *The levels of the spine model*

The spine model is useful for mapping human work systems to gain agreement on how things should work. In this case, the boundary of the human work system encompasses everyone who creates value from data in the organization. Tools are at the bottom of the spine, and there are many plausible choices and opinions on which is best. Going up the spine resolves the challenge of choosing between multiple options.

Tools facilitate getting our work done, and the right tools, used in the right way, help us apply our practices more efficiently than the wrong tools. Practices are the application of methods and ways of working to get things done in the system. To understand which practices to use, it is necessary to go up the spine again and define principles. Principles are propositions that guide behavior and evaluation. For example, the batch size feedback principle states that increasing batch size of work delays feedback, while reducing batch size increases feedback. To know which principles are useful requires an understanding of values in the system, which are further up the spine. Values are judgments on what is essential and are the standards optimized in the system. For example, Scrum values are focus, openness, respect, courage, and commitment. At the top of the spine are needs; adopting the right values makes meeting these needs more likely. Needs are the reason the system exists.

To keep the spine straight and ensure the tools meet needs entails starting at the top of the spine and working downward to define and align each vertebra of values, principles, and practices. There are two types of needs, those of the system and the people in the system. The reason the system exists is to help the organization make faster, better decisions leading to beneficial actions by extracting knowledge from data. People's needs are universal and include autonomy, meaning, physical well-being, contentment, honesty, and connection.

Once the reason the system exists and the motivations for people to want to be part of the system are understood, it is time to decide the values to optimize. The DataOps manifesto lists five values: individuals and interactions; working analytics; customer collaboration; experimentation, iteration, and feedback; and cross-functional ownership.[3] Inspiration for the values comes from the agile software development manifesto and DevOps. Successful DataOps depends on living these values.

By looking at values, it is possible to determine the fundamental principles. Principles should apply consistently regardless of context, scale, or level. For example, the Lean product development principle of *reuse reduces variability* applies to any type and size of organization and any level within it from an individual to the entire organization.[4] Principles can come from many disciplines, such as Lean thinking, agile software development, systems thinking, the theory of constraints, DevOps, queuing theory, economics, and *total quality management* (TQM).

Just as different agile frameworks have different principles, there are several takes on DataOps principles. Chapter 4 introduced the DataOps principles from the DataOps manifesto. As a reminder, here are the fundamental principles again:

- Continually satisfy your customer

- Value working analytics

- Embrace change

- It's a team sport

- Daily interactions

- Self-organize

- Reduce heroism

- Reflect

- Analytics is code

- Orchestrate

- Make it reproducible

- Simplicity

- Analytics is manufacturing

- Quality is paramount

- Reuse

- Improve cycle times

DataOps principles give rise to DataOps practices. Every practice employed must be rooted in one or more principles. For example, the agile XP practices of continuous integration and 10-minute build are driven by the XP principle of rapid feedback.

Implications for Practices and Tools

Some DataOps principles such as self-organization, daily interactions, embrace change, and reflect mostly determine practices for ways of working. However, other principles lead to technical practices and technology requirements to enable them.

One of the principles is to *improve cycle times* of turning data into a useful data product. Requesting data or access to infrastructure and waiting for permission and provisioning is a significant bottleneck and massive source of waste in organizations. The goal must be to maximize the availability of data through self-service and automation. However, self-service is not just about giving data consumers access to precanned data cubes through BI tools. Consumers of data need practices and tools that allow them automated self-service access to infrastructure, tools, packages, and all the data they need so they can choose how to use it. Automated self-service access to data and infrastructure, in turn, require practices and tools that allow data discovery and create trust in users by enforcing data security and privacy policies, infrastructure, and data access policies and monitoring of resource utilization.

Reducing heroism necessitates practices and tools that allow data analytics, data storage, compute infrastructure, and data pipelines to scale with ease and handle any workflow without the firefighting common to many teams. *Orchestration* involves implementing practices and tools that can streamline and orchestrate data pipeline tasks end-to-end across many potentially diverse data types, technologies, and languages. Borrowing from DevOps, practices and tools that enable frequent small changes instead of fewer but bigger changes support the principle of *continuously satisfying your customer*.

The principle of *reproducibility* requires practices and supporting tools that enable code, environments, and data to be reproducible so that development is safe to deploy in production. *Reuse* is a closely related principle to reproducibility and necessitates practices and tools that avoid waste through repetition. For example, the ability for data consumers to publish, discover, and reuse each other's datasets is important for reuse. Reuse also entails replacing tedious, error-prone, and inconsistent manual processes such as data munging and monitoring with automated alternatives.

Quality is paramount is a principle that requires practices that build trust in data. Tools are required to manage and monitor metadata, file validation, data integrity, data quality assessments, data cleansing, and track data lineage. The *it's a team sport* principle recognizes the value of combining the best tools for each task into a winning stack instead of using a single tool to cover ground and perform roles it is not capable of doing.

Analytics is code is a principle that encourages practices that use code-based tools. Although tools with drop and drag GUI interfaces initially have a lower barrier to entry and are faster to learn, ultimately, code is the best long-term abstraction for managing sophisticated data analytics and pipelines.

Code is preferable not because of any masochistic tendencies among people who can code or desire to keep work out of the hands of nonanalytics professionals, but because it is easier to apply software engineering best practice. Code is simpler than drag and drop development to version control, reuse, parameterize, base further abstractions upon, refactor for efficiency, self-document, collaborate on, test, reproduce across environments, customize, migrate between solutions, integrate with other development, and update with extended functionality. The best solution though is always a working solution that gets the job done, so any technology that enables DataOps is better than none at all.

The DataOps Technology Ecosystem

The promise of handing over a check to a single vendor such as IBM, Oracle, or SAS to build a complete data analytics stack from data ingestion to data consumption is long gone if it ever existed in the first place. Instead of a monolithic stack, the modern DataOps analytics technology stack is a modular ecosystem combining best-in-class technologies. The modular architecture is analogous with a microservices architecture where each technology is loosely coupled, does its job very well, and can change with little effect on the overall system.

The Assembly Line

There is no right or best DataOps technology ecosystem. Selecting a set of tools depends on the context. It is wasteful to spend lots of time and money building architectures and technologies that are cool because Google and Amazon use them, but are not the right tools for the job. Every architecture and technology stack is also imperfect at any given point in time, and future demands are hard to predict. Just as data products benefit from rapid feedback and iteration so do technology stacks. The ecosystem is designed for constant evolution and should change and adapt to new processes and requirements.

The key to understanding and building the DataOps technology ecosystem is not to think in traditional terms of architectural layers or the functional teams who support and use the technology. Conventional thinking results in multiple technology silos and barriers to data consumption. Instead, it is necessary to take a data-centric end-to-end view of the flow of data from source to consumption as an assembly line and then consider the technologies that support development and operations.

The best technologies to employ are those that support the DataOps practices that fulfill the ultimate need for the organization to make faster and better decisions that lead to beneficial actions by extracting knowledge from data. Figure 9-2 illustrates the technology considerations needed to create and operate data products.

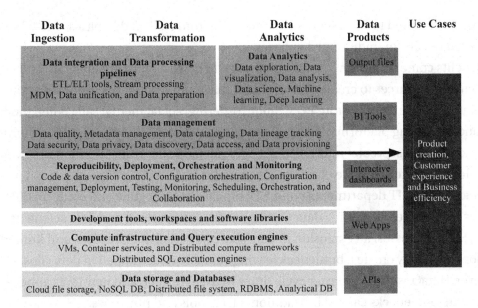

Figure 9-2. *DataOps technology components*

Although Figure 9-2 shows the flow of data as linear, in reality, the development process and production data flows are iterative with many datasets, artifacts, and technologies continuously managed and reused. There is also a data feedback loop back from use cases, which becomes another data source.

The following sections provide details of the technology requirements along the data assembly line. The DataOps technology landscape is rapidly evolving, and use cases differ between organizations, so it is not possible to be prescriptive about technologies and architectures. The technologies mentioned are not an exhaustive list of options or recommendations, but notable examples at the time of writing. In some cases, the technologies have multiple capabilities and could have appeared in more than one section.

Data Integration

The modern data analytics technology stack must support the ingestion of many heterogeneous internal data sources and data acquisition from external systems. Source data can come from web and mobile analytics tools, data warehouses and marts, supply chain systems, CRM and marketing platforms, ERP and financial reporting tools, and more. Adding to the complexity, source data also comes in a variety of types such as files consisting of structured, semi-structured, and unstructured data, event streams typically in a semi-structured format, semi-structured data from NoSQL databases, and tabular structured data from traditional databases.

Benefits come from allowing data analysts and data scientists to integrate and enrich disparate data sources to create data products that enable better decisions. For example, combining clickstream, in-store POS, online ordering, social media, call center, mobile app, and marketing platform data can help data scientists build ML models that improve supply chain plans, predict returns, target personalized offers and retention programs, and calculate customer price elasticity for a retailer.

Traditionally, IT departments build ETL pipelines to integrate and conform different sources into a schema within a data warehouse for data analysts and data scientists to use. Slow processes, an explosion in data sources, varied data formats, and limited developer capacity create a bottleneck leaving valuable data trapped in data silos. However, DataOps requires faster cycle times to useable data, and new tools appear that remove the bottlenecks caused by traditional ETL tools and processes.

Over the last few years, there has been an explosion in *software-as-a-service* (SaaS) ETL/ELT offerings that remove the heavy lifting effort involved with data movement between multiple data sources, destination data warehouses, and data lakes. The vendors offer dozens of prebuilt connectors to integrate data from applications including Salesforce and ERP systems, databases such as Oracle and SQL server, event streams such as webhooks and Kafka, file sources and stores, and data warehouses.

The products do the hard work of maintaining connectors, detecting data, preparing schemas, loading data, optimizing performance, and monitoring pipelines. The destinations supported by the products include popular databases including Amazon Redshift, Google BigQuery, Microsoft SQL Server, PostgreSQL, and Snowflake. With these solutions, it is possible to combine and query data in hours, not months.

Although they appear superficially similar, the new generation of ETL/ELT products typically falls into two groups. Some products such as Blendo, Fivetran, Segment, and Stitch (based on Singer open-source software) focus on synchronizing data between sources and destinations for ELT workloads. Other products, including Alooma, Funnel, Matillion, DataVirtuality, Etleap, Keboola, Xplenty, Azure Data Factory, and Google Data Fusion, also offer data transformation capabilities for ETL in addition to synchronization.

Often, the data ingested from the source comes from *online transaction processing* (OLTP) systems optimized for operations, but not analytical use cases. For data analytics, some data modeling in the form of flattened tables, *denormalized tables* with data from multiple tables bought together to avoid joins and speed up reading, and creation of *slowly changing dimension* to track history of dimensions such as customer address is very useful.

Well-modeled data makes it easier to reuse data without reinventing the wheel, which saves considerable time. If the data modeling transformations are not done before loading data, tools such as dbt (data build tool) or modeling layers in BI tools such as Looker's LookML allow data scientists and data analysts to create self-service transformations. Anyone comfortable using SQL can use dbt to apply software engineering best practices such as version control, automated testing, and peer review to develop transformations without relying on data engineers.

Storing data from multiple sources in a single location for analysis is of no use if it cannot be integrated. Conforming a large number of data sources into a data warehouse schema with ETL tools is not a scalable or fast solution. Every organization typically has primary entities such as customers, employees, products, and vendors that are linkable across data sources. However, the way independent tools and organizational units record entity values and field names for the same entity can vary enormously making matching difficult. For example, two different business units may record the same customer name and address in entirely different ways.

Often, it is left to data scientists to combine data themselves from a data lake. But without in-depth knowledge of every data source, integration becomes a nonscalable, time-consuming, and error-prone task. Master data management attempts to create one single master reference source from the multiple data items that may represent it. MDM software relies on data cleansing, transformation, and complicated rules to decide the single point of reference for integrating key entities across the organization. However, it soon becomes a challenge to create all the rules MDM software needs to maintain master records. To solve the problem of data integration, a new generation of data unification tools such as Tamr are emerging, which mix ML with human expertise to create automated and scalable solutions to combining data.

Data Preparation

Proper data preparation, sometimes also called data preprocessing or data wrangling, facilitates efficient data analysis by users. Data preparation is a multistep process to collect, clean, correct, combine, and transform data into a format data analysis and data science tools can consume for further analysis.

Examples of data preparation include filling in blank values, renaming fields to join data sources, and validating values to remove outliers. Data preparation accounts for 80% of data scientists' time, and 76% of data scientist regard it as the least enjoyable part of their work.[5] To reduce data preparation time and increase the time spent using data, several vendors offer data preparation tools including Trifacta, Talend, Altair, Alteryx, Paxata, and Datameer.

Unlike traditional ETL tools designed for professionals, data preparation tools are intended for self-service use by nontechnical users too and feature visual interfaces. Many data preparation tools also include data management features such as data discovery, data profiling, data lineage, and sensitive data masking. Some offer more advanced functionality such as version control, scheduling, intelligent data relationship inference, and metadata recommendations.

There are drawbacks to data preparation tools as they are built solely for data preparation by nonexperts. The tools may lack functionality for software engineering best practice, may not have connectors for some data sources, and can also run into scaling issues.

Data preparation tools work well for intermediary preprocessing steps between data sources, BI, and data science tools. However, the tools are hard to use as part of a more extensive automated end-to-end data pipeline unless they feature code generation export. Furthermore, unlike ETL tools that are metadata definition reliant, data preparation tools are data-centric and users work with data samples. Without robust data governance, it is possible for users to create multiple interpretations of the same data.

Stream Processing

Some data sources generate a real-time stream of event messages that are processed in a different way than files and tables of data. Examples include IoT devices and sensors, web clickstreams, and *event sourcing* (a type of design that logs state changes). Typically, message brokers such as RabbitMQ or a publish-subscribe stream platform such as Apache Kafka, Amazon Kinesis, or Google Cloud Pub/Sub handles messages. Messages can be loaded into offline data warehouses for future batch processing and analytics or processed in real-time.

Stream processing is the application of complex operations to multiple input streams or messages at the same time. Stream processing enables applications such as near real-time fraud detection that would otherwise not be possible because batch processing of files and tables takes too long.

Certain publish and subscribe platforms including Apache Kafka, Apache Pulsar, and Amazon Kinesis have some functionality for stream processing. Otherwise, when performance requirements are critical, specialized stream processing tools such as Apache Flink and Apache Samza process messages from Apache Kafka or other sources.

Spark structured streaming is a popular solution for stream processing when low latency is not vital as it offers users of Spark batch processing and ETL functionality a familiar API and shallow learning curve. Apache Beam also presents a unified programming model for ETL, batch, and stream processing data pipelines. Data pipelines in Apache Beam are defined using a Java, Python, or Go SDK and execute on one of several supported execution engines including Apache Spark, Apache Flink, Apache Samza, and Google Cloud Dataflow making them extremely flexible although the learning curve can be steep.

Data Management

Effective data management ensures that users can trust data and there is trust in users of data. Trust enables the self-service metadata-driven marketplace access to data by users without requiring constant requests to IT.

DataOps requires sophisticated metadata management, data cataloging, and data lineage tracking. Metadata management is critical to self-service analytics as it makes it possible for users to identify the data they want, where it came from, and understand how it can be used.

A well-documented data catalog is essential to help users find and interpret data. Data lineage tracking, where the data came from, where it has moved, and what has happened to it, is indispensable for data governance, compliance, and data quality management.

Off-the-shelf data management software is available from vendors such as IBM, Collibra, Alation, Manta, ASG Technologies, Informatica, Reltio, Timextender, Qlik, and Waterline Data to manage metadata, build data catalogs, track data lineage, and more. It is also possible to use open-source software such as Apache Atlas for data governance and metadata management in the Hadoop ecosystem or to create a data catalog using cloud services by extracting metadata from objects in cloud storage using AWS Glue Crawlers or Google Data Catalog.

Secure data must be provisioned to users in minutes not days or weeks. A self-service data culture requires robust, centrally controlled data security and privacy controls. Ideally, an automated service such as Amazon Macie or Google Cloud Data

Loss Prevention identifies and classifies sensitive data on capture. Otherwise, solutions such as Privitar can watermark data for auditing and lineage tracking, deidentify sensitive data while preserving useful patterns, and set privacy policies across datasets. Data consumers are then allowed self-service access to datasets in centralized data lakes or data warehouses in a format that adheres to security policies and regulations for their role. Alternatively, a tool such as Delphix can apply data masking on-the-fly and provides users a secure version of data for self-service consumption from multiple sources.

Auditing and monitoring are crucial to ensure compliance with laws, regulations, and data governance policies. Real-time alerts for abnormal behavior can be created by analyzing log files. Some data management software such as Global IDs can also perform data security classification and monitoring activities.

A unified IAM solution that defines granular role-based access control to data and resources supports self-service while preserving data privacy and security. IAM solutions are available for cloud and on-premise systems that integrate with access management platforms such as Okta, SecureAuth, and Auth0 to centrally manage access by users and groups.

Reproducibility, Deployment, Orchestration, and Monitoring

A primary requirement of the DataOps technology stack is the ability to automate and orchestrate the flow of data along potentially complex pipelines consisting of multiple technologies. Apache Airflow is the most popular open-source software for creating, scheduling, and monitoring DAGs. Alternatives include Luigi, Apache Oozie, or Azkaban for Hadoop and Google's managed Airflow service Cloud Composer.

DataOps teams must be able to reproduce infrastructure, data pipeline code, and pipeline orchestration in an automated way so they can safely develop, test, and deploy frequent small changes in identical environments. Terraform and AWS CloudFormation are two popular configuration orchestration tools for creating, modifying, and destroying infrastructure. Configuration management tools such as Puppet, Chef, and Ansible control installation and management of software on the provisioned infrastructure. Operating systems and applications are also reproducible. Shell scripts or products such as Vagrant can reproduce VMs easily. Docker is the most widespread platform for packaging code and dependencies as containers to run identically in different environments.

Reproducible environments require code and configuration files to be under version control. Git is the most prevalent version control software, while Github, Gitlab, and Bitbucket are the most common git repository hosting services. Once code and configuration files are in version control, automated deployment pipelines using CI/CD tools such as Jenkins, Travis CI, TeamCity, Bamboo, and Gitlab CI create environments and deploy data pipelines. The tools also run white box, black box, and regression tests written beforehand to ensure that no bugs are introduced.

Testing depends on proper test data management and commercial tools such as Informatica, Delphix, and CA Test Data Manager. These tools make the rapid provision of test datasets straightforward. Version control of ML models and data is a less mature field than code and configuration, but promising open-source libraries like DVC, ModelDB, Pachyderm, and Quilt Data are appearing.

DataOps teams rely on many orchestration, configuration management, deployment, and other tools to automate tasks. These tasks require scripts and secrets such as tokens, passwords, certificates, and encryption keys to work. Secrets management and software such as HashiCorp's Vault is essential to minimize the risk of secrets being exposed.

In production, automated testing and monitoring of data, infrastructure, and resources are critical functions in DataOps. Monitoring data pipelines and alerting when data quality problems are detected prevent bugs from traveling further down the pipeline where they can be much harder to fix.

Open-source package Great Expectations automates pipeline tests, the equivalent of unit tests for datasets, at batch run time. Commercial tools such as iCEDQ, RightData, and QuerySurge test data and validate continuous data flows in production in addition to providing automated testing during development.

The health of data products also needs monitoring, and open-source application monitoring solutions can be adapted to monitor data pipelines. Packages such as Prometheus can be set up to monitor data pipeline KPIs for timeliness, end-to-end latency, and coverage and then send the data to a time-series analytics dashboard such as Grafana for visualization and alerting.

Monitoring tools such as AppDynamics, New Relic, DataDog, Amazon Cloudwatch, Azure Monitor, and Google Stackdriver track metrics for resources and applications in data centers or the cloud. The tools integrate with incident management platforms such as PagerDuty to raise notifications.

The application performance management software Unravel is specialized for big data and monitors the performance of applications and platforms running data pipelines. The software includes more advanced features such as anomaly detection, insights into performance degradation, recommendations to optimize infrastructure and application configuration, and automated actions such as killing rogue processes.

Messaging and communication tools enable teams to collaborate effectively and raise alerts, signal data quality issues, answer questions, resolve issues quickly, and document knowledge. Tools in this space include Slack, Confluence, Microsoft Teams, Google Hangouts, and Google Groups.

Compute Infrastructure and Query Execution Engines

A computing resource is required to process data and run applications when third-party services are not used. The compute resource should exist on a scalable multitenant platform to deal with data no matter how big it is and support the development and production workloads of multiple users. The three common ways to supply the compute resource are VMs, distributed computing clusters, and container clusters.

VMs allow multiple OS environments to exist on the same physical infrastructure, which are all isolated from one another. The VM can provide different CPU, RAM, and local storage specifications than the underlying hardware allowing them to match the user need. VMs enable elasticity because they can be provisioned and discarded as needed to meet demand. VMs also support scalability to handle larger workloads. They can be scaled vertically by creating larger machines or horizontally by adding more VMs and sharing the workload between them.

Distributed computing systems take advantage of horizontal scaling by parallelizing workloads across a cluster of VMs. The two distributed computing systems with the greatest mindshare are Spark Core and Hadoop MapReduce. Both sometimes share components of the Hadoop ecosystem such as *Hadoop Distributed File System* (HDFS) for storage and *Yet Another Resource Manager* (YARN).

Spark is much faster at processing data than Hadoop MapReduce as it attempts to process data in RAM as far as possible and avoids the bottleneck caused by reads and writes to disk. Spark also has better libraries for SQL commands, machine learning, graph problems, and stream processing.

Increasingly, Kubernetes, referred to as K8s by the cool kids, is a popular way to scale data processing workloads and applications horizontally. Even Spark can now run on a cluster managed by Kubernetes. Kubernetes is an open-source container platform for managing deployment, scaling, and operations of containers across a cluster. Any application that runs in an *Open Container Initiative* (OCI) container will run on Kubernetes. In practice, however, it is mostly used with the Docker image format and runtime.

Kubernetes solves the problem of running a large number of containers in harmony across many different machines. Kubernetes can deploy containers, scale container numbers up or down with demand, distribute the load between containers (keeping storage consistent across multiple instances of an application), and self-heal failed containers. Most cloud providers offer hosted Kubernetes platforms such as *Google Kubernetes Engine* (GKE), *Amazon Elastic Container Service for Kubernetes* (EKS), and *Azure Kubernetes Service* (AKS).

A chief advantage of the cloud is that it allows painless separation of storage from compute. Previously, when analytical data was mostly stored in data warehouses, the only way to access the data was through the data warehouses' query interface and in the format the warehouse provided. With cloud object stores, many consumers and processes can simultaneously access the data in multiple formats via APIs and connectors and use the best tool for the job paying only for the time spent processing data. Tools to query data in cloud storage include the distributed SQL query engine Presto, Amazon Athena, Amazon Redshift Spectrum, BigQuery, Rockset, Dremio, and serverless cloud functions. Some of these solutions have numerous connectors making them a convenient self-service query interface for multiple data sources.

Data Storage

Storage is required to persist raw and processed data, temporarily store intermediate results of data pipeline operations, capture log data, and hold the artifacts required for the development and operation of data pipelines and analytics. Different use cases and data formats require multiple storage technologies.

A data lake is a common initial storage area for raw data before it's integrated and processed further. Data lakes are designed to store large quantities of data ingested from multiple sources in many different formats including unstructured data. The idea is that a data lake allows everyone to access a central repository of the organization's data without needing to extract it from multiple sources.

To prevent a data lake from becoming a disorganized data swamp, a typical pattern is to divide data lakes into layers to manage data governance and make consumption easier. A raw (or intake layer) is where data from batch and real-time stream sources is landed, basic data validation checks are undertaken, and data security and privacy policies are applied to classify, deidentify, or anonymize sensitive data. Role-based access controls highly restrict access to this zone.

In the management layer (also known as the trusted or conformed layer), processes extract metadata, standardize data, and clean it before making it available to consumers. In the consumption layer, data from the management layer is transformed into formats suitable for applications such as data warehouses or machine learning models.

Historically, data lakes leveraged *Hadoop Distributed File System* (HDFS) for storage, MapReduce or Spark for data processing, Apache Hive for data warehousing, and Apache Impala as a fast SQL query engine. However, cheaper object storage such as Amazon S3, Azure BlobStore, and Google Cloud Storage is far more prevalent for data lake storage in the cloud.

Unlike file systems that manage data in a file hierarchy, cloud object storage treats data as an object with metadata and a globally unique identifier. It is now increasingly common to query data in cloud storage using a distributed SQL query engine rather than use HDFS.

Data lakes have not made data warehouses redundant but are complementary. Data warehouses operate on the principle of *schema on write,* which transforms data to a fixed structure on writing to the database for optimized consumption. However, data warehouses are time-consuming to develop. Data lakes store data in a basic raw form and work on the basis of *schema on read*. A schema to transform data into a more useful form is applied on extraction. Schema on read puts the onus on the consumer to understand the data and transform it correctly, but the trade-off is that data lakes offer access to much more data than data warehouses alone.

Cloud data warehouses are evolving to handle massive analytical workloads by independently scaling compute or storage and adding the ability to handle multiple data types. Popular analytical data warehouses include BigQuery, Amazon Redshift, Snowflake, and Microsoft SQL Data Warehouse.

The development of analytical data warehouses is blurring the line between data lakes and traditional data warehouses, especially as many modern self-service ETL/ELT tools allow users to ingest data from multiple data sources into them directly. So, it is critical to enforce data management best practice such as sensitive data classification and masking, metadata management, data cataloging, and data lineage tracking, particularly as users should be encouraged to reuse and share datasets. Otherwise, there is a risk that analytical data warehouses will become the new data swamps.

In addition to data lakes and data warehouses, there is a need for specialist NoSQL databases. *Document databases* are key-value stores where the values are semi-structured documents in a format such as XML, YAML, JSON, or *Binary JSON* (BSON). Document databases such as MongoDB or Amazon DynamoDB are ideal for storing semi-structured data, metadata, or configuration information.

Column databases store columns of data together instead of rows as with an RDBMS. This storage pattern reduces the amount of data that is read by a query returning results much faster. Fast queries over large datasets make column stores such as Cassandra and Amazon Redshift ideal for data warehouses. Apache Druid is a column-orientated, distributed data store designed to handle and query high volumes of real-time data making it perfect for stream analysis.

Graph databases such as Neo4j store information about networks relationships and are popular for fraud detection and recommendation engines. *Search engines* excel at text queries. The search engine Elasticsearch is a lightning-quick distributed search and analytics engine ideal for near real-time operational analytics such as log analytics, application monitoring, and clickstream analytics.

DataOps Platforms

Specialist platforms to support DataOps are in their infancy but are beginning to grow in number and capability. These platforms bleed across traditional technology boundaries and provide multiple capabilities. Some platforms are designed to work with existing tools, while others are designed to replace multiple tools usually with a no-/low-code interface.

DataKitchen is a platform that supports the testing, deployment, and orchestration of data pipelines. The platform is designed to support the technologies an organization already uses as much as possible. Streamsets is a drag and drop UI platform for batch and streaming pipeline creation across multiple sources and destinations that features monitoring and sensitive data detection. Composable's DataOps platform features services for data orchestration and automation of data integration, data discovery, and analytics. Nexla's DataOps platform consists of low-code tools and no-code workflows for data integration, data management, and monitoring of data flows.

Lenses.io is a DataOps platform designed to work natively with Apache Kafka to manage and monitor streaming data flows. Saagie is DataOps platform for building and orchestrating data pipelines with many popular open-source technologies such as Spark, Kafka, and Hadoop.

Infoworks and Zaloni's data platforms sit as a layer between storage and compute services and consumers of data. Infoworks' DataFoundry and Zaloni's data platform automate data ingestion and data synchronization, capture metadata, provide self-service data preparation, data catalog and data lineage functionality, and orchestrate automated workflows.

The convenience of working inside an integrated platform that replaces several tools must be carefully weighed against the compromise of not choosing the best individual tools for a job. After all, a spork is a mediocre replacement for a fork and spoon.

Data Analytics Tools

The output of every analytics DataOps pipeline is data in a format that data scientists and analysts use for decision support or to develop and operate a data product in production. The requirements of the data scientists and analysts, toolset are diverse, ranging from creating charts to deploying and managing deep learning models.

Reports and dashboards are a standard output of analytics teams. The output of a data pipeline can populate every report or dashboard. QlikView, Tableau, Looker, Microsoft Power BI, Tibco Spotfire, and Thoughtspot are popular commercial BI tools. Data scientists often create interactive web applications using open-source tools including Apache Superset, RShiny, and Dash.

The data science workflow for model creation consists of several steps including infrastructure provision, data acquisition, data exploration, data preparation, feature engineering, model training and evaluation, model deployment and testing, and model monitoring. Getting data right is hard, but also the most crucial part of machine learning. DataOps practices and tools provide automated self-service access to deliver data scientists the data platforms and high-quality data in the format they need.

Many of the remaining steps in the data science workflow are often custom manual tasks using a variety of tools and libraries such as Jupyter notebooks, Pandas, scikit-learn, Tensorflow, Spark for feature engineering, model training, and model evaluation. The mix of tools and manual effort makes it hard to scale data scientist's contribution to tackling more problems.

Several companies are building tools to automate all or part of the machine learning workflow. These tools include Google Cloud AutoML, H2O's AutoML, Salesforce's TransmogrifAI, DataRobot, Auto-sklearn, and Auto-Keras. These tools automate the process of building models.

Other solutions are designed to support MLOps and the management of the model lifecycle. Example services include Amazon Sagemaker, Google Cloud AI Platform, and Microsoft Azure Machine Learning service, Seldon, MLeap, MLflow, Hydroshpere.io, Algorithmia, and Kubeflow with new solutions seemingly announced daily.

Data science and engineering platforms are an alternative to assembling a home-made technology stack. These platforms provide a one-stop self-service shop on top of native infrastructure to improve data scientist and data engineer workflows. The platforms roll up the capability to deliver the data science lifecycle into a single product for productivity benefits.

The platforms include popular data science languages, coding workspaces and their libraries, support multitenant scalable private or public cloud architecture, contain built-in collaboration and version control tools, allow for publication of production-ready ML models and interactive reports, have security and governance features, and more. Some commonly used platforms include Dataiku, Domino Data Lab, Qubole, Databricks, Iguazio, and John Snow Labs (which specializes in healthcare).

Challenges

Although there are significant benefits from modular data architecture, there are also challenges compared to monolithic systems. Every tool must be interoperable with those it interacts with because there are high orchestration efforts and significant complexity in handling multiple technologies. If not managed correctly, modular architecture can go against principles of simplicity and become a technology zoo.

Most technologies today are interoperable at the structural and syntactic level because they can exchange data in shared formats such as JSON, communicate via common protocols such as SQL or REST APIs, and exchange data while preserving data models, structures, and schemas.

However, the technologies are rarely interoperable at the metadata and *semantic*, or shared meaning, level. The lack of interoperability means valuable context, and metadata does not pass between tools. Data lineage tracking, data provenance identification, reproducibility, data unification, metadata-dependent execution, testing, and end-user interpretation are all much harder without semantic and metadata interoperability.

This problem is beginning to gain more prominence, and solutions are starting to appear. Dagster is a promising open-source Python library that adds a layer of abstraction above familiar technologies such as AWS, Spark, Airflow, and Jupyter through a standard API. Dagster treats ETL and ML pipelines as a single data application enabling subtasks to pass metadata between them.

Until more DataOps-centric solutions emerge, care must be taken to preserve boundaries between modular components especially when tools overlap in functionality. Transformation and analytics logic should reside within each tool as much as possible, so DevOps best practices for version control, testing, and continuous integration are simpler to apply. Avoid logic leaking into orchestration tools or configuration files as it leads to tight coupling and makes it much harder to debug pipelines or update the technology stack.

Build vs. Buy

Technology stacks should continuously evolve to meet the needs, values, principles, and practices of the organization. The theory of constraints tells us that there is always at least one constraint limiting the rate of goal achievement. At some point, part of the technology ecosystem will become a sizable enough bottleneck that it is worth the effort to upgrade it. Choosing technology and deciding if a custom in-house solution, commercial product, a paid-for service, or open-source software is best can be daunting. Each option has benefits and trade-offs.

Extend

The first consideration should be not to implement any new solution at all but to extend an existing solution. Instead of throwing away what you already have, determine if functionality can be extended. For example, a traditional relational database such as PostgreSQL can also natively handle semi-structured JSON data that potentially removes the need to install a NoSQL document database such as MongoDB.

The learning curve for extending existing technology may be shallow as there is likely to be an existing team who understands it well. There is also less architectural impact from extending rather than introducing new technology. The downside of extending is that the incremental benefits may not be significant and another solution may be needed sooner or later. Extending an existing solution may also build on shaky foundations and result in an accumulation of technical debt.

Build In-House

Building a custom solution in-house provides the ultimate opportunity to tailor the technology to your needs. In theory, any home-grown ML or deep learning model in production is a custom in-house solution and differentiator for the organization. However, many organizations go further and develop custom libraries and data science platforms to manage data product workflows. While there are benefits to home-grown solutions, there are also costs and risks.

Overoptimism is one of the 12 main cognitive biases that cause people to make errors in thinking.[6] The writer Douglas Hofstadter coined Hofstadter's Law to describe the difficulty of accurately estimating the time it takes to complete complex tasks.[7] Hofstadter's self-referential law states *it always takes longer than you expect, even when you take into account Hofstadter's law.* There is often a running joke within development teams that their product will be ready to ship 1 year from the point you ask for the completion date no matter when you ask.

While tools and platforms are in development, there are potentially high direct costs, opportunity costs, and costs of delay. Direct costs, such as developer time, are easy to quantify, but they are only the tip of the iceberg. Users forego the use of technology still in development leading to a cost of delay for products and projects that could have generated benefit and feedback. There is also an opportunity cost of developer resource because the time could be spent building brand new functionality instead of replicating an off-the-shelf product.

The costs do not end with the initial development of new technology. There are ongoing maintenance costs to fix defects and add new features.

Buy or Rent an Off-the-Shelf Product

Buying an off-the-shelf product has less risk than building a custom solution. In exchange for money, a user can take advantage of advanced functionality very quickly. A commercial vendor can take advantage of economies of scale to spread the cost of much more extensive development teams than most organizations can muster across many customers. Hence, in most cases, this makes it cheaper to buy than develop in-house even factoring in vendor profit margins.

A commercial vendor can offer support and frequent updates. A popular product will also have a community of users who can provide help in forums and potentially an ecosystem that extends the product with plug-ins and extensions.

Increasingly, vendors offer products as services on the cloud instead of installable software on local machines or data centers. The services range from *infrastructure-as-a-service* (IaaS), platform-as-a-service (PaaS), SaaS, and *function-as-a-service* (FaaS) to managed serverless platforms:

- **IaaS** is the most basic service and allows users to access fundamental infrastructure such as VMs over the cloud. An example is the Amazon EC2 service. However, users have to spend time provisioning the infrastructure, installing software, and configuring.

- **PaaS** adds complete development and deployment environments on top of infrastructure to allow application development without worrying about infrastructure, operating systems, development tools, or databases. Examples of PaaS include Google App Engine and Heroku.

- **FaaS** takes things a step further than PaaS with the provision of highly scalable environments for running code functions rather than entire applications making them ideal for building microservices or running code in response to events. Apache OpenWhisk, AWS Lambda, and Microsoft Azure functions are examples of FaaS. Frameworks like Nuclio have added support for data analytics workloads.

- With **SaaS**, a third-party hosts a fully functioning application and makes it available over the Internet. Github, Slack, and Dropbox are examples of SaaS applications.

- **Managed serverless platforms** remove the headache and complexity of managing infrastructure, configuring software, and scaling servers. Google BigQuery, Databricks Serverless, and Azure Stream Analytics are examples of managed serverless platforms.

The downside of commercial solutions is that the vendor is in control of the technology, and it may be challenging to influence the roadmap for future development. The customer may end up paying for functionality they do not want but miss some functionality they need. However, even if the preference is to build in-house, to buy or rent, commercial solutions can be considered an opportunity to learn. For instance, understanding what functionality is useful from actual usage can guide the development of in-house alternatives.

There must exist a high degree of trust that a third-party vendor will deliver on their promises, keep the product secure, and remain in business if they provide critical functionality. Vendor lock-in is a real risk if the provider makes it difficult to migrate to different technologies later. Lock-in can happen when a vendor insists on using their data models and proprietary data formats.

Borrow Open Source

Open-source software provides most, if not more, of the functionality and benefits of commercial products. A community of contributors undertakes development, maintenance, and bug fixes. The most popular open-source software projects have far more contributors than any single company can commit to a commercial or in-house product. For example, TensorFlow has over 2,000 global contributors.

A wide community of developers and users provides help through documentation, forums, and talks. In some cases, commercial support is available for open-source software. For example, Cloudera/Hortonworks and MapR provide enterprise services on top of the Hadoop ecosystem.

Well-known open-source software has many consumers, which makes recruitment of experienced users easier than proprietary systems. Open-source software licenses typically allow free usage and access to the source code, which results in lower up-front costs and avoids vendor lock-in.

Open-source software does have some of the downsides of commercial software. Development is under the control of third-party maintainers. So, there is no guarantee of quick bug fixes or development of the specific features you need. Often, open-source projects get abandoned entirely. However, access to source code mitigates some of the risks. Users can fork the project and move it in a different direction or contribute code via pull requests to add features or patches they need.

There are also drawbacks of using most open-source software compared to cloud-based FaaS, SaaS, and managed serverless platforms. The learning curve for open-source software can be steep as developers build it for technical users like themselves. Open-source software usually requires significant investment to explore how it will integrate and work within existing architectures and environments. The total cost of ownership for open-source software is not free. There are still ongoing and underestimated requirements to manage infrastructure, configure open-source software and environments, and handle updates that reduce its cost advantage.

Extend, Build, Buy, Rent, or Borrow

Going with what you know and extending existing technology is usually the best option to consider first. While shiny new technology may seem exciting to work with, it is better not to fall into the trap of *resume-driven development* (letting people choose technology that is best for their resume and not the problem). The idiom "if it ain't broke don't fix it" exists for a reason.

If extending existing technology is not an option, then pay-as-you-go services are usually the next best choice. Once you use SaaS or managed services, you will never want to go back to managing infrastructure and hardware again.

Building technology in-house should be a last resort. There is massive potential for waste going down the build-it-yourself route such as wasted time, wasted money, and wasted opportunity.

Data, and how it is used to create data products, is usually the source of competitive advantage rather than technology for most organizations. Only if the technology does not exist elsewhere and building a proprietary solution will be a source of competitive advantage should the in-house path be considered.

Cloud Native Architecture

Cloud native architecture should be the desired end state for DataOps because of the advantages it has for creating a self-service platform. However, it is essential to adapt to the unique opportunities and constraints the cloud offers; otherwise, as Damon Edwards famously remarked, "Without Self-Service Operations the Cloud Becomes Expensive Hosting 2.0."[8]

The cost of computing and storage technologies continues to decline, and growth in open-source code puts downward pressure on software costs. However, the cost of data analytics professionals continues to rise.

A good DataOps stack scales much faster than the expense data analytics professionals who maintain and use it. If the number of data products or size of data sets doubles, it should be possible for the DataOps stack to scale and handle the workload without requiring twice as many people or additional wait time.

Hitting capacity constraints or waiting months for a new server to be provisioned in a traditional data center is a bottleneck to efficiency. However, the cloud offers almost infinite scalability and elasticity. Elastic services can be spun up on demand and terminated when no longer wanted. Storage and compute can be scaled to handle any size workload.

Instead of worrying about the capacity constraints and resilience of fixed infrastructure, the cloud encourages automation to take advantage of elasticity, scaling, and cost savings by not paying for underutilized resources. The cloud also encourages self-service because services are available to users via APIs, and centralized role permissions allow access to all permitted resources without requiring multiple individual requests.

A centralized cloud platform promotes collaboration and helps break down organizational barriers because everyone is using the same platform and tools. The cloud also makes the perfect platform for central monitoring, governance, and controls for multiple resources.

Cloud native architecture favors managed services due to integration and efficiency benefits. Many organizations are wary of managed and serverless services because of the lock-in risk. However, this risk is often overstated.

Managed open-source services such as Amazon Elastic Kubernetes Service offer considerable benefits over self-management and are the lowest risk. Managed proprietary services such as Snowflake or Google BigQuery are still worth adopting because of the significant operational and performance benefits over alternatives. Proprietary managed services without an apparent performance or operational benefit over self-managed open-source software are a gray area and need to be considered case-by-case.

Evolving the Technology Stack

Keeping on top of rapid changes in technology to support DataOps is no easy task. There is a steady stream of new announcements from the technology community and plenty of tools and techniques team members want to try. It is easy to go down a dead end and adopt technologies that are not fit for purpose, or use custom solutions or products when better options exist. Fortunately, there are a couple of complementary techniques that help track technology evolution and timing of adoption – Wardley maps and technology radars.

Wardley Maps

Simon Wardley is a researcher and advisor who as VP of the software company Canonical helped its Ubuntu operating system become the dominant OS in the public cloud. Simon developed Wardley maps in 2005 as a way to plot user needs for a product or service to a value chain of components that deliver it in a way that could help understand the evolution of context and components.[9] Today, the UK government uses Wardley maps widely for strategic planning.

In the DataOps technology stack, components are the hardware, software, and service elements that combine in a chain of needs. Wardley maps consist of two axes – the y-axis plots the value of the component to the user and the x-axis measures the maturity of the component. The customer and their need form the anchor for the value chain and map.

A Wardley map is context-specific and dynamic as the position of components evolves over time. Figure 9-3 shows an example Wardley map for an interactive real-time analytics dashboard built using Imply's Pivot dashboard tool.

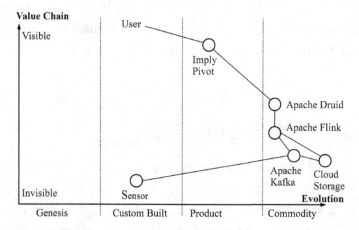

Figure 9-3. *A real-time time-series analytics dashboard Wardley map*

A component that creates highly visible value to the user appears high on the y-axis, while one that provides invisible value to the user appears low on the y-axis. For example, a recommendation model that makes movie recommendations is highly visible to a video streaming subscriber, but the electricity component to compute the model is invisible.

The x-axis of a Wardley map measures the maturity of the component in four stages including *genesis, custom-built, product,* and *commodity.*

Genesis is the territory components that begin their life through bespoke R&D efforts such as the first computer, the first cloud computing environment, or the first version of a programming language. There is great potential value of components in genesis, but also uncertainty about development direction and high risk of failure.

If the component shows promising benefit in the genesis territory, it will enter the custom-built stage. Several organizations will create their custom-built versions of the original component, a market or community will slowly form, and the ROI of further development becomes clear. However, the component is still leading edge and the preserve of experts, as it requires rare and specialist expertise to use.

Success in the custom-built stage will lead to the component entering the product stage. The product stage exhibits rapidly increasing consumption and the creation of product versions of the component that are user-friendly, widely used, and differentiated by their features. Consumers will demand more of anything that gives them a distinct benefit or advantage. An increasing number of suppliers compete to improve the product and add more features. Consumers creating their custom versions of components are at a disadvantage to those who use off-the-shelf products, which leads them also to adopt the product version of the component.

Unpopular ideas will die earlier, but high demand and competition will ensure that the most useful components reach the final stage of evolution, commodity. Eventually, product differentiation may plateau, and useful features are copied making products uniform. The high cost of products incentivizes the development of cheap, standardized commodity versions that are treated as a utility. Increasing demand leads to economies of scale, which further brings down costs. The component is no longer a differentiator but a cost of doing business.

It is often a new entrant to the market that initiates commoditization because it does not have the inertia of a company with a profitable product to protect. A well-known online bookseller disrupting the enterprise computing landscape is a famous example of a trigger leading to many computing components leaping from products to commodities.

Many of the most mature technology components are utility commodities that are well understood in the industry, standardized, and in widespread use. Examples include virtualization software, cloud storage, databases, operating systems, security libraries, version control software, and programming languages.

Utilities are not a bad thing. The commoditization of computing infrastructure and operating systems in the cloud enables the genesis of more advanced products at lower costs and faster pace due to not having to reinvent the wheel and deal with custom variation.

The distributed data processing framework Apache Hadoop is a great example of components passing through the four stages of evolution in the Wardley map. The genesis of Hadoop was a 2006 subproject within the Apache Nutch project after its cofounders, Doug Cutting, and Mike Cafarella read Google's MapReduce and Google File system papers. Hadoop was soon spun out into a separate open-source project that led to many custom-built installations notably at Yahoo, Facebook, and LinkedIn.

Several enterprising vendors saw the opportunity to standardize the implementation of Hadoop by turning it into a product and extending the ecosystem. Beginning in 2008, Cloudera, HortonWorks, and MaprR created enterprise Hadoop distributions that enabled organizations without deep expertise in Hadoop to create clusters in their data centers.

Today, Hadoop is a commodity offering by major cloud vendors. Amazon's Elastic MapReduce (EMR), Microsoft's HDInsight, and Google's Dataproc allow anyone with a credit card to create, resize, tear down a Hadoop cluster on demand, and pay by the second. The cloud vendor handles all security, tuning, configuration, bug fixes, and upgrades.

Using Wardley Maps

The benefit of Wardley maps is that they create a dynamic visual representation of components in a value chain that is useful in several ways. The simplest starting point is to plot components along the x-axis of evolution. Plot components as they appear in the market and not how you use them. For example, if you have built an in-house relational database, it is still a commodity since many open-source and managed service relational databases exist. Figure 9-4 shows the position of some standard components in the DataOps technology ecosystem.

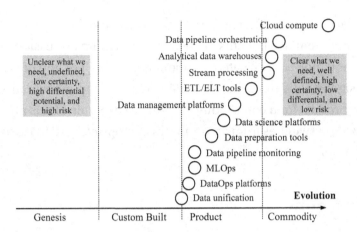

Figure 9-4. *The evolution of common components in the analytics stack*

Just as a builder uses commodity bricks instead of making them with clay and a furnace, the map highlights where custom-built or product solutions are replaceable with a more evolved component. The map also detects where custom solutions are useful because the customer values them and helps spot duplication of components across the organization.

Visualizing movement across the map identifies the components that are worthwhile considering and when, while avoiding hype or dead ends. There are weak signals that predict when a component is likely to make a jump in evolution and cross-over between stages. If a component does not display these weak signals or migrate through stages, then it is a red flag for adoption.

Components that are likely to jump the chasm between genesis and custom-built are associated with high levels of awareness. Examples of weak signals that indicate high levels of awareness are the appearance of many independent posts about the component on Medium, many stars and forks of any GitHub repository, and training courses, meetups, and conferences about the component emerging. For example, Spark showed these disruptive signals in 2014 and Tensorflow in 2016. Signs of these signals are the point to consider adopting the component.

The next set of signals emerges when multiple vendors see a business opportunity and create products with differentiated features that are easier to operate and maintain than a custom-built solution. For example, SaaS ETL/ELT, MLOps, and Data science platforms are currently at this stage with new offerings and features announced every day. An explosion in vendors and features is a signal to consider a product instead of a custom solution.

243

In the final stage, feature differentiation disappears, and there is less discussion of operational and maintenance benefits. Instead, there is more discussion on how to use the component, and more complicated components are built on top of it. At this point, no one will pay significantly more for one version of the component than another, and it is time to ditch a product for a commodity version. An example of this phenomenon is when an organization switches from an on-premise proprietary RDBMS to an analytical database in the cloud.

Technology Radar

The pioneering technology consultancy ThoughtWorks developed the Technology Radar visualization tool to capture information on tools, techniques, platforms, and frameworks and facilitate conversations.[10] The radar is a metaphorical graphical tool to assess and pick the best technologies for different use cases objectively and operates at a more granular level than Wardley maps.

The technology radar is a list of technologies categorized according to an adoption lifecycle from *hold*, *assess*, *trial* to *adopt* plotted as rings on a radar chart. The technologies in the outer hold ring are not recommended because they are not mature enough or are otherwise problematic.

Moving inward, technologies in the assess ring are promising with potential and thereby worth tracking, but not yet worth trialing. The next ring is trial, which encompasses technologies that are capable of broader adoption because they have solved problems in limited use cases, but require more experience to understand risk and build competence. The innermost ring is adopt, which uses these technologies because there is high confidence that they serve their purpose.

The radar chart consists of four quadrants, which is a way to organize the technologies into related areas. Unlike the adoption lifecycle, the naming and positioning of the quadrants are not important. In the current version of ThoughtWorks Technology radar, the four quadrants are techniques, languages and frameworks, platforms, and tools. Figure 9-5 shows a suggested way to group technology for DataOps.

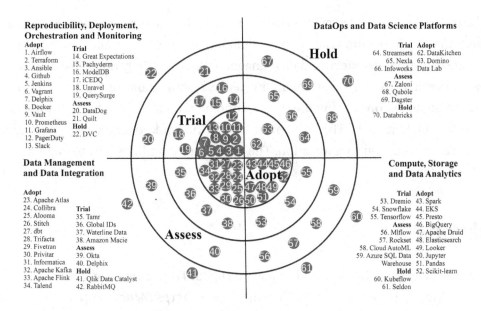

Figure 9-5. *An example DataOps technology radar*

The radar is not the outcome of a top-down directive but results from discussions among a representative group of senior data professionals and technologists. The group discusses and votes on the technologies to include and their position on the radar tool regularly. Ideally, the group follows this process twice a year. The scope of technologies to include is not the entire market but those worth paying close attention to because they may be useful day-to-day.

People should be encouraged to try new technologies, but they also have a responsibility to demonstrate value or share the lack of it honestly and openly. The technology radar is a way of collectively cutting through the hype to adopt the best technologies rather than trying cool tools that are not the best way of getting the job done.

Summary

Data products and pipelines have different considerations for software applications when it comes to developing solutions in an agile way and delivering at DevOps velocity. Traditional IT application-centric processes and technology are a bottleneck to productivity because they were never designed to handle the diverse range of data sources, data formats, and use cases that exist today. However, the right technology, as part of an interoperable modular best of breed ecosystem, can successfully support DataOps practices.

The technology in the DataOps ecosystem must allow self-service access to data and tools to reduce friction, scale to meet demand, orchestrate complex processes, and encourage trust through effective data management. Technology must also allow an increase in velocity through reproducibility, reuse, testing, monitoring, and automation. Only when organizations exploit the right technology can it go from being a bottleneck to an enabler of their goals. The ideas presented in the book so far may seem a long way from the activities in your organization. The next chapter outlines how to implement DataOps in steps.

Endnotes

1. Accelerating the Pace and Impact of Digital Transformation, Harvard Business Review, November 2016. *https://hbr.org/ sponsored/2016/11/accelerating-the-pace-and-impact-of- digital-transformation*

2. Kevin Trethewey and Danie Roux, The Spine Model. *http://spinemodel.info/*

3. The DataOps manifesto. *www.dataopsmanifesto.org/*

4. Donald G. Reinertsen, The Principles of Product Development Flow: Second Generation Lean Product Development, March 2012.

5. Gil Press, Cleaning Big Data: Most Time-Consuming, Least Enjoyable Data Science Task, Survey Says, Forbes, March 2016. *www.forbes.com/sites/gilpress/2016/03/23/data- preparation-most-time-consuming-least-enjoyable-data- science-task-survey-says/*

6. Christopher Dwyer, 12 Common Biases that Affect How We Make Everyday Decisions, Psychology Today, September 2018. *www.psychologytoday.com/us/blog/thoughts-thinking/ 201809/12-common-biases-affect-how-we-make-everyday- decisions*

7. Douglas Hofstadter, Gödel, Escher, Bach: An Eternal Golden Braid, 1979.

8. Damon Edwards, Without Self-Service Operations, the Cloud is Just Expensive Hosting 2.0, DevOps Summit 2014, Nov 2014. *www.slideshare.net/dev2ops/with-selfservice-operations-the-cloud-is-just-expensive-hosting-20-a-devops-story*

9. Simon Wardley, Wardley maps, Topographical intelligence in business, March 2018. *https://medium.com/wardleymaps*

10. Technology Radar, ThoughtWorks, *www.thoughtworks.com/radar*

CHAPTER 10

The DataOps Factory

Data science and analytics are in a broken state. A 2016 KPMG study of 2000 global data analytics decision-makers revealed that only 10% believe they excel in data quality, tools, and methodologies, and 60% say they are *not* very confident in their analytical insights.[1] For every organization that finds measurable success from data science and analytics, several others struggle with data quality, the ability to get work into production, and generate meaningful ROI on investments in people or technology. DataOps is a cure for many of the problems facing data science and analytics today. By adopting DataOps, organizations can deliver data products in a consistent, reliable, fast, scalable, and repeatable process just like a factory.

Unless dealing with a greenfield situation, it is not possible to jump straight to the end state of all analytical work following the DataOps methodology. Respecting the principles of agile and DevOps, the movement to the end goal must be in iterative, small, and frequent steps.

There is no out-of-the-box solution for a DataOps transformation, only continuous discipline in applying practices, following principles, and living values. Every organization has a different starting point and capabilities. The following sections illustrate suggested actionable steps to take. The journey is not always sequential; modify or skip steps according to your context.

The First Steps

The journey must begin with outcomes in mind because achievement comes from collaborative contributions to a common goal. DataOps is not the product. It is an enabler of success. Data science and analytics must serve the strategic mission, vision, and objectives of the organization. Without alignment with the rest of the organization, data science and analytics initiatives are unlikely to succeed.

© Harvinder Atwal 2020
H. Atwal, *Practical DataOps*, https://doi.org/10.1007/978-1-4842-5104-1_10

Start with a Data Strategy

The journey of DataOps adoption begins with a big-picture view and the creation of a data strategy. A 2017 McKinsey & Company survey found the companies with the most successful analytics programs are 2.5 more likely to report having a clear data strategy than their peers.[2]

A data strategy is an analysis of the organization's internal and external environment culminating in a roadmap for closing the gap between the current state of data analytics fitness and where it needs to be to meet the organization's objectives. A data strategy helps the organization make decisions and choices grounded in its goals, and DataOps is a crucial component in delivering the strategy. DataOps articulates how people, processes, and technology work together to remove the mismatch between data production and data consumption to meet the organization's strategic aspirations.

Unless you know where you are, you cannot know which direction to travel. The situational analysis element of the data strategy captures the organizations' mission, vision, objectives, strengths, weakness, and the external environment. The analysis provides critical awareness of how decision-makers use data, the depth of talent and skills, current and planned technology capability, level of process maturity, and state of data management.

Identifying stakeholders and decision-makers sympathetic to adopting new ways of working is critical as it avoids wasting time trying to convert conservative managers. A data strategy also generates a set of potential analytical initiatives that become strategic themes, a portfolio vision, and epics for delivery through agile teams and practices. Such insight is extremely valuable to kick-start the transition to DataOps.

Leadership

A data analytics leader or group of leaders should lead the transformation to DataOps. Strong leadership makes change much easier to achieve. The DataOps leaders should have the capacity to make a case for change, set the vision, have the authority to remove obstacles or change processes, and have credibility with the rest of the organization especially IT and business stakeholders. Typically, the leadership comes from a Chief Data Officer or the most senior individuals responsible for data science, data analytics, or data engineering in the organization.

The first task of DataOps leaders is to identify senior executives who can support the transformation and people in the organization that will be impacted by the introduction of DataOps because they are essential to the data production process or are data consumers. Once identified, the relevant people in the organization must be convinced of the need to change.

The case for change is demonstrated in two ways – external threats and internal shortcomings. Most organizations operate in a competitive environment or are at risk of disruption by nimbler organizations. Presenting examples of how competitors are making better use of their data assets or innovating faster creates a sense of urgency. Highlighting internal problems builds the case for a better future state. Considering both types of threats makes a compelling argument that the status quo is untenable.

Lean thinking tools such as value stream maps are a great way of highlighting existing problems because they visualize and quantify waste and bottlenecks in current processes. Socializing the output of the measurement exercise with as many teams involved in the process as possible from IT Operations and data management to data science can be very revealing. Team involvement can highlight where the chasm between data production and data consumption is most significant, whether that is waiting months for approval of a software package, remedying bad data quality, leaving machines running overnight because there is no access to the right computing resource, configuring software, or waiting for permission to use data.

The focus on product development instead of process innovation in most organizations means most people are not aware of the need for change unless it is made evident. For many people involved, exposure to value stream mapping and supporting data may be the first time they have seen the end-to-end process for turning raw data into a data product and the inhibiting processes and policies that stifle value creation.

Most organizations implement outdated zombie processes and policies for reasons that are no longer valid but still apply them as an end in themselves because that is what they have always done without question. To remedy this problem, leaders should collect and share the costs of poor data quality, the impact of the cost of delay, and low ROI on data investments.

Leaders must make a compelling case for change and begin the process of cultural transformation. No one should want to be part of an unhealthy process. They should want to be part of identifying improvements to make.

Alongside the case for change, DataOps leaders must communicate the vision for change. The vision for change articulates where you are trying to go and motivates people to head in that direction.

The vision can include more data-driven decision-making, increased productivity, faster time to market, greater confidence in data, reduced costs, improved customer engagement, and quicker innovation. Finally, DataOps should be introduced as the methodology to deliver the vision and solve many of the current problems identified.

Minimum Viable DataOps

When the case for change is accepted, the data strategy is complete, and even a rudimentary data strategy is better than none at all the difficult work begins. Even after teams and organizations recognize the need to change, they struggle to transition to a better position because habits and culture are deeply ingrained leading to organizational inertia. Organizations may also fail because they try to run before they have learned to walk.

The answer is not to think too big but start with a minimum viable DataOps solution as a way to maximize the chances of success. Minimum viable DataOps aims to experiment, learn, and show value to the organization quickly.

The First Initiative

Minimum viable DataOps is a way of avoiding two common mistakes organizations make in data science and analytics. Monica Rogati's famous AI hierarchy of needs diagram illustrates the deep layers necessary for the successful delivery of AI and deep learning.[3] Figure 10-1 illustrates the AI hierarchy of needs and the minimum viable DataOps approach.

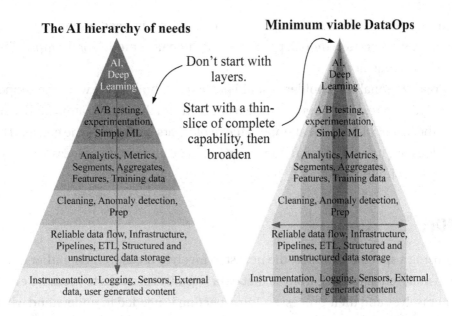

Figure 10-1. *The AI hierarchy of needs and minimum viable DataOps*

Most organizations that want to make better use of data analytics assume that they must start at the top of the hierarchy with AI. So, they adopt a *hire PhDs and hope* strategy that fails because they lack the proper foundations for success. Other organizations build the layers one at a time through waterfall project management and functional teams in a slow process that leads to misalignment of layers.

Minimum viable DataOps avoids both these mistakes by focusing on a single analytical initiative and delivering an end-to-end solution in the most agile and Lean way possible before widening capability in future iterations. This approach is the right route to take even if there is high-level sponsorship and a generous resource budget as it avoids the risk of overengineering project plans and solutions.

The data strategy informs the starting point for minimum viable DataOps by identifying the options for the initial analytical initiative. The starting initiative dictates the stakeholders and teams who will be involved, data requirements, the difficulty of execution, and benefit if successful.

The goal should be to pick something that can demonstrate a measurable early win, provides learning and confidence that can be replicated elsewhere in the organization, and has the support of receptive organizational stakeholders, that is, stakeholders who benefit from the outcome. The output should be a data product that can be iterated and improved such as a customer churn prediction model, social media sentiment analysis dashboard, fraud detection model, predictive maintenance model, or a supply chain demand-forecasting model.

The organizational stakeholders should be people who actively want the support of data analytics to reach their goals, have respect within the organization, and can influence the rest of the organization to remove blockers and spread the gospel. The initiative does not have to be something new. It can be an existing process that has significant room for improvement.

Measure

After choosing a specific initiative, the next step involves measurement rather than rushing to make changes. The irony is that data scientists use data to measure everything except themselves and their processes. Introspection is needed to understand what to alter before transformations can take place. Lean thinking tools such as value stream maps may help visualize and quantify waste and bottlenecks in the current initiatives's end-to-end processes.

In the early stages of the DataOps transformation, the focus should be on the last mile to deliver the right data product to solve the right problem in the most efficient way. It is not possible to change an organization's culture, amend data management practices, transform operations, or re-platform the technology infrastructure overnight. However, from the value stream mapping exercises, it should still be possible to identify acute pain points to fix by adopting DataOps practices and increasing collaboration.

The First DataOps Team

The next step is to create a dedicated domain team that forms the prototype for future teams. DataOps leaders should choose individuals who are most enthusiastic about adopting new ways of working as they will become change agents who help future teams successfully transition to DataOps. In return, the DataOps leader coaches and guides the DataOps team through the transformation and helps remove roadblocks from its path. DataOps will be a new concept for most team members, so the first contribution of the DataOps leader is to educate the team members and motivate their involvement.

Effective team contribution goes beyond specialist skillsets. Team members must be closely aligned to domains and their outcomes and see the bigger picture so they can contribute outside their comfort zone. The DataOps team should ideally be dedicated to the initiative and have as many cross-functional skills as possible to independently develop, test, productionize, and monitor data products. The team must make the transition from siloed working to interdisciplinary collaboration with each other and organizational stakeholders who benefit from the outcomes.

The formation of the team provides an opportunity to create a self-organizing team and adopt agile ways of working. The team must contain the expertise and have the confidence to make fast decisions autonomously.

Teams have a choice of agile frameworks to choose from including Scrum, Scrumban, and Kanban. These frameworks are very valuable because they create a cadence for delivery through regular meetings and continuous improvement through retrospectives. Ideally, the team should physically colocate within a dedicated space.

The analytical initiative should be assigned a product owner who is responsible for managing progress by working with stakeholders and the cross-functional DataOps team. A portfolio Kanban can be useful for DataOps leaders to track progress. The product owner creates epic hypothesis statements for the initiative by articulating the problem the epics will solve, how they are to be measured, and their data and non-functional requirements. If there are competing options for the first epic, an epic prioritization matrix can help inform the decision.

Data science and analytics consists of two processes – data product development and ongoing production. So, the ambition for the team is to break down any barriers between the two to enable faster iteration.

The goal for the DataOps team is to begin implementing practices such as testing, scaling, reproducibility, reuse, deployment, and monitoring that can be shared and reused by other initiatives and teams later. Full automation is not a priority at this juncture because it is crucial to first get fundamental practices and collaboration right.

The DataOps team should begin by building trust in data by watermarking data, adding checks for file validation, integrity tests, data quality, data completeness, data correctness, data consistency, data accuracy, and data uniformity. The team should actively monitor data quality to handle unexpected changes and failures. With data checks and data product monitoring in place, the team can deal with missing data, schema changes, failed processes, and many other glitches before they cause costly downstream problems.

After checks and monitoring are in place, version control for code, configuration files, and datasets are adopted. Version control has many benefits. It allows multiple people to collaborate on the same code base, makes reuse of artifacts easier, and provides a way to understand changes over time through version descriptions. Version control is also the first step in support of continuous integration and continuous delivery.

Some of the tools and techniques used by the DataOps team may be new to them. So, leaders should allocate resources for ongoing training. Standardizing on the software used elsewhere in the organization, particularly in IT operations, is also helpful. A by-product of adopting software used by technology teams, such as Git, Jira, Confluence, Jenkins, Vault, or Puppet, is that it brings greater credibility to data science and analytics teams.

Ultimately, beneficial results are the measure of data analytics. If a data science or analytics team disappeared, people in the organization should notice. Data science and analytics should be a core organizational capability with a measurable positive impact.

Developing benefit measurement and product health monitoring is a high priority for the team. Alignment to organizational benefit objectives also avoids the trap of starting with data rather than with the problem, which may deliver interesting insights but no real value to others outside the team. With measurement in place, the team can set itself improvement goals.

Creating feedback loops is critical to improving results. Feedback from internal customers in the form of organizational stakeholders who benefit from the outcomes is also critical to prevent the team from getting off-track. Regular service delivery review meetings are an opportunity for the DataOps team to discuss with organizational stakeholders how well they are meeting expectations.

Rapid feedback can be achieved by following the batch size feedback principle to reduce batch sizes of work. The team can show value quickly and avoid overoptimization by building a simple ML model or dashboard first and following up with small frequent iterations. Rapid feedback will also alert the team to changes they need to make, which can include choosing a different initiative for minimum viable DataOps if the original hypothesis turns out to be a lousy testbed.

It is vital to publicize early benefits from adopting DataOps practices as frequently as possible to create curiosity and excitement among other teams. Continuous measurement and small frequent iterations should create a regular stream of metrics to share from improvements in benefits of KPIs, time savings, resource efficiency, and data quality improvements.

Starting small reduces risk and fear, while still creating the opportunity to learn and demonstrate gains. With a minimum viable end-to-end DataOps pipeline to prove value, it is easier to gain buy-in from the rest of the organization.

Expand Across Teams

DataOps is not a project. The first iteration of DataOps is not the last. With minimum viable DataOps in place and benefits publicized, the next stage is to expand practices to more domains and epics. The second objective is to get to a tipping point where it becomes more compelling to continue the journey of implementing DataOps practices, principles, and values than to resist them. Results speak louder than words. It remains essential to avoid diversions into time-consuming political battles with hard-to-change departments or to waste time developing a large-scale change management program.

Achieve Critical Mass

From the data strategy, it is possible to identify the next set of epic initiatives and domain teams from which to expand DataOps. There will still be skeptics and detractors who do not recognize the need for change. Therefore, an invitation-only strategy may be appropriate.

If the first DataOps team has managed to publicize its success well, it should not be difficult to find volunteers for team membership and additional organizational stakeholders who want to benefit from new ways of working. Organizational stakeholders do not need to be influential stakeholders and decision-makers in the organization. It is more important at this stage to generate success throughout the organization and make DataOps the most common approach to deliver data science and analytics in the organization. The more teams that deploy DataOps practices, the higher the return on investment in data analytics and the more effective the organization becomes.

Successfully scaling DataOps requires more than getting practices right. There are implications for culture, organization, ways of working, and processes. The same care and attention devoted to the first DataOps team must be lavished on subsequent teams by the DataOps leaders.

Regular retrospectives and team health checks are an excellent way to ensure teams remain on track to transform. However, with more than one DataOps team, explicit coordination is needed to continue the momentum and prevent teams from slipping back into bad habits.

Coordinate Teams

Chapter 8 described how coordination through a center of excellence, guilds, or coordinating roles ensures that domain-orientated teams do not become silos, but benefit from cross-fertilization of best practice and career progression opportunities. Coordination and collaboration across teams are active forces for the dissemination of best practice and continuous improvement.

Teams can use coordination to consult with others and standardize on the best technology and practices. Over time, this process enables scaling of expertise, reduces complexity, and results in greater standardization.

Active coordination enables enthusiastic leaders to share knowledge and guide transformation. For example, a DataOps center of excellence is a way to construct a permanent hotbed of learning, communication, and continuous improvement.

Senior members of functional teams serve in the center of excellence and operate as an agile team with the DataOps leaders acting as product managers and senior stakeholders. The center of excellence actively coaches individuals and teams to help them acquire new skills, establish DataOps practices, build roadmaps, and foster an agile DevOps Lean thinking culture.

Culture

The creation of coordinated domain-orientated DataOps teams is the first step in the journey to structure teams around the ideal data journey in the organization and not functional skills or technologies they traditionally organize around. Equally important is the establishment of the right culture and data governance.

The DataOps leaders must reinforce cultural change through the many months it takes to complete the transformation. DataOps teams must be encouraged to stop thinking of data engineering, data science, and analytics as discrete tasks performed by separate vertically aligned functional teams. Instead, they must learn to think of their work through the factory metaphor as a horizontal end-to-end flow that is everyone's responsibility.

The DataOps leaders and their change agents must actively create a culture of continuous improvement and innovation. The teams must become more accountable by setting service level agreements (SLAs) for consumers of their data product that define the team's responsibility for quality, availability, and resolution time. Teams must benchmark data flow cycle times and data quality KPIs to identify bottlenecks so they can optimize value by changing processes.

The DataOps leaders should adopt many DataOps practices by incorporating agile and Lean thinking into their ways of working so they can act as role models for change. The most senior DataOps leader acts as the product manager for the leadership team and owns the vision, roadmaps, and program backlog for the DataOps transformation and prioritizes work against outcome-orientated goals to maximize the chances of success. The DataOps leaders should recognize teams for innovation, process improvement, and collaboration as well as their outputs.

Data Governance

Strong data governance and security must be in place before DataOps is scaled further to reduce the risk of poor data quality and exposure of sensitive data that may cause problems for the organization. If a data governance framework is too strict, it will reduce data availability and kill the ability to create faster data cycles. Creating a collaborative culture between organizational stakeholders, data producers, data consumers, data owners, and data stewards strikes the best balance.

Sensitive data needs to be identified, encrypted or masked, and monitored. A data classification policy should be created so that data owners can use it to develop access, storage, transmission, and processing policies for different types of data. Organizational stakeholders should be involved in data governance discussions as they can help identify trade-offs between benefits, costs, and risks.

Much of the data cleaning, data discovery, and data provisioning analytics depends on or requires a metadata solution to be in place. Now is also an excellent time to start considering data catalogs, data lineage tracking, data dictionaries, and business glossaries if they are not already in place.

Trust in data is another foundational requirement before DataOps can be scaled. Trust in data should be built as soon as it is ingested from batch or real-time sources. Data consumers should work with data stewards to define KPIs for good-enough data quality, which become the requirements to certify data and monitor data pipelines, and triggers to fix issues.

By demonstrating benefit, trustworthy processes, and a broad base of support among organizational stakeholders, it becomes easier to gain C-suite buy-in for the final stages of implementation. The final steps are the riskiest and test the organization's commitment to becoming genuinely data-driven, which is why a big bang implementation is not recommended.

Extend

With the foundational elements in place and increasing benefit to the organization, DataOps leaders can begin to tackle other pain points. The changes made so far will cause the output of the domain-orientated DataOps teams to exceed the capacity of data platform teams and data management processes that provide data and infrastructure access. So, we should tackle these bottlenecks next.

Organize for Success

DataOps is about building high-velocity low-risk organizations that are able to take advantage of the vast amounts of heterogeneous data they capture. As described in Chapter 8, the organizational structure has a massive impact on what teams create, the quality of output, and the velocity of delivery. Cross-functional domain-orientated teams break down some silos to improve efficiency, but there is a need to integrate all teams responsible for the journey from raw data to the finished data product.

IT data teams are typically responsible for data capture, data access, data infrastructure, and operations. And, they sit between the data and data consumers in most organizations. Unfortunately, these teams are organized by skill or legacy technology. So, they do not have insight into how data is used or can be used by the organization.

The teams are incentivized to minimize costs and change because they fear the implication for budgets, operations, security, and compliance. Hence, they become a roadblock for data consumers. However, it is possible to overcome these risks with the right data management processes and technologies.

Bringing together those who manage data and platforms with those who consume data breaks down the final silos. The initial step should be to build bonds and integrate people from these teams into DataOps teams' rituals such as planning meetings, retrospectives, and service delivery reviews as well as sharing Kanban/Scrum boards, monitoring, and benefit measurement outputs. The aim is to help the teams understand the DataOps team's culture and daily work so they can proactively make improvements to reduce pain points and maximize the work not done by removing any work that does not add value.

Ultimately, cultural change becomes much simpler to achieve if all the teams involved in the data factory report to the same senior leaders such as a CDO or CAO. Through a common reporting structure, it is easier to create a data-centric and outcome-orientated culture that shares commitments, objectives, and rewards. Teams that manage platforms and data begin to treat the consumers of data and infrastructure as customers to satisfy rather than users who introduce risk.

Centralize Platforms

One way to make domain-orientated teams more productive is for data platforms and operations teams to create a centralized and highly scalable platform with access to all the data and standardized tools they need. Doing this enables teams to spend more time creating data products in the most efficient way possible instead of spending time provisioning infrastructure, building their own services, and waiting for data access.

Migrating data analytics to the cloud and cloud-native architecture is the best solution to build a centralized platform for DataOps teams if it has not already happened. With the cloud, it is easier to design architecture and processes for growth and heterogeneous data and use cases.

However, it can be a challenge to maintain existing legacy applications concurrently. Centralizing analytics is still the best solution because existing databases and processes can offload data and workload to the cloud to rationalize data sources, break down silos, and create a single environment where all datasets and artifacts can be easily shared.

The difference between centralized monolithic applications of old such as databases, analytical applications such as SAS or SPSS, and BI tools is that modern centralized cloud platforms can support an ecosystem of hundreds of technologies from virtual machines to Python packages. With a cloud platform, it is simpler to deploy best-of-breed modular technology that supports DataOps practices from metadata management to BI tools.

Different people may have different needs and tool requirements. So, there should be a period of experimentation to discover tools that are worth adopting. However, technology cannot be a point solution. It must fit the rest of the architecture and be interoperable.

To avoid a return to silos caused by incompatible technologies that create barriers for the movement of data and people between teams, centralized platform teams should encourage standardization of the tools with the highest adoption and interoperability. Standardization enables reuse of successful patterns and enables teams to contribute improvements to each other.

Automate All the Things

With modern cloud technology, the ability to store and process data scales exponentially. However, the ability to consume it doesn't unless we have automation and monitoring. Once teams, practices, and technology are in place, the next step is automation.

Creating data products at speed requires automation of infrastructure, environments, security, data access, deployment, data pipeline orchestration, and more. So, the organization must put in place processes and (if necessary) acquire the tools to automate as many activities as possible.

Automation of the identification, categorization, security, provision, quality assessment, and cleansing of data moves data management teams from being gatekeepers to shopkeepers. Sensitive data can be classified and encrypted automatically. IAM and role-based access control can also regulate the access to data and resources to help automate security policies. Decentralized metadata management combined with software automation can tag data to help build data catalogs, which saves data scientists and analysts' time investigating datasets.

Automation can then extend to the development and monitoring of data pipelines. The goal is to continuously integrate, test, deploy, and monitor the production pipeline automatically.

Automation of data pipeline development requires that infrastructure, data pipeline tools, and pipeline orchestration configuration are in a configuration management tool and under version control along with the data pipeline and pipeline orchestration code.

Black box, white box, and regression tests must also be in version control so they can be run as part of an automated CI process every time changes are made to data pipeline code. Automated test data management solutions are needed to provision data for the CI process that mirror production data. Otherwise, it is not possible to determine if bugs are due to changes in code or data.

Automation can also extend beyond data pipelines to productionizing machine learning algorithms through MLOps. MLOps combines elements of DataOps and DevOps to automate model development, deployment, release, and retraining. Using MLOps, organizations can deploy and refresh many more models than possible with manual approaches.

Once the production data pipeline is operating, the automated black box and white box used for CI can monitor it on an ongoing basis. On discovery of new defects in the data, new tests can be appended to existing tests to catch problems earlier in the development cycle.

Automated monitoring of pipelines removes the constraints imposed by the bottleneck of manual testing and catches more data bugs before they impact data consumers. As a result, organizations can maintain many more data pipelines.

Organizations can also create many more data pipelines because reusable components of pipeline development and monitoring are available for data scientists and analysts to use not just data engineers. As Jeff Magnusson stated in his article "Engineers Should Not Write ETL," data scientists should have end-to-end ownership of their work, which frees up data engineers to focus on platforms, services, abstractions, and frameworks that enable others to work with more autonomy.[4]

Knowledge transparency across the organization is vital. Automated monitoring is not just for DataOps teams. Organizational stakeholders must also have access to functional monitoring so they are alerted of errors that may affect decisions such as missing data and concept drift in models.

Often, stakeholders are unaware of the problems in the data assembly line or with data products. At the tactical level, the lack of visibility results in poor decision-making, finger-pointing, and blame. At the strategic level, senior stakeholders are unlikely to support and prioritize improvement initiatives until they can see the problems for themselves.

Other forms of automated monitoring are also needed to prevent platforms from descending into chaos. Automated monitoring is vital for governance, security, budgeting, and performance. Monitoring tools can alert for anomalies in resource utilization in data centers or the cloud. Budget alerts prevent teams from racking up uncontrollable costs. Cloud compliance frameworks tied to audit tools allow organizations to adhere to regulations. Monitoring of sensitive data, data encryption, data and platform access, firewalls, storage, and other services keep data secure.

With comprehensive monitoring in place, problems are detected early. Monitoring data also promotes continuous improvement because teams can set targets for performance.

Provide Self-Service

By this stage, multiple teams have moved from responding to requests like a service desk to collaboration and subsequently proactively identifying new opportunities to meet the organization's objectives using data. The previous steps taken to create trust and deliver automation with monitoring can now enable self-service capabilities. Only the pace they can set themselves limits teams because they are free of bureaucracy and manual overhead.

Centralized governance and platforms enable decentralized data and infrastructure access. Instead of many siloed platforms, a single or a limited number of central platforms allow data analytics professionals to access self-service infrastructure that is less demanding to administer, control, monitor, audit, and secure. Self-service makes DataOps development faster while reducing risk because access to data, tools, and infrastructure is in sync with the organization's security and operational policies.

Self-service is the final stage of eliminating the gap between data producers and data consumers. The time and effort to take an idea, develop it into a data product, safely deploy it into production, measure benefits, iteratively improve, and reuse it is reduced to the absolute minimum. The changes that self-service DataOps creates lead to a high-velocity data-first culture with better decision-making and more innovation with lower risk and greater sustainability.

Figure 10-2 summarizes the suggested steps to building the DataOps factory.

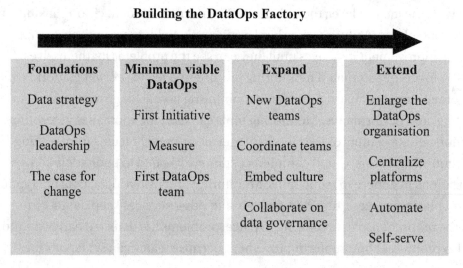

Figure 10-2. *The steps to building the DataOps factory*

The path to building the DataOps factory is not easy as the inertia, habits, and culture of organizations are hard to change. Remember to use DataOps values, principles, and practices to guide you toward always taking steps forward no matter how small.

Summary

Getting data science and analytics right can seem intimidating. There are many factors to consider. Hire (PhDs) and hope is not a strategy. Recruitment, people development, culture, organization, prioritization, collaboration, data acquisition and ingestion, data quality, processes, algorithms, technology, reproducibility, deployment, operations, monitoring, benefit measurement, governance, data security, and privacy must all be mastered.

It is incredibly challenging to get everything right, especially when organizational culture is rarely data-centric and many existing data management practices are no longer fit for purpose. In today's competitive environment of big data, data science, and AI, old ways of working designed for data warehouses and BI are a liability. Not only are they a constraint, they also invite risk by encouraging shadow IT with weak governance.

DataOps methodology is the best way to eliminate barriers, collaborate, and maximize the chances of success. DataOps turns data science and analytics from the craft industry it is today in most organizations into a slick manufacturing operation. DataOps enables rapid data product development and creates an assembly line that converts raw data from multiple sources into production data products with a minimum of waste.

Even if an organization is not excited by the opportunities data science presents for better decision-making, it should worry that competitors and consumers are. Exponential growth in data production and demand for consumption is inevitable. Only those organizations who recognize the need for the new way of DataOps will succeed in taking advantage of the future.

Carrying on like it is 1999 is not an option. I hope this book has prepared you to take the initial steps. If you are already implementing some of the steps, congratulations you are already ahead of most organizations. Good luck on your DataOps journey.

Endnotes

1. Building trust in analytics, KPMG International Data & Analytics, 2016 *https://assets.kpmg/content/dam/kpmg/xx/pdf/2016/10/building-trust-in-analytics.pdf*

2. Peter Bisson, Bryce Hall, Brian McCarthy, and Khaled Rifai, Breaking away: The secrets to scaling analytics, McKinsey Analytics, May 2018. *www.mckinsey.com/business-functions/mckinsey-analytics/our-insights/breaking-away-the-secrets-to-scaling-analytics*

3. Monica Rogati, The AI Hierarchy of Needs, Hackernoon, June 2017. *https://hackernoon.com/the-ai-hierarchy-of-needs-18f111fcc007*

4. Jeff Magnusson, Engineers Shouldn't Write ETL: A Guide to Building a High Functioning Data Science Department, March 2016. *https://multithreaded.stitchfix.com/blog/2016/03/16/engineers-shouldnt-write-etl/*

Index

© Harvinder Atwal 2020
H. Atwal, *Practical DataOps*, https://doi.org/10.1007/978-1-4842-5104-1

Printed in the United States
By Bookmasters